art / shop / eat

LONDON

Alison Hartley

Covent Garden, Piccadilly

Bloomsbury

Bankside

Westminster

South Kensington

introduction

London is one of the most culturally rich cities in the world. Its past as the capital of an empire has endowed it with superb collections of antiquities and Old Masters, yet it has also recently become a focal point for contemporary art, helped by the global renown of the YBAs (young, and not-so-young, British artists). Its commercial galleries regularly play host to internationally acclaimed artists and many shops and restaurants display art on their walls.

This guide describes in detail five of the most important collections in London: the National Gallery, British Museum, Tate Modern, Tate Britain, and Victoria and Albert Museum. All five are rich enough to deserve repeat visits and, encouragingly, their permanent collections are free to enter. Not resting on their laurels, most have recently embarked on ambitious building programmes, too, and are constantly improving their displays and visitor facilities. Each of these main collections is surrounded by other public and commercial venues where you can enjoy art of all kinds.

The districts around the museums also have their own distinctive character and include some of Europe's most famous shopping quarters, from the high fashion of Knightsbridge to the funkier boutiques of Covent Garden and Soho, from bustling Borough food market to the second-hand bookshops of the Charing Cross Road.

Don't forget that London has also become one of most gastronomically varied world cities, where you can as easily find Michelin-starred foodie temples as cheap but filling noodle bars.

The planning chapter will help you negotiate public transport - a useful river ferry between the Tates has recently opened - and there are maps of each featured area. The entertainment chapter lists major musical and theatrical venues, while the glossary provides background on some of London's artistic and literary personalities past and present.

Armed with this guide I hope you will Art, Shop, Eat - and above all, Enjoy - London this and many future visits.

COVENT GARDEN
PICCADILLY

National Gallery

OPEN	Daily 10.00-18.00, Wed till 21.00; for late opening of special exhibitions in the Sainsbury Wing, ask at the information desk; Lower Gallery A Wed 14.00-17.30 only
CLOSED	1/1, 24-26/12
CHARGES	Admission free to galleries; charge for special exhibitions, with lower rates for senior citizens, students and children 12-18, unwaged and disabled visitors, and NACF members, children under 12 free
TELEPHONE	**020 7747 2885**
WWW	**nationalgallery.org.uk**
MAIN ENTRANCE	Trafalgar Square (Portico and Sainsbury Wing)
UNDERGROUND	Charing Cross, Leicester Square
DISABLED ACCESS	Wheelchair access is via the Sainsbury Wing, which has lifts to all floors. The nearest car park is in Whitcomb Street; holders of a disabled parking badge can book a parking space at the rear of the Gallery, **T 020 7747 2854**
GUIDED TOURS	Guided tours introduce the collection (daily at 11.30 and 14.30, also 18.30 Wed, free); there are also free lunchtime lectures (13.00), children's trails and family events (Sat 11.30 and 14.30). Four themed audio-guides each look at about 20 works. The more comprehensive Gallery Guide Soundtrack, in seven languages, is available for a voluntary contribution; it has Braille numbering and can be used with a hearing aid (Soundtrack desks close at 17.00)
SERVICES	Sainsbury Wing: information desk and cloakroom on the ground floor; toilets on the way to the basement and on the first landing. In the first-floor Micro Gallery you can plan a visit or research a painting. Main Wing: information desk and cloakroom in vestibule; toilets on the lower floor
SHOPS	Main shop, with an extensive range of art books, in the Sainsbury Wing, ground floor; the Room 3 Shop, off the Central Hall in the main building, sells mainly postcards and posters
EATING	Restaurant in the Sainsbury Wing; self-service café in the East Wing

The Gallery presents regular special exhibitions in the basement of the Sainsbury Wing (tickets from the desks on the ground floor), and small-scale, free shows in the Sunley Room in the Main Wing.

The National Gallery houses the British public collection of Western painting from 1250 to 1900 (Tate Modern takes over for the 20c). Over 4 million visitors each year come to see many of the most instantly recognizable images in Western art.

The nucleus of the collection was a group of 38 pictures owned by a banker, John Julius Angerstein. They were bought by the British government in 1824 to create a gallery for all, centrally located and free. At first, acquisitions followed the Trustees' personal tastes but after reforms in 1855 the Director travelled Europe buying works to a more considered plan. As the collection expanded, its British art began to be exhibited elsewhere, which eventually led to the establishment of the Tate. During the Second World War all the paintings, except for a 'picture of the month', were hidden in a slate mine in Wales. The National Gallery now holds over 2300 paintings.

THE BUILDING

The paintings were first displayed in Angerstein's own house in Pall Mall, a very modest building by the standards of the Louvre in Paris, a fact not lost on the press. In 1831, Parliament agreed to build a more suitable venue and chose Trafalgar Square, at the heart of London. The Gallery was designed by William Wilkins, a Greek Revival architect. He had to cope with a very narrow site and use elements from two of George IV's failed projects - the Corinthian columns in the portico from the demolished Carlton House and statuary from the Marble Arch. His building, draped ineffectually along the top of the square, was not much liked, but it escaped being replaced; instead, new galleries were added over the years. The Sainsbury Wing, a Postmodern design by husband-and-wife

National Gallery

team Robert Venturi and Denise Scott Brown, was opened in 1991 to house the early Renaissance paintings. Its façade mimics features of the original building. To coincide with the pedestrianization of the northern side of Trafalgar Square, a new development of the East Wing is underway, its first phase scheduled for completion in 2004.

HIGHLIGHTS

Hans Holbein's double portrait of *The Ambassadors*	Room 4
Venetian paintings by Titian, Tintoretto and Veronese	Rooms 9-11
Portraits and biblical scenes by Rembrandt	Room 23
Velázquez's *Rokeby Venus*	Room 30
British paintings by Hogarth, Gainsborough, Reynolds, Turner and Constable	Rooms 34, 35
Impressionism and Post-Impressionism, with works by Monet, Renoir, Degas, Van Gogh and Cézanne	Rooms 43-46
Early Renaissance paintings including works by Van Eyck, Uccello, Piero della Francesca, Botticelli, Bellini, Leonardo, Michelangelo and Raphael	Rooms 51-66

Almost the entire collection is arranged on one floor, in the three wings of the main building and in the separate Sainsbury Wing. All works not in conservation or on loan will be on display, although at present, the reserve collection in Lower Floor Gallery A can be seen only on Wednesday afternoons. The organization is chronological: the earliest pictures are in the **Sainsbury Wing**. The **West Wing** contains the later Renaissance pictures and is linked to the **North Wing**, where Northern European paintings predominate. The **East Wing** contains the later works, including British portraiture and landscape and the French Impressionists. The Central Hall gives access to the Lower Galleries, the café and smaller shop, and the **Sunley Room**.

SAINSBURY WING: PAINTING 1250-1500

ENTRANCE The **grand stair** up to the main floor is an uplifting experience in more ways than one. The names of Renaissance greats above your head were carved by Michael Harvey (1990). Here you begin to see that natural light is a key feature of the

THE NATIONAL GALLERY

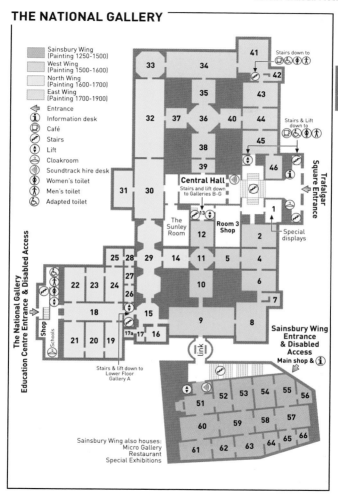

Sainsbury Wing. The feeling of ascent continues in Botticini's *Assumption of the Virgin* (c 1475-6) at the top of the stairs, where you can pick up a Soundtrack guide and begin your tour of the early Renaissance paintings, to the left, or turn right into the West Wing via a bridge.

ROOMS 52, 53 The first room (51) you will see starts with the biggest names, Leonardo and Michelangelo; for a gentler, chronological introduction to the period, turn left and walk through to Room 52. The paintings in this room and the next were made before 1400, and show how the rather static, frontal style we recognize from Byzantine icons gradually incorporated greater realism, through the influence of **Giotto**. In *Pentecost* (c 1306-12), attributed to him, a real space is shown by the recession of the ceiling and at least some of the figures appear to interact naturally. Many of the works are from Siena: its most famous artist of this period, **Duccio**, is represented by small panels from his *Maestà* (c 1311), a huge altarpiece showing the Virgin in majesty, and by a well-preserved triptych of the *Virgin and Child with Saints* (c 1315). Colours are intense and gold dazzles.

Room 53 is dominated by Jacopo di Cione's altarpiece for San Pier Maggiore in Florence, featuring the *Coronation of the Virgin* (1370-1). In the middle of the room is the *Wilton Diptych* (1395-9), an exquisite portable altarpiece demonstrating the refinement of Richard II's court. On the back is the king's personal badge, a white hart, as worn by the attendant angels on the front.

ROOMS 54, 55 The snaking hemlines and intricate throne architecture seen in Lorenzo Monaco's *Coronation of the Virgin* (c 1407-9) exemplify the decorative International Gothic style, while the small figures in **Fra Angelico**'s *Christ glorified in the Court of Heaven* (c 1423) have his characteristic sweetness. Slightly later, **Masaccio** attempted a more serious exploration of individual psychology. In his damaged *Virgin and Child* (1426), bulky figures cast shadows. Masaccio may have studied classical statuary, as part of the first flourishing of the Italian Renaissance when the arts of ancient Greece and Rome were being rediscovered.

Room 55 has two of the very rare known paintings by the great medallist **Pisanello**, the *Virgin and Child with St George and St Antony Abbot* (c 1438-41) and the *Vision of St Eustace* (c 1440). In the latter, one of the saint's hunting dogs bears its teeth at the apparition, another is undistracted from the hare it chases. **Paolo Uccello**'s fascination with the workings of perspective is evident in his painting of the *Battle of San Romano* (c 1438-40), with its pattern of lances and carefully drawn, awkwardly shaped objects. In the contest between *St George and the Dragon* (c 1460) Uccello's beast is hindered by having only two legs but the atmosphere is appropriately threatening, and there is more play with perspective in the vegetation laid out like the groundplan of a building.

ROOM 56 Straight ahead is a small room of paintings from the Netherlands, where a revolution in the visual arts was taking place at roughly the same time as in Italy. The two countries were connected by trade and the subject of one of the Gallery's most famous works, the *Arnolfini Portrait* (1434) by **Jan van Eyck**, was an Italian merchant. The details of this painting are so clear and familiar that it is surprising to find how small it really is. Beside it is a possible self-portrait by Van Eyck, wearing an elaborate red turban (1433). **Rogier van der Weyden** is represented by several workshop paintings but the most striking is a fragment by his own hand from a larger altarpiece (before 1438), in which the figure of Mary Magdalene sits reading, now isolated and tranquil.

ROOMS 57, 58 To stick with the Italians, turn right from Room 55 to see work from Florence at the peak of the early Renaissance; antique ruins are everywhere. The new understanding of human proportion achieved by drawing from life is evident in the huge *Martyrdom of St Sebastian* (1475) by the brothers Pollaiuolo. Three basic poses were drawn from different angles for the figures of the archers; the artists were also sculptors. Fra Filippo Lippi had a softer manner, as seen in the *Annunciation* and *Seven Saints* (c 1450-3). Among several works by **Sandro Botticelli**, the *'Mystic Nativity'* (1500) is the most intriguing: a composition full of circles, pyramids and straight lines, with an awe-inspiringly large Virgin.

Its strange atmosphere may derive from the time of spiritual unease in which it was painted.

A secular Botticelli is seen in the next room. His post-coital *Venus and Mars* (1485) hangs over a magnificent cassone, a type of storage chest often given on marriage. Also in mythological mood are Antonio Pollaiuolo's tiny *Apollo and Daphne* (1470-80) and Piero di Cosimo's *Satyr Mourning a Nymph* (c 1495), accompanied by an even more downcast dog.

ROOM 59 The artists featured here have a character quite distinct from those working in Florence. The Venetian **Carlo Crivelli** drew with a wiry line and conjured metallic surfaces out of paint. The *Annunciation with St Eumidius* (1486) includes his trademark scattering of fruit and veg, and his altarpiece for San Domenico in Ascoli Piceno (1476) even features raised ornament and jewels.

ROOM 51 Take this opportunity to go back to Room 51 to see the next generation of Florentine artists. The sculptor, goldsmith and painter **Andrea del Verrocchio** had a successful studio where his pupils included Botticelli, Perugino and **Leonardo da Vinci**. Andrea's own *Virgin and Child with Two Angels* (1470s) and the workshop's *Tobias and the Angel* (1470s) demonstrate his skill in depicting textiles, jewels and charming, elegant figures; young Leonardo may even have painted the little dog trotting at the angel's side.

Leonardo's much later *Virgin of the Rocks* (c 1508) is one of two versions of the subject (the other is in the Louvre) and is typical in its mysterious gestures and relationships. In a little, darkened room behind the painting is another Leonardo, a full-size drawing or cartoon of the *Virgin and Child with St Anne and St John the Baptist* (c 1499-1500). It was never used for the painting it was designed for but remains a fascinating record of an artist's second thoughts: his reworkings give it a shadowy, mystical quality. Leonardo was the key rival and influence in the early career of **Michelangelo** in Florence: the *Virgin and Child with St John and Angels* (c 1497) is a very early and rare painting by an artist who regarded himself primarily as a sculptor. Its unfinished state, showing initial drawing and the grey-green underpainting of flesh, gives another insight into an artist's creative processes.

ROOM 60 Now **Raphael** appears on the scene, with works from his early period in Florence; this city of artistic pre-eminence is seen in the background of Francesco Granacci's splendid *Portrait of a Man in Armour* (c 1510), where you can just pick out the statue of David by Michelangelo. Raphael's altarpiece of the *Crucified Christ* (c 1503) - a rather static composition despite the angels' curling sashes - is very much still under the influence of his teacher, Perugino. The twisting pose of *St Catherine of Alexandria* (c 1507/8) shows how much Raphael had learned by the time of his departure for Rome.

ROOM 61, 62 The next rooms focus on Venice and its provinces. **Giovanni Bellini**'s *Assassination of St Peter Martyr* (c 1507) and *Madonna of the Meadow* (c 1500) take place in meticulously rendered but dreamlike landscapes, where everyday agricultural labour continues undisturbed by sacred dramas. The work of **Mantegna**, Bellini's brother-in-law and court artist in Mantua, is even more distinctive, featuring clinging drapery and unusual colour combinations in the *Virgin and Child with the Magdalene and St John the Baptist* (1490-1505). He was particularly skilled in imitating carved stone friezes with marble backgrounds, as in *Samson and Delilah* (c 1500). Room 62 has more by both artists, including Bellini's famous image of the hawkish *Doge Leonardo Loredan* (1501-4).

ROOM 63 Among several works by Gerard David, *Christ nailed to the Cross* (c 1480-9) demands an extraordinary engagement, as Christ catches the viewer's eye. **Hieronymous Bosch** also asks us to contemplate patient suffering in *Christ Mocked* (c 1500), in which he is surrounded by grotesques. A contrasting delicacy is seen in *St Giles and the Hind* (c 1500) by the Master of St Giles, with a foreground of vegetation of incredible freshness and accuracy: you can see what inspired the Pre-Raphaelites. The art of the Netherlands was popular in Portugal and Spain, and Bartolomé Bermejo, painter of the burnished *St Michael triumphant* (1468), may have trained there.

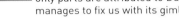

ROOMS 64, 65 From **Germany**, the long-fingered, often contorted figures of the Master of the St Bartholomew Altarpiece seem vigorously alive: note the man perched precariously at the top of a *Deposition* (c 1500-5) and characterful *St Peter and St Dorothy* (c 1505-10). The dominant figure at the end of the 15c was **Albrecht Dürer**, whose *St Jerome* (c 1495) was painted just after his first visit to Italy. It has a visionary intensity despite its tiny size. Though only parts are attributed to Dürer, *The Painter's Father* (1497) manages to fix us with its gimlet eye at a distance of 500 years.

Piero della Francesca *The Nativity* (1470–5)

ROOM 66 Finally, back in Italy, we see works by Domenico Veneziano and his much more famous pupil, **Piero della Francesca**. The stony grey spaces of the Sainsbury Wing complement Piero's trance-inducing paintings: the *Baptism of Christ* (1450s) takes place by the glassy Jordan; the *Nativity* (1470-5), perhaps unfinished, is full of unheard angel music.

WEST WING: PAINTING 1500-1600

On leaving the Sainsbury Wing by the circular link room, you are immediately confronted by a vast expanse of Titians and Tintorettos in Room 9. To follow a chronological route through the collection of paintings from 1500 to 1600, turn right into Room 8 and left through the next rooms to Room 4. Alternatively, you may have approached from the Gallery's main entrance.

ENTRANCE AND CENTRAL HALL Beyond the vestibule, stairs to East and West Wings lead off the landings. The **floor mosaics**

(1928-52) by Boris Anrep depict the labours, pleasures and virtues of what was then modern life: Churchill stars as defiance, Virginia Woolf and Greta Garbo are among the Muses. Look back to see Frederic Leighton's re-creation of *Cimabue's Madonna carried in Procession* (1853-5), and up to see J.D. Crace's original ceiling decoration restored. Desks for advance ticket sales and Soundtrack guides are also here.

The Central Hall is a kind of grand waiting room, lined with all-too-comfortable leather benches. It is to be restored as a picture gallery. Concerts are given here on Wednesday nights. Doors at the far end lead to the **Sunley Room**, which presents excellent free exhibitions. A door in the centre of the left-hand wall leads to the West Wing, but take the one from the staircase landing to continue this tour.

ROOM 2 **Sebastiano del Piombo**'s enormous picture of the *Raising of Lazarus* (1517-19) is the first item in the National Gallery's inventory, coming from the Angerstein collection. Some of its figures were based on drawings by Michelangelo, and there are other paintings based on his work here, including a 16c copy of his *Leda*. But *The Entombment* (c 1500-1) is probably the real thing, showing the unblemished body of Christ within a grid of interlocking vertical figures and horizontal linen bands. Michelangelo may have abandoned it to bid for the marble block that became the *David*. His later rival in Rome was Raphael, in whose portrait of *Pope Julius II* (1511-12) the bearded sitter looks worn out by cares - or perhaps he was just pondering new ways to antagonize Michelangelo.

ROOM 5 Go through Room 4 to Room 5 for artists from other Italian centres. In Andrea Solario's *Man with a Pink* (mid-1490s) the flower is a sign of betrothal and it may have been an engagement picture. The man, with a touch of grey in his fringe, might have been a daunting prospect for the bride. Lorenzo Costa's portrait of the medical writer *Battista Fiera* (c 1509) has great immediacy, the sitter's red hair well contrasted with his plum-coloured coat.

ROOM 4 Here is another array of incisive portraits, this time from Germany. The centrepiece is the recently restored *Ambassadors* (1533) by **Hans Holbein**, featuring meticulously observed musical and scientific instruments and an anamorphically distorted skull (view the painting from the right-hand edge to see this spring into shape). Also by Holbein are a full-length portrait of *Christina of Denmark* (1538) - made for Henry VIII, on the lookout for a fourth wife; *Erasmus* (1523); and the pensive *Lady with a Squirrel* (c 1526-8). No less impressive are portraits by **Lucas Cranach the Elder** and Hans Baldung Grien. Cranach's *Cupid Complaining to Venus* (c 1530) is a model of negligent parenting.

ROOMS 6, 7 A particular type of soulful soldier-scholar - dressed in moody black and looking thoughtful amid classical ruins - was established in late 16c Italian portraiture. **Giovanni Battista Moroni** is represented by expressive paintings of a *Gentleman* (late 1560s) and a humbler man known as *The Tailor* (c 1570), and **Lorenzo Lotto** by the formidable *Lady inspired by Lucretia* (c 1532).
  Tiny Room 7 brings together Old Testament scenes (c 1515) painted for the bedroom of Florentine banker Pierfrancesco Borgherini by **Pontormo** and Bacchiacca, in heady salmon and rose pinks.

ROOM 8 Here is Andrea del Sarto's tense, almost monochrome *Portrait of a Young Man* (c 1517), but most of the paintings are of imaginary scenes. **Correggio** was admired for his misty treatment of classical and religious subjects, as in *Mercury instructing Cupid* (mid-1520s). Parmigianino made the towering, mannered *Madonna and Child with St John and St Jerome* (1527). Visual clarity and thematic opacity characterize the *Allegory with Venus and Cupid* (mid-1540s) by **Bronzino**, a jigsaw puzzle of gestures that resists a complete explanation. Next to it is his relatively straightforward *Portrait of a Young Man* (1550s), perhaps a member of the Medici family, his patrons.

ROOMS 9, 10, 11 The watery soft-green walls of Room 9 are a fitting backdrop to the art of 16c Venice, and pre-eminently of

Titian. These rooms show several important earlier works - including the swaggering *Man with a Quilted Sleeve* (c 1510); an exquisitely poised *Noli me Tangere* (c 1514); and *Bacchus and Ariadne* (c 1522) with the god's unearthly leap - as well as the magnificent group portrait of the *Vendramin Family* (1543-7) and the late, finger-daubed *Death of Actaeon* (c 1565-76). In Jacopo Bassano's *Purification of the Temple* (1580), a chaotic stream of people and animals, the cowering moneylender on the right is supposed to be the avaricious Titian!

In the four *Allegories of Love* (1570s) by **Veronese**, pearly-skinned blondes enact scenes of 'Happy Union', 'Respect', 'Faithlessness' and 'Scorn' - though not necessarily in that order. The paintings' assumption of a low viewing-point shows they were designed to appear high up (as they are sometimes hung in Room 11). Tintoretto strikes a darker note in his strangely unbalanced *Christ washing the Feet of his Disciples* (c 1556) - from the far end of the gallery you feel you can walk into it. In **Giorgione**'s mysterious *Sunset* (1506-10), distance is ambiguous and activities are lost in shadow. Palma Vecchio's *Blonde Woman* (c 1520) is another Venetian bombshell, with a blue ribbon cupping her exposed breast.

ROOM 12 The last room shows 16c art of the Netherlands. In his *Adoration of the Kings* (c 1500-15) **Jan Gossaert** depicts weeds and broken paving as lovingly as golden chalices and velvet robes: after visiting Italy he made less appealing attempts to copy classical statuary, like the lumpen *Adam and Eve* (c 1520). The tiny *Portrait of a Lady* (1551) is by Catherina van Hemessen, one of the Gallery's rare female artists. **Quinten Massys**' *Grotesque Old Woman* (c 1525) may have been based on a drawing by Leonardo and inspired John Tenniel's illustrations to *Alice in Wonderland*. In complete contrast is his beautiful *Virgin and Child with St Barbara and St Catherine* (c 1515-25); painted in glue size on cloth, it is one of the few survivors of a type common in the 16c Netherlands and seems to disappear before your eyes.

In Room 13 you will see a staircase to the left down to the Lower Floor Galleries B-G (see below).

National Gallery Central Hall

NORTH WING: PAINTING 1600-1700

From the Sainsbury Wing, walk from the link bridge straight through Rooms 9 and 10 and turn left in Room 11. From the main entrance, take the door in the left-hand wall of the Central Hall, go through Room 12 and turn right in Room 11.

ROOM 14 The Gallery's collection of 17c Dutch works is one of the most comprehensive in the world. Here is **Pieter Bruegel the Elder**'s *Adoration of the Kings* (1564), an almost comic collection of caricatures, and an introduction to Dutch artists' pre-eminence in still-life painting with Joachim Beuckelaer's *Four Elements* (1570), with biblical scenes in the background of markets for fruit, fish and meat.

ROOM 29 This space is devoted mainly to the extraordinary talents and workrate of the Flemish artist **Peter Paul Rubens**. *The Massacre of the Innocents* (1609-10), which set a new auction record for an Old Master painting in 2002, has been loaned to the National Gallery for three years before leaving for Canada. With *Samson and Delilah*, painted around the same time, it shows what Rubens learned in Italy about painting the heroic male nude and dramatic lighting. Besides biblical and classical scenes there are Rubens' often beautiful oil sketches, rapidly drawn designs for tapestries, silverware and the ceiling frescoes in the Banqueting House at Whitehall; portraits such as *Susanna Lunden* (1622-5); and influential outdoor scenes including *Autumn Landscape with a view of Het Steen* (c 1636), his country estate, with a huge expanse of terrain and the lights on at home. There is also work by Rubens' pupil **Antony van Dyck**, including a stunning portrait of *Cornelis van der Geest* (c 1620). For more Van Dycks, walk to Room 31 via Room 30.

ROOM 15 The 17c French artist Claude Lorrain, whose *Seaport with the Embarkation of the Queen of Sheba* (1648) is seen here, was hugely influential on later landscape painting. The painter J.M.W. Turner bequeathed his *Dido building Carthage* (1815) and *Sun rising through Vapour* (before 1807) to the Gallery on condition that they were hung between two works by Claude, as in this small space.

ROOMS 16, 17A, 17 Take the right-hand exit ahead of you to begin a sequence of small rooms displaying 17c Dutch painting. Room 17a shows a fascination with minutely observed natural objects, flowers, shells, insects and even vegetables. In Room 17, there is an unusual peepshow of a spartan Dutch interior, made by the painter Samuel van Hoogstraten (1650s); around it are interior scenes by *fijnschilders* ('fine painters') including **Gerrit Dou**.

In Room 16 next door are more superlative interiors, in particular two rare paintings by **Jan Vermeer**, both showing a young woman playing a virginal (both c 1670) in a light that seems liquid and cool. Also superb are Gabriel Metsu's studies of figures in domestic settings, Pieter Saenredam's airy white church interiors and outdoor scenes by Pieter de Hooch, especially *Courtyard of a House in Delft* (1658).

ROOMS 23-28 Emerging at Room 15 once more, walk ahead to a lobby with stairs descending to Lower Gallery A (see below). Turn right into Room 26 for more Dutch portraits and genre scenes, including merry-makers by **Jan Steen**. The diplomat *Constantin Huygens* (1627) looks authoritative in his picture by Thomas de Keyser, one of Amsterdam's most popular portraitists before Rembrandt's arrival.

Room 27 has Dutch landscapes and cityscapes. Look out for Hendrick Avercamp's circular *Winter Scene with Skaters near a Castle* (c 1608-9), in which tiny figures enjoy themselves on the ice.

Flemish paintings in Room 28 contrast the often bawdy behaviour in the work of **David Teniers**, and especially in Adriaen Brouwers' *Tavern Scene* (c 1635), with the more refined pastimes of *Cognoscenti in a Room Hung with Pictures* (c 1620).

In Room 25 to the left are *vanitas* paintings, reminders of mortality. *Young Man holding a Skull* (1626-8) by **Frans Hals** carries this message despite the energy of its broad brushstrokes. Even Judith Leyster's cheeky *Boy and Girl with a Cat and an Eel* (c 1635) can be read as a warning against mischief-making. Hendrick ter

Brugghen's *The Concert* (c 1626) takes its style and subject from Caravaggio: ter Brugghen was one of a number of Utrecht painters influenced by the Roman artist.

Turn into Room 24 for more Hals, including a *Portrait of a Man* (c 1660) looking squiffily from under a rakishly angled hat. Pieter Lastman created mythological scenes such as *Juno discovering Jupiter and Io* (1618), the type his pupil Rembrandt aspired to paint. There are works by Rembrandt's own pupils Nicholas Maes, Aert de Gelder and **Carel Fabritius**, whose open *Self-Portrait* (1654) was painted the year he died in an explosion in Delft.

Take the side exit into Room 23 for a representative selection of work by **Rembrandt** himself, from the small and meticulous *Anna and Blind Tobit* (c 1630), painted before he left Leiden, to the touching *Self-Portrait at the Age of 63* (1669), the last year of his life. The face of the elderly *Margaretha de Geer* (c 1661) looks as fragile as her old-fashioned white ruff but her hands reveal the indestructible matriarch. The theatrical *Belshazzar's Feast* (c 1635) was an attempt to make a splash as a history painter.

ROOMS 21, 22 Room 22 covers a generation of Dutch landscape artists, including **Jacob van Ruisdael**. In his *Landscape with a Ruined Castle* (late 1660s) sunlight breaks out over a distant windmill. His pupil, Meindert Hobbema, painted the famous, serene view of the *Avenue at Middelharnis* (c 1689). The Dutch were famous in Britain for their paintings of the sea and there are several examples here by Willem van de Velde, Jan van de Capelle and others.

Cut across Room 18 to see more Dutch painting in Room 21. **Aelbert Cuyp** developed his Mediterranean lighting effects under the influence of colleagues who had spent time in Italy, so while his *River Scene with Distant Windmills* (1640-2) lies under realistically grey northern clouds, later works such as *A Distant View of Dordrecht, with Five Cows ...* (c 1650-2) have a golden glow.

ROOMS 18-20 Move back to Room 18 for an overview of 17c French painting. At the end a huge portrait of *Cardinal Richelieu* (1633-40) by Philippe de Champaigne presides over the gallery as

Richelieu did over France - even the pink damask walls match his robes.

The key artist of the century was **Nicolas Poussin**, and Room 19 is devoted to him alone. It contains five of his original paintings of the *Seven Sacraments* (1637-42), in which Poussin used different permutations of gesture and ringing colour accents to achieve compositions that become more beautiful the longer you look. Also here are serene views of the Roman countryside, classical and biblical scenes, and the racy little *Nymph with Satyrs* (c 1627).

Room 20 shows more French paintings influenced by Rome, its countryside and antiquities, including those by Gaspard Dughet and **Claude**. His lovely little *Landscape with Hagar and the Angel* (1646) was admired by Constable.

ROOMS 30 Retrace your steps to Room 29 and leave it at the other end, into Room 30. This covers the rich period of Spanish painting in the 17c. Among the wonderful works by **Diego Velázquez** is the *Toilet of Venus* ('The Rokeby Venus'; 1647-51), a very rare female

Diego Velázquez *The Toilet of Venus* ('The Rokeby Venus'; 1647-51)

nude for this time in Spain, exchanging glances with the viewer via a mirror. In a portrait of *Philip IV in Brown and Silver* (c 1631-2) the king looks awkward under the artist's scrutiny: in another made 25 years later he just looks exhausted. *Kitchen Scene* (c 1618) combines still life, genre and religious painting in one.

Bartolomé Esteban Murillo is known for his paintings of children - as in his *Infant St John the Baptist with the Lamb* (1660-5). Francisco de Zurbarán used limited colours and stark lighting to focus on saintly sacrifice in *St Francis in Meditation* (1639), while the elongated figures and flickering colours of El Greco's *Purification of the Temple* (c 1600) have a hallucinatory quality.

ROOM 31 Here are a number of paintings connected with the court of Charles I in England, including **Van Dyck**'s huge *Charles I on Horseback* (c 1638) in which the king towers over us looking regal, as intended. The same artist depicted the effortlessly superior *Lord John Stuart and his Brother Lord Bernard Stuart* (c 1639), later victims of the Civil War. The captivating portrait of *A Woman and a Child* (1620-1) is from Van Dyck's earlier period around the time he went to Genoa.

ROOMS 32 AND 37 Room 32, the largest in the Gallery, is devoted to 17c Italy. *Supper at Emmaus* (1601) is the miraculous imagining by **Caravaggio** of the resurrected Christ's appearance to two disciples, whose thrusting elbow and outflung hand seem to extend into our own space. *Salome receives the Head of St John the Baptist* (1607-10), painted in the last years of his life, is grim: Salome cannot bear even to look at her trophy. There are a number of altarpieces by Guido Reni, including the huge *Adoration of the Shepherds* (c 1640), and shadowy paintings by Guercino and Salvator Rosa.

Room 37 (strictly speaking in the East Wing) has smaller paintings by some of the same artists. A stormy night illuminated by flares and bursts of moonlight is held in a tiny oil on copper, *St Paul on Malta* (c 1600) by Adam Elsheimer, a German who worked in Italy.

EAST WING: PAINTING 1700-1900

ROOMS 38-40 From the Central Hall, take the door on the right into Room 39. On one side are paintings from **18c Venice**. Pietro Longhi's *Exhibition of a Rhinoceros at Venice* (probably 1751) before masked carnival-goers is typical of his memorably simple scenes of such entertainments. Antonio Guardi makes the city seem breezier than in the older Canaletto's work. On the other side of the room are paintings by **Francisco de Goya**, including one of his portraits of the victorious *Duke of Wellington* (1812-14), loaded with military honours, and the sensuous *Doña Isabel de Porcel* (before 1805) wearing a skilfully scribbled mantilla.

Room 38 is full of work by **Canaletto**, reflecting his popularity with English patrons of his own time. *The Stonemason's Yard* (c 1728) is a record behind the scenes in the glittering tourist trap of Venice. The showier reality is seen in *Venice: Basin of San Marco on Ascension Day* (c 1740), in which the Doge's magnificent state barge is about to move off into the lagoon, accompanied by a shoal of gondolas.

Turn right in Room 36 to get to Room 40 and more 18c Venetian painting, this time made to please the locals. **Giovanni Battista Tiepolo**'s *Allegory with Venus and Time* (c 1754-8) was intended for a ceiling and is accordingly airy, in light, sweet colours.

ROOMS 34-36 The octagonal space of Room 36 shows 18c British portraits. Two early presidents of the Royal Academy are represented: their institution was at the forefront of efforts to improve the reputation of British art at home and abroad. *Colonel Banastre Tarleton* (1782) must surely have approved of his heroic action-man figure in his portrait by **Joshua Reynolds**. *Queen Charlotte* (1789-90) was less appreciative of Thomas Lawrence's efforts to make her look cheerful after the diagnosis of George III's dementia.

Walk straight on to Room 35 for more modestly scaled English 'conversation pieces', in which two or more figures are shown. Here **Thomas Gainsborough** has *Mr and Mrs Andrews* (1748-9) presiding a little stiffly over their chunk of Suffolk. Joseph Wright of Derby's marriage portrait for *Mr and Mrs Thomas Coltman* (c 1770-2) presents a much livelier couple. Coltman was the heir of a London coffee-house, an urban milieu familiar to William Hogarth, whose absorbing series *Marriage à la Mode* (c 1743) hangs nearby. In these theatrical little scenes every detail charts the terrible consequences of a loveless marriage contracted through greed. By contrast, his *Shrimp Girl* (c 1745) is a breezy, informal portrait of someone from a very different layer of the social orders.

Room 34 is hung with more British landscape and portraiture from 1750 to 1850. Here you might see famous Gainsboroughs, such as his late *The Morning Walk* (c 1785) with its feathery brushstrokes, but also some of the less familiar landscapes that he subsidized with earnings from his portraits. Besides the placemat-friendly *Hay Wain* (1821) there are beautiful sketches by **John Constable** of *Weymouth Bay* (1816-17) and *Salisbury Cathedral and Archdeacon Fisher's House* (1821), and a view of *Salisbury Cathedral from the Meadows* (1831) with a rough texture animated by slashes of paint from a palette knife. Among several iconic images by **J.M.W. Turner** are the *Fighting Téméraire* (1839), contrasting the elegant, ghostly warship to the squat tug towing it upriver to be broken up, and *Rain, Steam and Speed* (c 1844), evoking the excitement of travel on the Great Western Railway. But the single most eye-catching image in the whole gallery is *Whistlejacket* (c 1762) by **George Stubbs**. This Arab stallion was only a moderately successful racehorse but a very effective artist's model: the blank background against which he rears makes a large painting almost overwhelming.

ROOM 33 Leave Room 34 at one end to find 18c French painting, contrasting the Rococo frills of the court with more restrained domestic still lifes exemplified by *The Water Cistern* (c 1734) by **Jean-Simeon-Baptiste Chardin** and the cool greys and browns of his *House of Cards* (c 1736-7). The emergence of Jean-Honoré Fragonard's trademark eroticism is seen in *Psyche showing her Sisters her Gifts from Cupid* (1753). This style was favoured by *Madame de Pompadour*, Louis XV's powerful mistress and patron of the luxury arts, shown by François-Hubert Drouais in the year of her death (1764). Elisabeth Vigée-Lebrun also flourished at this time as a painter of women and children. Her artfully casual *Self-Portrait in a Straw Hat* (1782 or later) was inspired by Rubens' portrait of his sister-in-law Susanna Lunden in the Gallery.

ROOMS 41, 42 Return through Room 34 to reach Room 41 for French painting of the early 19c. The Gallery has few large-scale works but plenty of examples demonstrate the basic divergence of the Neoclassical and Romantic. The smooth surfaces and composure of *Madame Moitessier* (1844-56) represent the first of these. The enigmatic and ornamental Madame M. was ten years older by the time **J.-A.-D. Ingres** was content with his painting. *A Horse frightened by Lightning* (1813-14) by Théodore Géricault, on the other hand, is all about spontaneity and drama while the later twilit landscapes of **Camille Corot** evoke mood rather than a specific place. At the end of this period the realism of Gustave Courbet and **Jean-François Millet** wrenched attention towards political and social realities. Millet's *The Winnower* (c 1847-8) was his first major depiction of hard peasant life and its sale allowed him to continue painting.

Small Room 42 has Caspar David Friedrich's haunting, symbolic *Winter Landscape* (1811).

ROOMS 43, 44 The final rooms in this sequence are likely to be the most crowded, being devoted to Impressionism and Post-Impressionism, two of the most popular schools in the 20c. (Wednesday evenings seem to be a good time to get them to yourself.) There are a number of works by **Claude Monet**, including two of his 19 views of the Houses of Parliament, painted 30 years apart. Works from France show his interest in both the urban and rural - the *Gare St-Lazare* (1877) and *Poplars on the Epte* (1891), from one of his earliest series. Others span his career, from *La Pointe de la Hève, Ste-Adresse* (1864), a beach seen on a grey afternoon, to the sweeping, intensely coloured brushstrokes of *Irises* (c 1914-17).

Auguste Renoir captured the excitement of the big night out in *At the Theatre* (1876-7), while **Edouard Manet**'s *Corner of a Café-*

Concert (1877-9) and *Music in the Tuileries Gardens* (1862) glimpse two more aspects of 19c Parisian entertainment. Alongside these famous names is that of Gustave Caillebotte, who supported the Impressionists through purchases and exhibitions. His *Man at his Bath* (1884) is a bold attempt at depicting the male nude.

The broken brushstrokes and bright colour of **Camille Pissarro**'s work, including *Felix Pissarro* (1881), influenced the younger **Georges Seurat**. His Pointillist style used tiny dots of colour that he hoped would mix 'in the eye': it is seen in one of the figures in *Bathers at Asnières* (1883-4), a surprisingly cool painting for a supposedly hot sunny day, but is more evident in *Le Bec du Hoc, Grandcamp* (1885, reworked 1888), where Seurat even painted in a frame.

ROOMS 45, 46 The last two rooms show more of the Post-Impressionists, a more independent bunch than the closely knit Impressionists. Some were self-taught, such as **Henri Rousseau** whose hallucinatory *Tiger in a Tropical Storm* (1891) shows off his naive but imaginative style - he never saw a real jungle. **Vincent van Gogh** also had an unconventional art education and his images are some of the most famous in the Gallery. They include one of his paintings of *Sunflowers* (1888), made to welcome Gauguin to his house in Arles, and *Wheatfield with Cypresses* (1889), painted at the asylum where he recovered from the crisis the visit brought about. The colours are fresh but the clouds and hills seem to writhe. **Paul Gauguin** travelled further and further from the art world, eventually ending up in Tahiti. His dreamy *Vase of Flowers* (1896) was painted there. Also in self-imposed exile from Paris, **Paul Cézanne** spent his later years rebuilding the physical world in blocks of colour, as in *Hillside in Provence* (1886-90): his *Bathers* (1900-6) became a touchstone for the Cubists.

Finally, Room 46 returns us to Paris and the 50-year career of **Edgar Degas**, from an early mythological scene via dancers, bathers, cafés and the circus to *Combing the Hair* (c 1896), its intense colour reflecting the intimacy of the action.

LOWER FLOOR GALLERIES Above the stairs from Room 13 in the

West Wing, and in Room F immediately at the bottom, are a series of frescoes of the *Story of Apollo*, painted by Domenichino (1616-18) for a country villa near Rome. Rooms B-E and G display much of the reserve collection and are worth exploring if you cannot find a favourite painting in the main displays. Room A, accessible via the lobby of Room 15 in the North Wing, holds less important works and is open only on Wednesdays, 14.00-17.30.

Courtauld Gallery

OPEN	Mon-Sat 10.00-18.00, Sun and PH 12.00-18.00
CLOSED	1/1, Good Friday, 24-26/12
CHARGES	£5, concessions £4, free Mon 10.00-14.00 except PH, free for UK students, under 18s and unwaged.
TELEPHONE	**020 7848 2526**
WWW.	**courtauld.ac.uk** and **somerset-house.org.uk**
MAIN ENTRANCE	Somerset House, Strand
UNDERGROUND	Temple, Embankment, Charing Cross
DISABLED ACCESS	Lift to all floors, one bookable car parking space

The Gallery has a café and the shop an extensive stock of art books.

This world-class array of Western art, based on several private collections, begins with medieval pieces including carved ivories. The first-floor 'fine rooms' open with Renaissance painting and sculpture, including works by Botticelli and Giovanni Bellini, followed by Northern European masters, among them Lucas Cranach, a rare work by Pieter Brueghel the Elder, and landscapes and portraits by Rubens. 17c and 18c portraits include images by Van Dyck, Gainsborough and Goya.

On the second floor the Impressionist and Post-Impressionist masterpieces include Manet's *Bar at the Folies Bergère*, Van Gogh's *Self-portrait with Bandaged Ear* and haunting late Gauguins.

Somerset House was built in the 18c as offices for the navy and royal societies. The 18c King's Barge can be seen at the original river entrance. The fountain-filled courtyard has a café, holds concerts and family events in summer and becomes a skating rink in winter.

The **Gilbert Collection**, of over 800 items of silver and gold, hardstone and portrait miniatures is also housed here (entrance charge, *T* 020 7420 9400, www.gilbert-collection.org.uk), as are the **Hermitage Rooms**, which re-create interiors and display exhibits from the famous St Petersburg museum (entrance charge, timed tickets, *T* 020 7845 4630, www.hermitagerooms.com).

Somerset House The Nelson Stair

National Portrait Gallery

OPEN	Daily 10.00-18.00, Thur, Fri till 21.00
CLOSED	1/1, Good Friday, 24-26/12
CHARGES	Admission charge for special exhibitions
TELEPHONE	**020 7306 0055**
WWW.	**npg.org.uk**
MAIN ENTRANCE	St Martin's Place
UNDERGROUND	Charing Cross, Leicester Square
DISABLED ACCESS	Wheelchair access at Orange Street entrance

The shop has a good array of postcards and gifts inspired by the collection, and there is a bookshop in the basement.

Founded in 1856 to celebrate 'the most Eminent Persons in British History', the Gallery reflects the enduring popularity of portraiture as an art form in Britain. It now holds more than 10,000 paintings and sculptures - and 50,000 photographs - of Britons from monarchs to models. The displays are chronological, beginning with the Tudors on the second floor. They include some iconic images of personalities from Shakespeare to Blur, Elizabeth I to Churchill. Artists as various as Holbein, Sickert and David Bailey are represented, but the emphasis is on the sitter and amateurs - including Jane Austen's sister Cassandra, who made the only known portrait of the novelist from life - also have their place.

There are regular temporary exhibitions on the ground floor, including popular annual open competitions for painted and photographic portraits. Recent development has given the Gallery a grand new atrium and a restaurant with great views across Westminster.

View from restaurant at the National Portrait Gallery

on route

Banqueting House, Whitehall, entrance charge, Mon-Sat 10.00-17.00, **T** 0870 751 5178, www.hrp.org.uk. Designed by Inigo Jones (1622) and decorated by Peter Paul Rubens, this is the last remnant of the old Whitehall Palace and was the site of the execution of Charles I in 1649. It is occasionally closed for state occasions. **U** Charing Cross

Covent Garden The piazza (1639), the first square in London, and St Paul's church were designed by Inigo Jones. When aristocratic residents moved west it became a rather chaotic market, eventually housed in an elegant 1830s building which now shelters craft stalls and shops. Street performers and musicians play to large crowds. *U* Covent Garden

Institute of Contemporary Arts, The Mall, gallery daily 12.00-19.30, bar, restaurant and cinema Mon 12.00-22.30, Tues-Sat 12.00-01.00, Sun 12.00-23.00, *T* 020 7930 3647, www.ica.org.uk. For a daily membership you can see a contemporary art show or a film, hear a lecture, or use the bar and restaurant. *U* Charing Cross

Leicester Square Long a centre of entertainment - Turkish baths and oyster rooms in the 19c, and now nightclubs and some of the capital's largest cinemas - its status as a tourist magnet is inexplicable but you will probably find yourself crossing it anyway. *U* Leicester Square

London Transport Museum, Covent Garden Piazza, entrance charge (over 16s), daily 10.00-18.00, Fri 11.00-18.00, *T* 020 7379 6344, www.ltmuseum.co.uk. Not just a garage for old buses, trams and trains, but displays on everything from tunnelling to advertising, interactive exhibits, and a range of logo-emblazoned souvenirs. *U* Covent Garden

Photographers' Gallery, 5 and 8 Great Newport Street, Mon-Sat 11.00-18.00, Sun 12.00-18.00, *T* 020 7831 1772, www.photonet.org.uk. See a varied programme of exhibitions or use the reference library and café. Potential purchasers can receive advice. *U* Leicester Square

Royal Academy of Arts, Burlington House, Piccadilly, entrance charge for special exhibitions, daily 10.00-18.00, Fri till 22.00, *T* 020 7300 8000, www.royalacademy.org.uk. Britain's oldest institution devoted to the fine arts carries on its teaching and supportive role and presents important exhibitions on its main floor and in the Foster-designed Sackler Gallery. Its self-service café/restaurant is popular. *U* Green Park, Piccadilly Circus

St Martin-in-the-Fields, Trafalgar Square, *T* 020 7766 1100, box office *T* 020 7839 8362, www.stmartin-in-the-fields.org. Landmark church (1722-6) designed by James Gibb. Free lunchtime concerts most Mon, Tues, Fri at 13.05, and ticket-only evening concerts, especially of Baroque music (Handel played here). Outside is a craft market and the crypt houses a café, shop and brass-rubbing centre. *U* Charing Cross

Trafalgar Square Planned by John Nash in the early 19c and still a focal point for national celebrations and protests alike, the square is famous for Nelson's Column, and notorious for its gangs of pigeons. Pedestrianization of the northern half has eliminated some of the traffic.

Look out for the bronze of Charles I by Hubert Le Sueur (1633), looking down Whitehall to the place of his execution. *U* Charing Cross

commercial galleries

St James's and Mayfair, to the west of Trafalgar Square, are still London's prime art-dealing areas, with too many galleries to mention here. The greatest concentration lies along Cork Street and adjacent Albemarle, Clifford and Old Burlington Streets, with more up New Bond Street. South of Piccadilly, try Duke Street and Ryder Street. Opening times are generally Mon–Fri 10.00–17.30, Sat 10.00–13.00. The following list is intended to give an idea of their variety.

Alan Cristea Gallery, 31 Cork Street, *T* 020 7439 1866, www.alancristea.com. Prints by modern masters including Matisse and Picasso, and by living artists including David Hockney, Howard Hodgkin and Julian Opie. *U* Green Park

Chris Beetles, 8 and 10 Ryder Street, *T* 020 7839 7551, www.chrisbeetles.com. Selling exhibitions of 19c and 20c British oils, Louis Wain and great modern book illustrators. *U* Green Park

Contemporary Ceramics, 7 Marshall Street, *T* 020 7437 7605. Showcase for contemporary craftsmen and women, mostly from Britain, with a shop selling pieces at affordable prices. *U* Oxford Circus

Gagosian Gallery, 8 Heddon Street, *T* 020 7292 8222, www.gagosian.com. An international gallerist showing major contemporary artists from the YBAs Damien Hirst and Jenny Saville to Cy Twombly and Richard Serra. *U* Piccadilly Circus

Jill George Gallery, 38 Lexington Street, *T* 020 7439 7319, www.jillgeorgegallery.co.uk. Figurative and abstract work by British artists including the sculptor David Mach. *U* Piccadilly Circus

James Hyman Fine Art, 6 Mason's Yard, *T* 020 7839 3906, www.jameshymanfineart.com. 20c British (Cecil Collins, Bridget Riley) and international (Nan Goldin, Thomas Struth) art on show in the former

Indica Gallery, where John Lennon met Yoko Ono. **U** Green Park

Marlborough Fine Art, 6 Albemarle Street, **T** 020 7629 5161, www.marlboroughfineart.com. Paintings and sculpture by modern British and international artists, including Frank Auerbach, R.B. Kitaj and Paula Rego; also deals in modern master prints. **U** Green Park

Mayor Gallery, 22a Cork Street, **T** 020 7734 3558, www.artnet.com/mayor.html. The first gallery to open in Cork Street (1925), exhibiting 20c and contemporary work by British, European and American artists, including the Surrealists, Pop Artists and 'Kitchen Sink' school. **U** Green Park

Proud Galleries, 5 Buckingham Street, **T** 020 7839 4942, www.proud.co.uk. Popular shows of contemporary photography, often themed around music, fashion and sport. **U** Charing Cross

Rocket Gallery, 13 Old Burlington Street, **T** 020 7434 3043. You might see artists' books, contemporary photography or abstract work by established artists. **U** Piccadilly Circus

Sadie Coles HQ, 35 Heddon Street, **T** 020 7434 2227, www.sadiecoles.com. Contemporary British and American artists including Sarah Lucas and Elizabeth Peyton. **U** Piccadilly Circus

Waddington Galleries, 11 Cork Street, **T** 020 7581 2200, www.waddington-galleries.com. Major London gallery dealing in 20c masters - Josef Albert, Ivon Hitchens - and contemporary artists including Fiona Rae. **U** Green Park, Piccadilly Circus

eating and drinking

AT THE GALLERIES

NATIONAL GALLERY

£ **Gallery Café**, **T** 020 7747 2860. Serves sandwiches, cakes, teas and coffees in an unlovely but spacious basement. Current development plans will improve refreshment facilities. Self-service.

££ **Crivelli's Garden**, **T** 020 7747 2869. Named after Paula Rego's striking mural. Simple, modern Italian food. Lighter snacks (pizzas and panini) served at the bar. Waiter service.

COURTAULD GALLERY/SOMERSET HOUSE
£   **Gallery Café** (Courtauld), hot and cold food, waiter service; **Deli**, cold snacks to take away; **Courtyard Bar**, snacks and drinks in summer.

££   **River Terrace Restaurant** (Somerset House). Glamorous location by the riverside during summer months, serving a range of hot and cold dishes.

£££ **The Admiralty** (Somerset House), *T* 020 7845 4646. Sophisticated French cuisine, with a surprisingly good range of vegetarian options.

NATIONAL PORTRAIT GALLERY
£   **Portrait Café**. Slotted between the basement and the pavement, this is handy for a break between galleries. Small and can be very busy.

£££ **Portrait Restaurant**, *T* 020 7312 2490. Unorthodox views over gallery rooftops to Nelson's Column provide a spectacular backdrop to reliable modern European cuisine and a great oasis for gallery-goers. There is a lounge area for lighter snacks.

SURROUNDING AREA
£   **Bar Italia**, 22 Frith Street, *T* 020 7437 4520. Panini and coffee are available 24 hours a day at this Soho landmark. *U* Leicester Square

Café in the Crypt, St Martin-in-the-Fields, *T* 020 7839 4342. Atmospheric bolthole under the church, serving coffee, afternoon teas and a range of hot and cold meals and snacks. Its central location makes it a good place to meet. *U* Charing Cross

Café Amato, 14 Old Compton Street, *T* 020 7734 5733. A great range of reasonably priced patisserie overshadows the savoury dishes also available. *U* Leicester Square

Café Apogée, 3 Leicester Place, *T* 020 7437 4556. Good, Mediterranean-style salads, grilled meats and salads, and great juices. You can eat at tables outside. *U* Leicester Square

Food for Thought, 31 Neal St, *T* 020 7836 9072. Good-value vegetarian food at this cosy basement favourite. It may be hard to find a seat. No credit cards. *U* Covent Garden

Gaby's, 30 Charing Cross Road, *T* 020 7836 4233. Well-located outfit selling Middle Eastern staples and New York salt beef sandwiches, take away or eat in. No credit cards. *U* Leicester Square

India Club, 143 Strand, *T* 020 7836 0650. Well-placed for visitors to Somerset House, this unique 1950s throwback does good, simple and exceptionally cheap Indian food. *U* Temple

Maison Bertaux, 28 Greek Street, *T* 020 7437 6007. Quirky patisserie (founded in 1871), serving excellent croissants, cakes, tea and coffee at pavement tables. *U* Leicester Square

Paul, 29-30 Bedford Street, *T* 020 7836 3304. French teashop offering high-quality light lunches, fresh breads and tempting pastries to eat in or take away. *U* Covent Garden, Charing Cross

Pâtisserie Valerie, 44 Old Compton Street, *T* 020 7437 3466. This small patisserie chain is a good place for a continental breakfast, cakes and savoury snacks. There is another branch at 8 Russell Street in Covent Garden. *U* Leicester Square

Photographers' Gallery Café, 5 Great Newport Street, *T* 020 7831 1772. A 'nice, wholesome' retreat from Covent Garden shopping. *U* Leicester Square

Mezzo Café, 100 Wardour Street, *T* 020 7314 4000. Good-value Mediterranean-style light lunches (don't go into the neighbouring, and much more expensive, gastrodrome by mistake). It becomes a bar in the evening. *U* Piccadilly Circus

Mildred's, 45 Lexington Street, *T* 020 7494 1634. Popular vegetarian restaurant with a constantly changing menu of tasty soups, stir fries and pasta dishes. No credit cards. *U* Piccadilly Circus

Wagamama, 14A Irving Street, *T* 020 7839 2323. Branch of the canteen chain serving generous portions of noodles and rice in clattering minimalist surroundings. Set meals are good value. There is a Covent Garden branch at 1 Tavistock Street and a Soho branch at 10a Lexington Street. *U* Leicester Square

Zilli Café, 42-44 Brewer Street, *T* 020 7287 9233. Recent addition to chef Zilli's growing empire, with fresh pasta, sandwiches and soups to eat in or take away. It doubles as a food store. The more expensive fish restaurant is next door. *U* Piccadilly Circus

££ **Andrew Edmunds**, 46 Lexington Street, *T* 020 7437 5708. Great-value bistro food well-served in a relaxed, romantic setting. Recommended. *U* Piccadilly Circus

Cork and Bottle, 44-46 Cranbourn Street, *T* 020 7734 7807. This basement wine bar - intimate or cramped depending on whether you can get a table - is a reliable refuge from the fast-food hell at ground level, with a good wine list and menu of old favourites. Don't wander into the next-door sex shop by mistake. *U* Leicester Square

Gordon's Wine Bar, 47 Villiers Street, *T* 020 7930 1408. Layers of lovingly preserved dust cocoon London's oldest wine bar, lurking in a Thameside basement. It specializes in port, sherry and madeira but also has good-value wine, less good-value food and a terrace open in summer. *U* Charing Cross

Itsu, 103 Wardour Street, *T* 020 7479 4790. Tiny but tasty oriental dishes (sushi, noodle salads) served from a conveyor belt, to eat in or take away. *U* Piccadilly Circus

Kettner's, 29 Romilly Street, *T* 020 7734 6112. Oscar Wilde once ate here and some of his glamour lingers in the attractive ground-floor dining-room. The food (pizzas and burgers) is a cut above the usual fare from owners Pizza Express. *U* Leicester Square

Joy King Lau, 3 Leicester Street, *T* 020 7437 1132. Reliable Chinese with a wide choice of dim sum. *U* Leicester Square

Pizza Express, 450 Strand, *T* 020 7930 8205. This branch of the ubiquitous chain has a street-level bar and huge basement dining area. Branch at 10 Dean Street has live jazz nightly. *U* Charing Cross

Woodlands, 37 Panton Street, *T* 020 7839 7258. Vegetarian Indian food. The fixed-price lunch and pre-theatre buffets are good value in this district. *U* Piccadilly Circus

Zizzi, 73-75 Strand, *T* 020 7240 1450. Chain contending with Pizza Express for the area's hungry tourists, serving generous portions of pasta and pizza. Child-friendly. *U* Charing Cross

£££ **Alastair Little**, 49 Frith Street, *T* 020 7734 5183. Once ground-breaking and still great eclectic modern cuisine. *U* Leicester Square

L'Estaminet, 14 Garrick Street, *T* 020 7379 1432. Traditional French cooking at a long-established restaurant, with good pre-theatre deals. Wine bar downstairs. *U* Charing Cross

Gay Hussar, 2 Greek Street, *T* 020 7437 0973. Famous and still atmospheric Soho haunt serving Hungarian food. *U* Tottenham Court Road

Incognico, 117 Shaftesbury Avenue, *T* 020 7836 8866. Classy outpost of Nico Ladenis' restaurant empire, serving reliable, classic French food and a range of wines by the glass, with excellent set lunches and pre-theatre deals. *U* Tottenham Court Road

Lindsay House, 21 Romilly Street, *T* 020 7439 0450. Top British cuisine by Irish chef Richard Corrigan, served in a Georgian townhouse. Prices are stratospheric: try the set weekday lunch or pre-theatre meal. *U* Leicester Square

Quo Vadis, 26-29 Dean Street, *T* 020 7437 9585. Mediterranean-style food at one of Marco-Pierre White's stable of restaurants. Try not to think of Karl Marx and family starving in the garret above. *U* Leicester Square

Rules, 35 Maiden Lane, *T* 020 7836 5314. London's oldest restaurant, founded in 1798, is papered with memorabilia of famous patrons from Dickens to Edward VII and still serves a meaty menu including game and British beef. *U* Covent Garden

J. Sheekey, 28-32 St Martin's Court, *T* 020 7240 2565. This recently revived Theatreland restaurant now offers seriously good fish dishes, worth the money. There are cheaper set lunches at the weekend. *U* Leicester Square

LATE-NIGHT BARS

Lab, 12 Old Compton Street, *T* 020 7437 7820. The Lab in question being the London Academy of Bartenders, so expect supreme cocktails. Open Mon-Sat till 24.00, Sun till 10.30. *U* Piccadilly Circus

The Player, 8 Broadwick Street, *T* 020 7494 9125. Small, relaxed basement bar (under the lingerie shop Agent Provocateur) with friendly staff and a wide cocktails list. Pre-book and note it's members-only after 23.00. Open Mon-Thur till 24.00, Fri, Sat till 1.00. *U* Oxford Circus

Sak Bar, 49 Greek Street, *T* 020 7439 4159. Moodily lit Soho bar/lounge with low sofas and tables. Professional staff mix pricey cocktails. Crowded at weekends. Open Mon till 24.00, Tues till 1.00, Wed-Sat till 3.00, Sun till 10.30. *U* Leicester Square

shopping

This section makes no apologies for focusing on books: Charing Cross Road is known to bibliophiles the world over. Denmark Street, or 'Tin Pan Alley', is still a magnet for musicians, while further east Covent Garden is the place for some great fashion and food shops.

ACCESSORIES

American Retro, 35 Old Compton Street, **T** 020 7734 3477, www.americanretro.com. Whacky urban accessories (French Kitty, Paul Frank, Emily), cards and clothes. **U** Leicester Square

Stephen Jones, 36 Great Queen Street, **T** 020 7242 0770, www.stephenjonesmillinery.com. Couture and bridal headgear from one of London's top hatmakers. **U** Covent Garden, Holborn

Kirk Originals, 29 Floral Street, **T** 020 7240 5055, www.kirkoriginals.com. Old-established opticians making limited-edition frames in retro styles. **U** Covent Garden

BOOKS

Cecil Court, between Charing Cross Road and St Martin's Lane. A tiny street of shops full of books and printed ephemera, from Victorian music hall posters to Beatles memorabilia, maps and prints. **U** Leicester Square

Dover Bookshop, 18 Earlham Street, **T** 020 7836 2111, www.doverbooks.co.uk. Devoted to the famous publications of copyright-free images, paper dolls and other treats. **U** Covent Garden

Foyles, 113-119 Charing Cross Road, **T** 020 7437 5660, www.foyles.co.uk. Huge and famously eccentric old store, now more customer-friendly (even bland) but still carrying a huge stock. Women's bookshop Silver Moon is now on the top floor. **U** Tottenham Court Road

Hatchards, 187 Piccadilly, **T** 020 7439 9921, www.hatchards.co.uk. Founded in 1797 and on this site since 1801, this well-stocked store offers both creaky atmosphere and good service. **U** Piccadilly Circus

Helter Skelter, 4 Denmark Street, **T** 020 7836 1151, www.helterskelterbooks.com. Fanzines and rock-related books from biographies to lyric-writing guides, on the site of the Regent Sounds studio where the Rolling Stones, Kinks and Hendrix once recorded. *U* Tottenham Court Road, Leicester Square

Murder One, 71-73 Charing Cross Road, *T* 020 7734 3483, www.murderone.co.uk. Blood-curdling array of fictional and true crime books, magazines and videos. Horror, fantasy and SF lurk in the basement. *U* Leicester Square.

Shipley's, 70 Charing Cross Road, *T* 020 7836 4872, www.artbook.co.uk. Towering shelves of new, second-hand and rare books on art, architecture, and much more. *U* Tottenham Court Road, Leicester Square

Sports Pages, Caxton Walk, 94-96 Charing Cross Road, *T* 020 7240 9604, www.sportspages.co.uk. Britain's first specialist sports bookshop with plenty of overseas titles, so you'll find baseball and petanque besides cricket and pigeon-racing. *U* Tottenham Court Road

Edward Stanford, 12-14 Long Acre, *T* 020 7836 1321, www.stanfords.co.uk. Packed with inspirational travel guides, maps and globes; recently refurbished and now on three floors. *U* Covent Garden

CLOTHES

Agnès B, 35-36 Floral Street, *T* 020 7379 1992, www.agnesb.fr. Understated French clothes for men and women. *U* Covent Garden

Beau Monde, 43 Lexington Street, *T* 020 7734 6563, www.beaumonde.uk.com. Classy made-to-measure clothes (and matching handbags) 'for the busy woman'. *U* Piccadilly Circus

Carhartt, 56 Neal Street, *T* 020 7836 5659, www.thecarharttstore.co.uk. Trendy American workwear for men. *U* Covent Garden

Duffer of St George, 29 and 34 Shorts Gardens, *T* 020 7379 4660. Own-brand clothes and other designer labels including Pringle, vintage Levis and Clements Ribeiro. *U* Covent Garden, Leicester Square

Koh Samui, 65-67 Monmouth Street, *T* 020 7240 4280. Stocks pieces by young British designers (Julien Macdonald, Luella Bartley) and as-yet-unknowns. *U* Covent Garden, Leicester Square

Nicole Farhi, 11 Floral Street, *T* 020 7497 8713. Grown-up French fashion for men and women in muted colours and fine fabrics. *U* Covent Garden

Paul Smith, 40-44 Floral Street, *T* 020 7379 7113, www.paulsmith.co.uk.

Colourful shop with witty clothes for men and women by the renowned British designer. **U** Covent Garden

Souvenir, 47 Lexington Street, **T** 020 7287 9877. Chic clothes, shoes and accessories by designers including Dior and Marc Jacobs. **U** Piccadilly Circus

COSMETICS & HEALTH

Lush, Unit 11, Covent Garden Market, **T** 020 7240 4570, www.lush.co.uk. Handmade soaps that look and smell good enough to eat (don't). **U** Covent Garden

Neal's Yard Remedies, 15 Neal's Yard, **T** 020 7379 7222, www.nealsyardremedies.com. Essential oils, herbal teas and natural concoctions with which to pamper skin and hair. **U** Covent Garden

Pout, 32 Shelton Street, **T** 020 7379 0379, www.pout.co.uk. Try out a new you at this fun-loving beauty parlour, offering manicures, makeovers, own-name and international products. **U** Covent Garden

Space.NK Apothecary, 4 Thomas Neal Centre, Earlham Street, **T** 020 7379 7030, www.spacenk.co.uk. Tranquil store offering advice on make-up, skincare and haircare as well as beauty products from around the world for men and women. **U** Covent Garden

DEPARTMENT STORES

Fortnum & Mason, 181 Piccadilly, **T** 020 7734 8040, www.fortnumandmason.com. The Queen's grocer (founded 1707) occupies an elegant building with famous window displays. Inside the premium goodies include fine teas and hampers. Clothes and luxury items are upstairs and household goods below. **U** Green Park

FLOWERS

Wild Bunch, 17 Earlham Street, **T** 020 7497 1200. A good range of flowers and plants from an extensive roadside stall. **U** Covent Garden

FOOD

Carluccio's, 28A Neal Street, **T** 020 7240 1487, www.carluccios.com. Excruciatingly tempting (and expensive) Italian provisions, plus sandwiches, quiches and cakes to take away. **U** Covent Garden

Fresh and Wild, 71-75 Brewer Street, **T** 020 7240 1487, www.freshandwild.com. Organic and Fairtrade produce for the virtuous, plus natural remedies, grocery, coffee and juice bar. **U** Piccadilly Circus

Lina Stores, 18 Brewer Street, **T** 020 7437 6482. Delectable Italian deli, specializing in fresh pasta; recommended by Jamie Oliver. **U** Piccadilly Circus

Monmouth Coffee House, 27 Monmouth Street, **T** 020 7836 5272. Small, fragrant shop said to supply the finest coffee in London. **U** Covent Garden

Neal's Yard Dairy, 17 Shorts Gardens, **T** 020 7240 5700. Fine British cheeses (and chutneys and yoghurts), lovingly cared for. You can nibble before buying. **U** Covent Garden

GIFTS

Anything Left-Handed, 57 Brewer Street, **T** 020 7437 3910, www.anythingleft-handed.co.uk. There is also an extensive mail-order service for all things sinistral. **U** Piccadilly Circus

G. Smith & Sons, 74 Charing Cross Road, **T** 020 7836 7422. Trying to give up nicotine? The display in the alluring red-and-gold window of this 'noted snuff shop' (founded 1869) won't help at all. **U** Leicester Square

The Tintin Shop, 34 Floral Street, **T** 020 7836 1131, www.thetintinshop.co.uk. Books, posters, T-shirts, DVDs and even crockery starring the Belgian sleuth. **U** Covent Garden

JEWELLERY

florence-b, 37a Neal Street and 25a Old Compton Street, **T** 020 7240 6332. Showcase for new designers. **U** Covent Garden

KIDS

Benjamin Pollock's Toy Shop, 44 Covent Garden Market, **T** 020 7379 7866, www.pollocks-coventgarden.co.uk. Old-fashioned toys, especially paper theatres and dolls. **U** Covent Garden

Child, 49 Shelton Street, **T** 020 7240 6060. Clothing and accessories, for the fashionable 0-6s. **U** Covent Garden

LINGERIE

Agent Provocateur, 6 Broadwick Street, *T* 020 7439 0229, www.agentprovocateur.com. Raunchier than your average undies. *U* Oxford Circus

MUSIC

Ray's Jazz Shop, Foyles (see above), *T* 020 7440 3205. Jazz and world music from long-established shop saved from closure by Foyles. Nice. *U* Tottenham Court Road, Leicester Square

Rose Morris, 11 Denmark Street, *T* 020 7836 0991. A six-floor music store with books, tutorial videos (deconstructing Metallica basslines, for example), guitars and recording equipment. *U* Tottenham Court Road, Leicester Square

Macari's Musical Instruments, 92 Charing Cross Road, *T* 020 7836 2856, www.macaris.co.uk. Everything to make a noise with, from saxophones to mandolins. *U* Leicester Square

Vintage and Rare Guitars, 6 Denmark Street, *T* 020 7240 7500, www.vintageandrareguitars.com. A window to press your nose against even if you can't play a note. *U* Tottenham Court Road, Leicester Square

SHOES

Camper, 39 Floral Street, *T* 020 7379 6878, www.camper.es. Comfy and colourful bowling shoes from Spain. *U* Covent Garden

Dr Marten Department Store, 1-4 King Street, *T* 020 7497 1460, www.drmartens.com. Superstore for this world-famous brand, with a range of clothing too. *U* Covent Garden

Natural Shoe Store, 21 Neal Street, *T* 020 7836 5254, www.thenaturalshoestore.com. Comfy and ecologically sound footwear. *U* Covent Garden

BLOOMSBURY

British Museum

OPEN	Exhibition areas and Reading Room Sat-Wed 10.00-17.30, Thur-Fri 10.00-20.30 (some rooms till 17.30); Great Court Sun-Wed 9.00-18.00, Thur-Sat 9.00-23.00
CLOSED	1/1, Good Friday, 24-26/12
CHARGES	Admission free to exhibition areas, Great Court, Reading Room; charge for special exhibitions, some guided tours and audio tours
TELEPHONE	**020 7323 8181** for tickets to special exhibitions and events
RECORDED INFO	**020 7323 8000**
WWW.	**thebritishmuseum.ac.uk**
MAIN ENTRANCE	Great Russell Street; northern entrance on Montague Place
UNDERGROUND	Holborn, Russell Square, Tottenham Court Road
DISABLED ACCESS	Most rooms accessible to wheelchairs, which can be borrowed at the entrances; to book parking spaces **T 020 7323 8299**
GUIDED TOURS	Guided tours introduce Museum highlights (daily at 10.30, 13.00 and 15.00, £8, reduced price £5); shorter EyeOpener tours focus on specific galleries (daily at various times, free but donation recommended). Audio tours of highlights or the Parthenon sculptures, or offering family activities, are available at the ticket office in Great Court (£3.50). There are induction loops for talks and tours and regular sign-interpreted talks
SERVICES	Information desk in Great Court. Cloakrooms inside main and northern entrances. Toilets throughout building; baby-changing only on main and lower floors
SHOPS	Large bookshop, souvenir and children's shops in Great Court; smaller shops for items related to exhibitions in Rooms 5 and 90; Grenville Shop off the atrium sells more expensive gifts - good replicas, jewellery, silk scarves; as does the British Museum Shop at the corner of Great Russell Street and Bloomsbury Street
EATING	Cafés in the Great Court; Gallery Café off Room 12 in the west wing; Court Restaurant above the Reading Room on Level 3

The Museum presents regular special exhibitions and events (details and tickets from the desks in Great Court).

British Museum Great Court

The British Museum is one of London's oldest free tourist destinations, and still the most popular. Each year close to 6 million people come to see its vast collection of artefacts - which include some of the most famous archaeological discoveries ever made - from cultures around the world, and since the recent opening of the Great Court it has become an architectural attraction, too.

It was founded in 1753 at the instigation of Sir Hans Sloane, whose will offered his personal collections of art, antiquities and natural history to the nation at a bargain price. At the same time two collections of books and manuscripts were bought from the Harley and Cotton families. Funds to house this embryonic national museum and library at Montagu House in Bloomsbury were raised by a lottery and in 1759 it opened, although the general public were admitted only in 1879.

The Museum was continually augmented by all kinds of donations, from the Royal Library given by George II in 1757 to artefacts picked up by Captain Cook on his travels in the South Seas. The explorers, soldiers, missionaries and merchants of the expanding British Empire supplied natural curiosities, ethnographical items, art and antiquities; in the 20c, it received the spectacular archaeological finds from Sutton Hoo and Mildenhall. Parts of the original collection have been diverted over the years (pictures to the National Gallery, botanical and zoological specimens to the Natural History Museum, books and manuscripts to the British Library) but acquisition continues and there are now more than 6 million items.

THE BUILDING

The original collections rapidly outgrew Montagu House, and in 1823 work began on a much more impressive building on the same site. Its designer, Robert Smirke, had travelled in the Mediterranean to study classical buildings and the Museum's huge portico of Ionic columns advertises his brand of Greek Revival architecture. The whole edifice was completed in 1847, by which time Smirke had retired and been replaced by his brother, Sydney.

The sculpted figures huddling under the pediment represent the progress of civilization. They overlook a forecourt that manages to look bleak at most times of year. This was Sydney's work, but he compensated by installing the exquisite circular Reading Room (see below) in the Great Court in the 1850s. Over time, the spaces around the Reading Room were filled with functional buildings to house the book stacks and the Great Court effectively disappeared. Only in 2000, after the long-delayed removal of the new British Library to St Pancras, did it become accessible to the public. The Great Court is now the largest covered public square in Europe, with a high-tech roof designed by Foster and Partners and a replica portico (in controversial French stone) completing Smirke's original plan.

HIGHLIGHTS

Rosetta Stone, key to ancient Egyptian hieroglyphs	Room 4
Sculpted door guardians and royal lion hunts from the Assyrian palaces at Nimrud and Nineveh	Rooms 6–10
Parthenon sculptures (the 'Elgin Marbles')	Room 18
Cast brass heads and wall plaques from Benin	Room 25
Europe's foremost collection of Chinese antiquities and Indian sculpture	Room 33
Spectacular pottery from Iran and Turkey	Room 34
Sutton Hoo ship burial	Room 41
Lindow Man, the Iron Age bog burial	Room 50
Treasures from the Royal Tombs at Ur	Room 56
Egyptian mummies and sarcophagi	Rooms 62, 63
Money Gallery, with over 750,000 coins	Room 68
Works on paper, especially Old Master prints and drawings	Room 90

In its entirety the British Museum is a daunting prospect: the following description is not intended as a tour but introduces each department - in alphabetical order - and points out some highlights. Certain rooms have limited opening hours: check ahead or at the information desk.

The collections are mainly arranged around the Great Court in the three wings behind the frontage. The west wing has galleries on three floors, the east wing on two; the north wing is divided into Levels -1 to 5. Ancient Greece and Rome and the Near East are covered in the **west wing**, mostly on the main floor, where you can also see Egyptian sculptures. More Near Eastern and Egyptian antiquities can be found in the **north wing**, on Level 3. At the top of this wing, on Level 5, are changing displays from the Japanese collections, and on Level 4 temporary exhibitions of prints and drawings. There is a room devoted to the arts of Korea on Level 2 and the Chinese and Indian exhibits occupy the whole of Level 1. The new ethnographic and American galleries are on the main floor and the Islamic arts on Level -1, by the north entrance. The African galleries are in the basement. The main floor of the **east wing** is occupied by the newly refurbished King's Library. Above it are more Near Eastern antiquities, a room on Bronze Age and Celtic Europe and one on Roman Britain, which leads into a loop of galleries dealing with Europe from the Vikings to the 20c. Finally, the **south wing**, which links to both east and west wings, has two more rooms on prehistory and the Money Gallery.

Doorways in each portico of the Great Court give access to the different wings of the building and provide escape routes and shortcuts around the labyrinth.

ENTRANCE AND GREAT COURT

FRONT HALL To the right of the doors a weathered statue of Sir Hans Sloane, on whose bequest the Museum was founded, surveys the entering crowds. Beyond this is the entrance to **The King's Library**. One of the finest Neoclassical interiors in London, it has been restored to house a new exhibition on the 18c

BRITISH MUSEUM
Main Floor

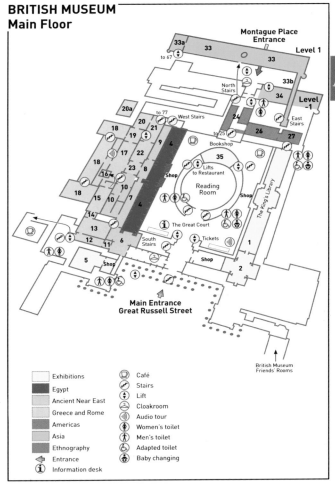

Montague Place Entrance

Level 1

Main Entrance
Great Russell Street

British Museum
Friends' Rooms

- Exhibitions
- Egypt
- Ancient Near East
- Greece and Rome
- Americas
- Asia
- Ethnography
- Entrance
- (i) Information desk

- Café
- Stairs
- Lift
- Cloakroom
- Audio tour
- Women's toilet
- Men's toilet
- Adapted toilet
- Baby changing

Enlightenment, the intellectual context for the Museum's foundation 250 years ago.

Turn left from the main doors to reach the special exhibitions galleries, Near Eastern and Classical antiquities, and eventually the Gallery Café. The recently restored coffered **ceiling** of the front hall is a colourful Victorian interpretation of Greek painted architecture.

GREAT COURT Move forward into the Queen Elizabeth II Great Court, the new centrepiece of the Museum. Foster and Partners covered the space with individually shaped glass panels held in a steel web, opening it to the rapidly changing London skies while offering protection to visitors all year round. Ancient sculptures are all around, but only the ancestral figure from Easter Island (c AD 1000) and a rugged Hellenistic lion (late 4c-early 3c BC) quite hold their own against the surrounding forest of signposts.

Most days the Great Court echoes to the babble of school children clutching clipboards, but even they respect the hush of the famous **Reading Room** that stands at the centre, cocooned in a white cylinder with staircases to an exhibition space and restaurant spiralling up each side.

The idea for a circular room is credited to Antonio Panizzi, who became Principal Librarian, and thus head of the Museum, in 1857. It was built by Sydney Smirke. At over 32m high and 43m in diameter the dome is only just smaller than the Pantheon in Rome. It is supported by 2000 tons of cast iron, which also forms the framework of the desks: the pipes below them were both footrests and part of the heating system. The beautiful ceiling is a kind of papier mâché. In its heyday, the Reading Room had 24,000 books for reference on the ground floor and 80,000 on shelves; the catalogue was kept at the central desk, from which the librarian supervised his clientele.

This magnificent room has been painstakingly restored and its research facilities are now open to all visitors. The viewing area is lined with books written by famous earlier users (Karl Marx, George Eliot, Arthur Conan Doyle and many more). To each side are screens for the COMPASS multimedia system, with information

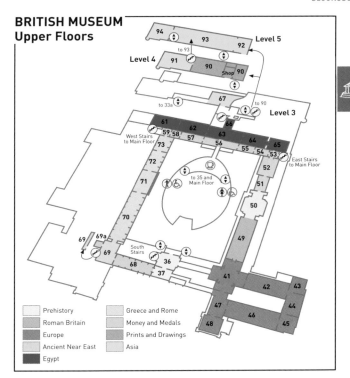

on around 5000 objects; you can plan your visit or order a print of a favourite item from here. Beyond is a new reference library of books and magazines on the cultures represented in the Museum.

The development of the Great Court has allowed for a separate **Young Visitors' Centre** to be built underneath, into which the tiny hordes descend for lunch. (This can be used by families at weekends and during school holidays.)

AFRICA AND THE AMERICAS

AFRICA *Room 25* Artefacts from Africa are found throughout the Museum, but the enthnography galleries in the basement of the north wing show the continuity of social and craft traditions on the modern continent. Many exhibits were made in the 19c and 20c and each room screens videos of traditional arts as practised today. In the first display by **contemporary African artists**, you may see a striking throne by Kester (2001), made of rusting debris from Mozambique's civil war.

Turn left into a room of **woodcarving**. Wood can be used to make domestic and ceremonial objects or figures with spiritual power. The two-headed dog Kozo, from the Congo, bristles with the iron nails that activate his intervention in human life. Items of **forged iron** signified status in trade, religion and war. One elegant display demonstrates the variety of design in the 'throwing knives' of Central Africa. In many societies, smiths are male and respected for their magical powers. By contrast, **pottery** is often an exclusively female art. Practical containers for water, beer and oil often have beautiful shapes and surface finishes but are also symbolically related to key events in life: pots may be made for a marriage and destroyed at death.

Double back to see a display on **masquerade**. This performance marks the transformation of men by the powers they wish to invoke - beasts, spirits, foreigners, witches and the dead; the costumes often reflect animal characteristics, as in the lethal-looking swordfish masks worn by young men. As with pottery, **textiles** play a vital practical and symbolic role in rites of passage and are made with a wide variety of techniques and materials, from mud and rafia to rayon and lurex. The highlight of the last room is the work of the Yoruba and Edo peoples of Nigeria. The former made a powerfully realized bronze head of the king or Oni (12c-14c), while the Edo's fine **cast brass figures**, heads and wall plaques were made in the 16c to decorate the royal palace.

WELLCOME TRUST GALLERY OF ETHNOGRAPHY *Room 24* Return to the main floor to see the recently opened centrepiece of the Ethnography Department's displays. It is named for Sir Henry

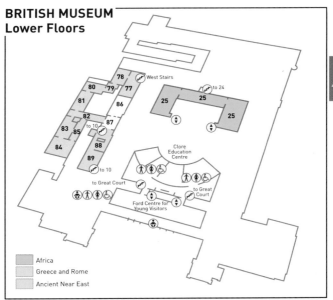

BRITISH MUSEUM
Lower Floors

78
80 79 77   West Stairs
81
86
82
87
83 85   to 10
84
88
89   to 10

25   25
25

Clore
Education
Centre

to Great Court

to Great
Court

Ford Centre for
Young Visitors

Africa

Greece and Rome

Ancient Near East

Wellcome whose medical trust continues research into health and medicine, and the exhibits look at the associated issues of **wellbeing and misfortune** in many cultures.

AMERICAS *Rooms 26, 27* Room 26, also on the main floor, focuses on **North America**, past and present, and the first contact between the different native peoples and European explorers in the 16c. Cultures from the Arctic to New Mexico are illustrated by a changing selection of clothes, domestic utensils, weaponry and religious items, and modern examples of traditional art forms. Some of the oldest objects here are stone arrow heads and pipes in the form of local birds and animals, which have survived from the settlements of the Woodland peoples (from 500 BC). The skills of the native peoples of the Arctic are represented by parkas made of gut and fox fur (the effectiveness of the former impressed the Royal Navy), and their close relationship with the animals they hunted by carved walrus ivory figures and tools and a decoy helmet in the form of a seal's head. Pueblo potters from New Mexico continue a tradition 2000 years old, making vessels with bold abstract patterns (and the occasional bird) in black or brown on white. From the Northern Plains comes a man's fringed, buffalo-hide cloak painted with his autobiography.

Room 27 holds spectacular artefacts from the earliest civilizations of **Mexico**, from the Olmecs (from 1200 BC) to the Aztecs (1300-1521). All the peoples of this region revered green stones, which were associated with water and thus with fertility, and some of the most striking artworks are jade masks carved by the Olmecs. The sophisticated city states of the Maya, in the Yucatan peninsula, produced the stone lintels displayed along one wall (AD 600-800): these depict bloodletting rituals and their controlled, compact designs are as unsettling as the subject matter. Mixtec craftsmen were employed by the Aztecs to make intricate gold jewellery and objects covered with turquoise mosaic – another green stone – including a fierce double-headed serpent (15c-16c). Aztec art revolved around propitiating their often

Mosaic mask of Tezcatlipoca (Aztec/Mixtec, 15c–16c, Mexico)

bloodthirsty gods: there are sculptures of imposing seated deities and the animals associated with them, such as a magnificent granite rattlesnake.

ANCIENT NEAR EAST

ASSYRIA *Rooms 6-10, 88, 89* Appropriately, the first sight to greet you in Room 6 is of two colossal **guardian figures** that stood outside the throneroom of Ashurnasirpal II (883-859 BC) at Nimrud, the city he founded. The details of their beards, fur and harnesses are still crisp. Ashurnasirpal and his son Shalmaneser were the two most important rulers of Assyria, now Iraq, which dominated much of Mesopotamia from the 11c to the 8c BC. The huge doors of the palace Shalmaneser built at Balawat have been reconstructed from their bronze fittings decorated with hundreds of tiny figures; look down at the stone doorsill, exquisitely carved to resemble a carpet. Room 7 contains an awe-inspiring sequence of **carved wall panels** from Ashurnasirpal's North-West Palace, depicting the king in religious processions, hunting, and conquering enemies. Though impressively stylized, the low-relief panels include naturalistic details; look out for the king's tank-like siege engine, and soldiers bobbing across a river on inflated animal skins.

Rooms 8 and 9 have carvings from later palaces. If short of time double back to Room 10 to find more magnificent panels depicting **royal lion hunts**, symbolic of the ruler's ability to protect his people, from the palace of Ashurbanipal (668-627 BC) at Nineveh. Panels showing the same king at war are in Room 89 downstairs, with smaller items including cuneiform tablets and a complicated mould for making arrowheads. Room 88 has a small display of finds from New Testament lands, and a column base from Persepolis, capital of the Persian empire (5c BC).

LEVANT *Rooms 57-59* Go up the West Stairs, past Roman mosaics from Asia Minor and North Africa, to Room 59. This introduces the civilizations of the Levant - Syria, Jordan, Lebanon and Israel. Room 58 re-creates a rock-cut tomb at Jericho from the Early or

Middle Bronze Age (1800-1700 BC), with grave goods, and part of a Jordanian palace scullery (3c BC) complete with the remains of a dinner party. Room 57 follows the invasion of the region by Egypt, the arrival of the **Philistines** - look out for their striking clay anthropoid coffin lids - and the influence of the Assyrians and Babylonians. It also explains the evolution from languages written in cuneiform, which had around 800 signs, to the Canaanite alphabet with around 24 - the foundation of the Greek and later all Western alphabets.

MESOPOTAMIA *Rooms 55, 56* Room 56 shows extraordinary artefacts from early Mesopotamia and Syria, where the first cities developed around 4000 BC and the Sumerians and Babylonians began to write and to count. The earliest cuneiform tablets (c 3000 BC) record rations of beer and barley rather than the doings of kings. The **Royal Tombs at Ur** (c 2600 BC) may in fact have been the final resting-places of religious officials. In any case the principals were accompanied into the afterlife by dozens of richly dressed attendants. Besides beautiful beads of precious stone and diadems of gold leaves, the grave goods include vessels for cosmetics, pieces of a board game and musical instruments. The Royal Standard of Ur may also have been part of an instrument: it is inlaid in shell, lapis and red limestone with scenes of war and peace. Room 55 has a masterpiece of Assyrian sculpture, the **Dying Lion** from Nineveh (c 645 BC) and some of the 20,000 clay tablets from Ashurbanipal's library, including the *Epic of Gilgamesh*.

ANATOLIA *Rooms 53, 54* These small rooms cover Anatolia from prehistory to Alexander the Great, including gold and ivory figurines from the **Hittite civilization** (1400 BC). This collapsed around 1200 BC but re-emerged in Syria where the city of Carchemish produced basalt lion heads (9c BC) and wall reliefs with hieroglyphic inscriptions.

IRAN *Room 52* At the top of the East Stairs, turn right into Room 52 to be confronted by a spear carrier modelled in coloured glazed brick, who introduces pre-Islamic Iran (6000 BC–AD 642). He comes from a palace at Susa, a key city in the Achaemenid empire (6c–4c BC), whose influence at one time stretched from the Aegean to Pakistan. The most striking objects here are thin plaques incised with human figures, a tiny model of a charioteer, a vessel in the realistic form of a fish, and magnificent armlets terminating in griffins' heads: all are of gold and from the **Oxus Treasure** (5c–4c BC) found in the 19c.

PALMYRA AND SOUTHERN ARABIA *Room 51* The lost oasis city of Palmyra (2c AD) in Syria was rediscovered in the 18c; its funerary sculpture demonstrates an angular take on the Roman style, with several **portrait busts** of women wearing elaborate jewellery. This room also contains religious objects from Southern Arabia (6c BC).

ASIA

ISLAM *Room 34* The other entrance to the Museum is in the north wing, from Montague Place. To the left, on Level -1, is the beautifully displayed collection of the arts of Islam. The first exhibits - a selected Koran in elegant script, a set of Iranian lustre tiles with a raised inscription (early 14c) - introduce the importance of **calligraphy**, which appears throughout the gallery. Also near the entrance is an astrolabe (17c) that was part of Sir Hans Sloane's collection and stands for the advanced scientific understanding in Islamic lands.

   Under the Mamluks (1250-1517), Cairo and Damascus were the main centres of power and cultural productivity. Especially impressive are their enamelled and gilded **glass mosque lamps**. Earlier pottery was inspired by Chinese imports; from Egypt there are beautiful jars and vases in blue, black and white, while 12c and 13c Iran introduced fritware painted with multicoloured enamels (*minai*). From the Ottoman empire there is a spectacular display of every period of **Iznik pottery**, from blue-and-white imitations of Chinese wares (1470s), to later pieces with a wider range of colours, including green and purple. A space set aside for

paintings and photographs is hushed by a specially made Turkish carpet (1989). A wonderful jade terrapin (c 1600) introduces the art of the Mughals in India (1453-19c) and their love of natural history, seen in every element of their decorative arts. The end of the gallery displays armour, coins, and more scientific instruments.

Head for the North Stairs, passing a small case which currently displays board games from India, where chess and even snakes and ladders originated. A set of red and green Indian chessmen (19c) demonstrate the game's roots in battlefield tactics.

CHINA *Room 33* As you enter the room from the North Stairs, the arts of China stretch out on your right: for a chronological tour, move round anti-clockwise, starting on the inner wall. The displays begin with axes and smooth, chunky discs of **jade**, from the Neolithic (4500-2500 BC). An impressive array of ceremonial objects in **bronze**, another revered substance, includes sturdy vessels, bells and drums from various periods. The Han dynasty (206 BC-AD 220), contemporaries of the Romans, created China's centralized bureaucracy and under them its material culture expanded, even into the afterlife: burial goods became more common and to discourage looters fierce ceramic **guardian figures** were placed in tombs. In a central case is an impressive entourage, including pairs of guardians, horses and laden camels (early 8c), from the dynamic Tang period (618-916).

The earliest **porcelain** was in wonderfully simple shapes, mostly monochrome with sparing decoration. Buddhism was in the ascendant by AD 450, and **Buddhist figures** are everywhere. At the end of the gallery, in faded pastel colours, is a painting on plaster of three Bodhisattvas from a temple at Xingtang Xian (15c). Before it sit three life-size figures of holy men, each projecting a very different personality. From here Room 33b leads to the East Stairs; it currently has a beautiful display of jade.

Displays on the other side of the room begin with one of **writing implements**, the tools of an official's trade. The Ming dynasty (1368-1644) is famous in the West for its porcelain, but other luxury items were perfected at this time, such as amazing **carved**

lacquer and enamelling. The Qing dynasty (1644-1911) continued to refine all this, producing porcelain in startling new colours (see the cups in pink and lime-green enamels), and collected the arts of the past.

SOUTH AND SOUTHEAST ASIA *Rooms 33, 33a* A gilded Tara with an impressive hourglass figure introduces the display. She was cast in one piece of bronze in Sri Lanka (7c-8c). On the inner wall there is a section on Indian prehistory and then the chief **Hindu deities** - Shiva, Vishnu, Indra - are introduced.

Seated Buddha (late 18c–early 19c, Burma)

All are illustrated with fine religious statuary in stone and cast bronze: do not miss the wondrously balanced figure of Shiva dancing in a ring of flames (c 1100). On the other side of the room are the arts of Vietnam, Thailand and the Himalayas. At the far end of the gallery, Room 33A contains impressive sculpture from the **Great Stupa at Amaravati** (3c BC-3c AD). Look out for lovely elephants on a section of railing, and a panel with a pair of feet, an early means of representing the Buddha.

KOREA *Room 67* Go further up the North Stairs to Level 2, passing four wooden Buddhist statues from China, including an exquisitely elegant and relaxed *Avalokitesvara* (11c-12c). Room 67 is a gallery devoted to the culture of Korea from prehistory to the present. The Koreans were printing Buddhist texts by AD 751 and there are some impressive early books. The largest exhibit is a study or **sarangbang**, where men would read or receive guests. The simplicity of this structure, linked to Confucian philosophy, is also seen in a globular white 'full-moon jar' (17c-18c) that was influential over 20c British art potters; and in bowls and flasks with a grey-green celadon glaze (12c).

On leaving the room, look down the stairwell to see a colossal Chinese figure of **Amitabha Budhha** (AD 585), nearly 8m tall.

JAPAN *Rooms 92-94* The rarefied atmosphere at the very top of the

Museum, on Levels 4 and 5, may be accounted for by sheer altitude but is at least appropriate to the contemplation of delicate prints, paintings and other decorative arts from Japan. Their fragility means that displays change frequently but may include carved **netsuke**, fans, armour,17c porcelain or contemporary ceramics.

BRITAIN AND EUROPE

PREHISTORY *Rooms 36, 37* At the top of the South Stairs is a new display of prehistoric artefacts, many from the British Isles. Among these is the **Mold cape**, a garment of embossed gold found in Wales (1900-1600 BC). Its precise use is unknown, and even ostensibly more practical items like the precisely chipped flint arrowheads and hand axes are thought to have been buried deliberately as 'objects of power', intended to mediate between man and his environment. Room 36 leads onto a balcony with a good view over Great Court.

BRONZE AGE AND CELTIC EUROPE *Room 50* To keep the tour chronological, go straight to Room 50. The earliest objects here belonged to people of the Bronze Age (1600-750 BC) concerned with defending themselves in war, proclaiming their tribe or rank, and discovering horsemanship. The two phases of the succeeding Iron Age were named after sites at Hallstatt in Austria (750-500 BC) and La Tène in France (500 BC to the Roman invasion): people of the latter period were called Celts by the Romans. Their unmistakable curvilinear decoration is seen in various types of object - the **Battersea Shield** (300-150 BC) found in the Thames is a fine example.

An amazing display of torcs in gold and silver found in Norfolk is just part of the **Snettisham Hoards** buried c 70 BC. The torc, a neck ornament, has been associated since antiquity with Celtic warriors but there is little evidence that they wore them. **Lindow Man** always draws a crowd to his new resting place here. Preserved in a peat bog since his violent death in the middle of the 1c AD, he may have been a Druidic sacrifice: there was mistletoe in his stomach contents.

ROMAN BRITAIN *Room 49* Britain felt the influence of the Romans many years before the conquest in AD 43; evidence from amphorae shows that in the 1c and 2c BC, as now, Britons had a taste for Italian wine and olive oil. Though they look insignificant, some of the most valuable items in Room 49 are slips of wood bearing faint writing: these are the **Vindolanda letters** - memos, lists and party invitations - written at a fort in Northumberland (AD 90-120). The Romans also transformed building: there are examples of their innovations from drains and central heating to roof tiles.

The **Hoxne Hoard** of gold coins, silver spoons and a fragile body chain was hidden after AD 407 at the time Roman control of Britain was slipping; and there is the 4c **Mildenhall Treasure** of tableware, including a massive silver dish. These hoards were not associated with graves and were probably buried to save them from an altogether different kind of horde.

EARLY MEDIEVAL EUROPE *Room 41* When the western Roman empire fell in 476 various northern peoples moved in: this room contains items made by Franks, Goths, Huns and Ostrogoths, including beautiful gold-and-garnet jewellery from the Ukraine (4c-6c). Among later raiders were the Vikings of Scandinavia, whose well-publicized talent for looting is illustrated by the **Cuerdale Hoard** of silver (buried c 905), including coins, bullion and jewellery - but Arabic coins also reveal them as

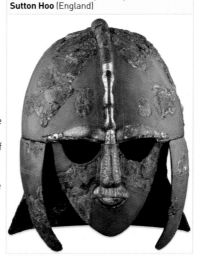

Helmet from the early 7c ship-burial at Sutton Hoo (England)

international traders. Highlights here are the masterpieces of Anglo-Saxon goldsmithing from the **Sutton Hoo ship burial** found in the 1930s, but do not miss the Franks casket (8c) of intricately carved whalebone; and Tolkein fans can look out for more objects inscribed with runes.

MEDIEVAL EUROPE *Rooms 42, 43* A loop of galleries deals with the development of modern Western culture. Room 42 covers the period 800-1500, starting with later Byzantine art, and includes the glum but appealing **Lewis chessmen** (mid-12c) which were probably made in Scandinavia. The gradual emergence in France of **Gothic art** - in the sense that it replaced classical art, as the Goths supplanted the Romans - is seen in reliquaries, chalices and other Christian apparatus; and in the very rare segments of wall painting (mid-14c) that survived the destruction by fire of St Stephen's Chapel, Westminster in 1834. The **Royal Gittern** (c 1280-1330) - the only important musical instrument to survive from the Middle Ages - is associated with Elizabeth I. An ancestor of the guitar, it has extraordinarily detailed carving of vines and huntsmen: look for the very startled rabbit clocking a fast-approaching arrow. On the exquisite **Royal Gold Cup** (c 1380), scenes from the life of St Agnes are picked out in intense enamel colours.

Some English wall tiles (1320-30) entertainingly tell of the infant Christ's 'unofficial' miracles. Room 43 contains more **medieval tiles and pottery** and explains how they were made and decorated.

CLOCKS AND WATCHES *Room 44* The room next door is filled with gentle ticking. Clocks were known in Europe by about 1300 and this display follows them through the development of the spring and pendulum, through tiny watches to huge long-case timepieces. The precision of the 'Congreve' Rolling Ball Timepiece (c 1810-40) is mesmerizing. There are regular 'please touch' sessions in this gallery.

WADDESDON BEQUEST *Room 45* This room is a darkened treasure trove of **ornamental curiosities** collected by Ferdinand de Rothschild of Waddesdon Manor, including elaborate

Renaissance pendants; enamels; goblets formed from shells, crystal geodes, ostrich eggs and even nuts; and a staggering Flemish miniature altar (early 16c) in wood, on which minute figures enact the Passion.

EUROPE 15C-20C *Rooms 46-48* These rooms illustrate the key historical developments that made modern Europe - from religious wars to voyages of discovery and the industrial revolution - through the decorative arts. The effect is of a mini-Victoria and Albert Museum.

At the start of Room 46, **15c-18c Europe**, we see the classical ideas rediscovered in Renaissance Italy spread throughout Europe by means of prints and travelling craftsmen. Roman art forms, such as the casting of bronze figurines and making exquisite portrait medals, were revived, and Venetian glassmakers carried new techniques over the continent. By contrast, the method for making Spanish lustre pottery had come from the Moors (c 1300). From England, there are fragments of lost Tudor palaces; part of the Cheapside Hoard of Jacobean jewellery, including delicate floral necklaces; and Royalist and Roundhead objects from the Civil War. Explorers and empire-builders brought back exotic new materials - coconut shells, mother of pearl and ivory. Europe struggled to emulate Chinese porcelain but finally succeeded in the 18c: there are examples from Dresden, Sèvres and Capodimonte, and Chinoiserie objects set beside genuine oriental pieces.

Room 47 deals with **18c and 19c Europe**. Napoleon may have caused political upheaval but he was also a keen patron of the arts and promoter of Neoclassicism, a revolt against royal Rococo. The Romantic fascination with nature is the background to some delicate jewellery in imitation of plants: a necklace set with hummingbird heads (1865-70) takes things a revolting stage too far. Industrialization provoked a renewed interest in handcrafting, as witnessed in objects designed by Christopher Dresser (1834-1904), one of the most famous names in the Arts and Crafts Movement. Meanwhile, international exhibitions and archaeological discoveries, many of which could be seen in the British Museum itself, created interest in the arts of other cultures.

Finally, Room 48 shows objects from **20c Europe and America**, from streamlined Art Nouveau cutlery and glass to abstract Suprematist porcelain (c 1923-4) celebrating the Russian Revolution.

EGYPT

EGYPTIAN SCULPTURE *Room 4* To begin this long gallery at the end with the oldest material, enter via Room 6, guarded by two seated figures of Amenophis III (c 1400 BC). To the left is the **Rosetta Stone**, one of the Museum's biggest attractions. Text panels explain how the unassuming stone (196 BC) allowed Egyptian hieroglyphs to be translated for the first time in the 1820s.

Opposite, next to a carved list of kings still bearing traces of colour (c 1260 BC), more text explains the periods of ancient Egyptian history: Pre-Dynastic, before Egypt's unification c 3100 BC; Dynastic, under the control of 30 ruling houses and sub-divided between the Old, Middle and New Kingdoms; and Ptolemaic, under Greek control after Alexander's conquest in 332 BC.

The Old Kingdom (2686-2181 BC) saw the building of the pyramids and the belief that the king was divine. Among a number of **false doors** from tombs, the largest is that for Ptahshepses (c 2400 BC), whose biography is carved upon it. Sometimes a statue would stand in for the mummy inside a tomb: a particularly well-preserved example is that of **Nenkheftka** (c 2200 BC). Look out for three expressive black granite statues of the powerful king of the Middle Kingdom (2050-1786 BC), Sesostris III. After a period of decline and invasion the 17th Dynasty founded the New Kingdom (1550-1070 BC), when great temples were built. Four striking statues of the lion-headed goddess **Sekhmet** (c 1400 BC) grasp the *ankh* or symbol of life. On a more intimate level are limestone figures of a man and wife, seated hand-in-hand (c 1350 BC).

Cross the hall leading to the Great Court. **Rameses II** set up more colossal statues than any other ruler: the upper half of one (1270 BC), in two shades of granite, stands above the crowd, as do two columns flaring into palm capitals (c 1250 BC). The Late Period

(661-332 BC) saw disintegration and eventually invasion by the Assyrians and Persians, but also a revival of earlier art forms. In this part of the gallery a number of animal statues show the Egyptians' continued powers of stylization. The room ends with the Ptolemaic and Roman periods: some forms seem never to have changed, such as the huge granite scarab (c 200 BC), but others, like the sphinxes (2c AD) that flank the exit to the West Stairs, are entirely Greek.

ANCIENT EGYPTIAN CULTURE *Room 61* At the top of the West Stairs, turn left into Room 61. The meaning of **hieroglyphs** (how to write the word 'cat', for example) is explained, and graffiti, spelling mistakes, and even puns are examined. Fragments of glazed tile reveal the sheer decorative beauty of hieroglyphs. The importance of the Nile is shown in the model boats and hippos, but there are also toys, cosmetics, jewellery, musical instruments and utensils. A case of votive statuettes includes the earringed **Gayer-Anderson cat** (664-332 BC), a streamlined bronze offering to the goddess Bastet.

FUNERARY ARCHAEOLOGY *Rooms 62, 63* These are probably the most crowded rooms in the Museum, particularly at weekends and in summer, for the very good reason that they tell you all you could ever want to know about the Egyptian way of death. For a roughly chronological overview, begin at the far end of Room 63.

The Egyptians believed that the physical being had to be preserved so that the spirit could pass into the next life. This involved **mummification**, which began as early as 3500 BC and is comprehensively explained with displays of embalmers' tools and chemicals. It also meant providing food and someone to do the work required in the next world. Models of mummified humans (*shabti*) left in the tomb gradually came to be regarded as servants to take on these tasks: eventually the deceased might be supplied with one for each day of

Inner coffin of the priest Hor (c 680 BC; Egypt)

the year, plus foremen. Carefully wrapped mummies were covered with elaborate shrouds and ornaments, including nets of turquoise-blue faience beads. Amulets and texts such as the *Book of the Dead*, with prayers and spells to help the deceased negotiate the afterlife, were also placed with the body. Earlier burials were in cedarwood boxes, but later the characteristically shaped outer sarcophagus was used. Perhaps the most splendid here is from the burial of **Lady Henutmehyt** (c 1279-1213 BC) of Thebes: her coffins are elaborately carved, painted and gilded.

The Roman period continued many traditions, including placing a portrait mask over the mummy's face: that of Artemidorus (AD 100-200) is one of a group in a particularly realistic style. Animals were also mummified, especially in the Late Period, as offerings to the gods with which they were associated: there are tiny bronze cases for a mummified eel and snake among the more familiar cats, ibises and crocodiles.

EGYPT AND AFRICA, COPTIC EGYPT *Rooms 64-66* Room 64 reaches back farther to the Pre-Dynastic period and the emergence of Egypt's characteristic architecture, writing and art. Look for the much less elaborate burials such as that of 'Ginger', preserved in the sand from 3400 BC, and for beautifully simple calcite vases (2890-2686 BC). Room 65 looks at the civilization of **Nubia** - now parts of Egypt and Sudan - which was the conduit for imports from equatorial Africa including ivory, spices and giraffe tails; a fragment from a tomb painting (c 1390 BC) shows these luxuries being presented by Africans. Backtrack to Room 66 to see textiles from Coptic Egypt, where **Christianity** supplanted paganism at the same time as in the wider Roman empire, until the Islamic conquest.

GREECE AND ROME

BRONZE AGE & ARCHAIC GREECE *Rooms 11-14* This is the most extensive collection in the Museum, comprising about 100,000 objects, and one of the best in the world. The highlights are mentioned here, but even relatively unfrequented rooms are filled with beautiful and revealing artefacts.

Rooms 11 and 12, reached via the cloakroom and Room 6, start with Bronze Age Greece (3200-1100 BC). The first small room focuses on the **Cyclades**, with simple marble and ceramic vessels and enigmatic human figures whose purpose is unknown: this civilization left no written records. Room 12 begins with the **Minoans** of Crete, associated with the Minotaur legend. The most striking leftovers of their culture here are perhaps the terracotta coffins shaped as baths or chests; gold jewellery and a cup with a spiral motif reminiscent of Celtic designs; and pottery decorated with stylized dolphins and octopuses. This marine imagery was shared with the **Mycenaeans**, from mainland Greece, who eventually overran the Minoans and were dominant in the 13c and 14c BC. Deadly looking bronze spearheads and swords attest to the warlike nature that took them to Troy, but their pottery was widely traded and their metalwork includes a strikingly modern bowl in sheet silver and others in gold and copper.

After the fall of the Mycenaeans around 1100 BC, Greece entered a Dark Age, forgetting many craft skills and even writing. Trade and the influence of eastern civilizations gradually helped them re-emerge. The **Geometric period** is named for the style of pottery with confident abstract patterns, painted or stamped. In the 7c BC the city of Corinth developed a fluid form of pottery decoration, but by the 6C BC, in the **Archaic period**, Athens had emerged as the key producer of pottery. Its distinctive 'black-figure' style against the natural red ground of the clay is demonstrated on a wide range of beautiful vessel shapes. Room 14 is devoted to the influence of Andokides, a leading painter or potter in Athens (530-500 BC) who helped develop **'red-figure' decoration**. This time, the clay provides the flesh-colour and the background is filled in black.

CLASSICAL GREECE *Rooms 15-21* After the defeat of the Persians in the 5c BC Greece entered its Classical era. Its far-flung influence is seen in Room 15 in marbles from the **Harpy Tomb** at Xanthos, the capital of Lykia in Asia Minor (480-470 BC). Room 16 shows the frieze - a vigorous struggle between Centaurs and Lapiths - from the **Temple of Apollo** at Bassae (420-500 BC) on the Greek mainland.

Room 17 reconstructs the east end of the **Nereid Tomb** (390-380 BC), the finest found at Xanthos. Of other fragments the most beautiful are three Nereids (daughters of a sea god), once borne on dolphins or birds above the spray that made the drapery cling to their bodies.

PARTHENON SCULPTURES *Room 18* is in fact three galleries devoted to displaying and explaining the Parthenon sculptures. Turn right to rent an audio guide or left for a **video reconstruction** of the great temple of Athena, built (c 447-432 BC) on a rocky outcrop in Athens to house a colossal gold-and-ivory statue of the goddess. The video explains where each type of sculpture - carved in the round or in relief - was placed on the building and demonstrates how Greek sculptors adapted perspective, fitting ranks of horsemen seven abreast into a plane of carving no more than 5 centimetres deep.

The main gallery is a cathedral-like space clearly intended to inspire a reverential attitude before these great, and controversial, works. This is not hard to muster, for despite their damaged condition they still have great presence and beauty. The **frieze** that once decorated the outside of the temple's main room is displayed along the side walls and shows impressive variety in depicting figures in a restricted space. At each end of the room are fragments from the sculptural groups that stood in each triangular pediment, among them a fine horse's head, and metopes showing Centaurs and Lapiths in single-combat.

Skirt round the back of the Nereid Tomb into Room 19 to see parts of two other temples on the Acropolis. From the **Erechtheum** come a single slender Ionic column and a graceful caryatid (c 415 BC): look at the back of the caryatid - serene despite her rather functional surroundings - to see her plaited and coiled hairstyle.

Room 20 is dominated by an example of the third type of **Lykian tomb**, a sarcophagus with a 'gothic' arch. It also has beautiful bronze vessels, including a water jar (*hydria*) of 350-300 BC found near Rhodes, and marble vessels imitating shells. Upstairs in Room 20a is the reserve collection of Greek vases (520-300 BC).

Room 21 displays some of the remaining fragments from the **Mausoleum at Halicarnassus** (now Bodrum in Turkey). Made for the 4c ruler Mausolus after whom elaborate graves are now named, it was one of the Seven Wonders of the World. Part of a magnificent horse, with its original bronze bridle, survives from a chariot group (*quadriga*) that surmounted the pyramidal roof; two impressive figures, once identified with the tomb's royal occupants, and sections of the frieze are also on display.

Rooms on the lower floors, accessible via Rooms 21 and 10, feature Greek and Roman inscriptions (78), the Archaic temple of Artemis at Ephesus (82) and the 18c **Townley Collection** of Roman sculpture (84).

THE HELLENISTIC WORLD *Room 22* On the ground floor, Room 22 concentrates on the Greek-ruled kingdoms from the death of Alexander the Great in 323 BC to the conquest of Egypt by the Romans in 31 BC. Alexander had forged city states into an empire, and its people now found independence in the creative rather than civic sphere. Rulers began to make use of portraiture, some of it very effective, in their coinage. The sculpture of the Molossian Hound demonstrates a new realism but idealized beauty and the grotesque were also expressed. Private wealth meant a market for **luxury goods** - dishes of coloured glass and jewellery made of sheet gold and precious stones, including exquisite necklaces and a belt and wreath of oak leaves with insect inhabitants (350-300 BC), probably for use in a religious ceremony and found in Turkey. The larger sculpture here includes a massive column drum from the **Temple of Artemis** at Ephesus (325-300 BC), another of the Seven Wonders.

From their rise to pre-eminence in the 3c BC, the Romans were enthusiasts of Greek sculpture: Augustus encouraged artists to copy 5c originals, believing that Classical Greece had had high moral values. Roman interpretations are sometimes the only records of lost Greek bronzes. Room 23 shows some of these, including the figure of an athlete by Polykleitos and the *Aphrodite of Knidos* by Praxiteles.

GREEK COLONIES IN ITALY *Room 73* Make your way to the upper floor of this wing, by the West Stairs (turn right at the top) or via the South Stairs and Money Gallery. Room 73 is filled with the artefacts - most found in tombs - of Greek colonies in southern Italy (from 750 BC), especially exquisitely painted pottery vessels.

ANCIENT CYPRUS *Room 72* The next room gives a comprehensive view of life in ancient Cyprus (4500 BC-AD 330) and its chequered history: it fell under the successive control of Greeks, Phoenicians, Assyrians, Persians, Romans and Egyptians. Its fine bronzework and gently smiling sculpted figures are particularly striking.

ITALY BEFORE THE ROMANS *Room 71* The Italian peninsula was home to many peoples, with their own languages and highly developed craft skills, but the culture of the **Etruscans** stands out (6c-1c BC). Look out for treasures from the 'Isis' tomb (c 570-560 BC), opened by Napoleon's brother Lucien and including an elegant gypsum statue of a woman and two carved and painted ostrich eggs. At first the Etruscans cremated their dead and there are different kinds of cinerary urn (one in the shape of a seated man); later they buried them in painted terracotta sarcophagi such as that of Seianti Hanunia Tlesnasa (c 150-130 BC). The sculptor of her effigy was kind, if the scientific reconstruction of her appearance is any guide. Real counterparts of the elaborate jewellery she wears are displayed nearby. Etruscan bronzes were collector's items to the later Romans.

REPUBLICAN AND IMPERIAL ROME *Room 70* A bronze head of Augustus (c 27-25 BC), the first emperor, greets you and there are more **sculpted portraits** around the room, at first in the unflatteringly realistic manner of the Republic, later in more idealising vein. In the later Empire a more florid style developed. There are displays on various outposts of the Empire: from Egypt, for example, a set of pots still containing a fresco artist's paints (1c AD). Roman practicality is shown everywhere, from ubiquitous clay lamps to quite large sheets of window glass; by contrast, there are delicate wall paintings and stucco reliefs that reveal a love of domestic finery. The chief masterpiece in the room must be the **Portland Vase** (AD 5-25), with a mythological scene in blue-and-white cameo glass. Smashed by an 'intemperate' vandal in 1845 it has been painstakingly conserved. Nearby is the racy **Warren Cup** (mid-1c AD), a silver vessel with homoerotic scenes.

Finally, Room 69 arranges the objects we have just seen to explore **daily life in Greece and Rome** (1400 BC-AD 500), from childhood games - rag dolls, lead animals, hoops and marbles - to water supply.

OTHER GALLERIES

MONEY AND MEDALS *Rooms 68, 69a* Room 68, the long **Money Gallery**, covers the form, use and abuse of cash since the first coins were minted in Lydia in the 6c BC to modern electronic transactions. The **Fishpool Hoard** of gold coins, buried around 1463 to avoid being stolen during the Wars of the Roses, glitters invitingly; alternative currencies include cowrie shells and bars of salt. This gallery and others hold **handling sessions** at different times each day, enjoyable opportunities to learn more, including how to spot fakes.

PRINTS AND DRAWINGS *Room 90* In Room 90 in the north wing, handily bisected by a shop, are temporary displays from the Museum's mind-blowing collection of almost 3 million Western **prints and drawings** from the 15c to the present. You might see Michelangelo's *Epifania* (c 1550-3), his only surviving full-scale preparatory drawing, prints by Dürer, Rembrandt or Goya or watercolours by Turner and Constable. There are also large numbers of popular prints and ephemera including playing cards and toy theatres. You can look at all but one of the images in the collection in the Study Room on production of some identification. One of the largest prints ever made is at the other end of the Museum, outside the Gallery Café: the Triumphal Arch (1515) was designed by Albrecht Dürer among others, so is worth a look if you are in the vicinity.

Wallace Collection

OPEN	Mon-Sat 10.00-17.00, Sun 12.00-17.00
CLOSED	1/1, Good Friday, 1/5, 3/6, 24-26/12
CHARGES	Admission free
TELEPHONE	020 7563 9500
WWW.	wallace-collection.org.uk
MAIN ENTRANCE	Hertford House, Manchester Square
UNDERGROUND	Bond Street
DISABLED ACCESS	Full access, large print and audio plans, access coordinator

An 18c building in a quiet square near chic Marylebone High Street houses one of the finest private art collections ever amassed in Britain, by the extremely wealthy Marquesses of Hertford and the illegitimate son of the 4th, Sir Richard Wallace, whose widow left it to the nation in 1897. All the rooms contain richly decorated furniture that set off the other exhibits. On the ground floor you can see Renaissance paintings and jewels, majolica and Venetian glass, but chiefly a magnificent array of arms and armour, including matching outfits for a 15c German knight and his horse, and rows of oriental helmets. The stairs to the first floor are overlooked by Boucher fantasies, introducing a fine array of 18c French paintings by Watteau and Fragonard, followed by the Great Gallery where work by Rubens, Van Dyck, Rembrandt, Titian, Poussin, Velázquez, Reynolds, Gainsborough and, most famously, Frans Hals' *Laughing Cavalier* hang. Other rooms have small Dutch genre scenes, Sèvres porcelain and gold snuff boxes. The courtyard has recently been roofed by Rick Mather to create an airy restaurant and a lower ground floor with an entertaining display on fakes and forgeries and rooms for temporary exhibitions and lectures.

Sir John Soane's Museum

OPEN	Tues-Sat 10.00-17.00 (first Tues of month also 18.00-21.00)
CLOSED	1/1, 24-26/12 and all other PH
CHARGES	Donation suggested. Tours Sat 14.30 (£3)
TELEPHONE	**020 7405 2107**
WWW.	**soane.org**
MAIN ENTRANCE	13 Lincoln's Inn Fields
UNDERGROUND	Holborn, Chancery Lane
DISABLED ACCESS	Special wheelchairs provide access to ground floor. Telephone first to discuss arrangements in detail

This remarkable building, complete with caryatids, was built by England's foremost architect of the early 19c, John Soane (1753-1837), the designer of Dulwich Picture Gallery and the Bank of England. He lived in it with his family, used it to demonstrate his ideas to students, and bequeathed it to the nation (with no.12 and part of no.14 alongside) with the stipulation that it should be kept as nearly as possible in the state in which he left it. The result is a uniquely atmospheric, labyrinthine space of niches and domes, mirrors and sudden illumination through coloured glass, a fitting corollary for Soane's complex personality. The walls are encrusted with fragments of classical sculpture or unfold to reveal drawings by Piranesi and paintings by Hogarth and Canaletto. In the cellar are a Gothic 'monk's cell' and the 'crypt' containing the sarcophagus of Pharaoh Seti I (1303-1290 BC). The exhibition space, with cases designed by Eva Jiricna (1995) draws on the Museum's collection of 30,000 drawings by Soane and other great architects including Adam and Wren. The rest of no. 14 has recently been acquired and is now being refurbished to create better facilities, including a room for Soane's collection of architectural models.

on route

British Library, 96 Euston Road, Mon-Fri 9.30-18.00, Tues till 20.00, Sat, Sun, PH till 17.00, **T** 020 7412 7332, www.bl.uk. The new national library with 12 million books, exhibitions of 'treasures' (from Magna Carta to Beatles' lyrics) and stamps, and regular changing shows, in a red-brick pile by Colin St John Wilson. **U** King's Cross St Pancras, Euston

British Library

Dickens House Museum, 48 Doughty Street, entrance charge, Mon-Sat 10.00-17.00, Sun 11.00-17.00, **T** 020 7405 2127, www.dickensmuseum.com. First editions, ephemera and personal items belonging to the great novelist, who lived here for a couple of productive years. Ideal for enthusiasts. **U** Russell Square

Foundling Museum, 40 Brunswick Square, entrance charge, **T** 020 7841 3600, www.coram.org.uk/heritage/museum.htm. In 1739 Captain Thomas Coram founded a hospital to care for abandoned children. Its museum now comprises London's first art gallery, created by Hogarth to raise funds with work by Reynolds and Gainsborough, and touching mementoes of the children. **U** Russell Square

Percival David Foundation, 53 Gordon Square, Mon-Fri 10.30-17.00, **T** 020 7387 3909, www.soas.ac.uk/PDF. Little-known but well-presented collection of high-quality Chinese ceramics. **U** Euston Square

Petrie Museum, Malet Place, Tues-Fri 13.00-17.00, Sat 10.00-13.00, **T** 020 7679 2884, www.petrie.ucl.ac.uk. Comprehensive range of archaeological finds from all periods of ancient Eygptian history, including the world's oldest dress. **U** Goodge Street

Pollock's Toy Museum, 41 Whitfield Street, entrance charge, Mon-Sat 10.00-17.00, **T** 020 7636 3452, www.pollocksweb.co.uk. Eccentric museum in two 18c and 19c houses crowded with toys, models and games. Toy theatres and plays are also sold here. **U** Goodge Street

Royal Institute of British Architects, 66 Portland Place, Mon-Fri 8.00-18.00 (Thur till 21.00), Sat 8.00-17.00, **T** 020 7580 5533, www.riba.org. Extensive architecture library, bookshop, free exhibitions and café in a handsome 1930s building. **U** Great Portland Street

St George's Bloomsbury, Bloomsbury Way, www.stgeorges bloomsbury.org.uk. Designed by Wren's assistant, Nicholas Hawksmoor. Its pyramidal spire was inspired by the Mausoleum of Halicarnassus, bits of which you can see in the British Museum. **U** Tottenham Court Road

Senate House, Malet Street. The daunting white tower that houses the library of the University of London was designed by Charles Holden in the 1930s. George Orwell understandably used it as the model for his Ministry of Truth in the novel *1984*. *U* Goodge Street

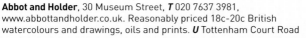

commercial galleries

Abbot and Holder, 30 Museum Street, *T* 020 7637 3981, www.abbottandholder.co.uk. Reasonably priced 18c-20c British watercolours and drawings, oils and prints. *U* Tottenham Court Road

Austin/Desmond, Pied Bull Yard, 68-69 Great Russell Street, *T* 020 7242 4443, www.austindesmond.com. Prints and paintings by modern and contemporary British and Irish artists. *U* Tottenham Court Road

Bloomsbury Workshop, 12 Galen Place, off Bury Place, *T* 020 7405 0632, www.bloomsburyworkshop.com. Art of the Bloomsbury Group (Vanessa Bell, Duncan Grant, Roger Fry et al). *U* Tottenham Court Road, Holborn

Contemporary Applied Arts, 2 Percy Street, *T* 020 7436 2344, www.caa.org.uk. Britain's largest crafts gallery - glass, ceramics, jewellery, textiles and furniture. *U* Goodge Street, Tottenham Court Road

Focus Gallery, 3-4 Percy Street, *T* 020 7631 1150, www.focusgallery.co.uk. 20c and contemporary British photographers, internationally known and up-and-coming. *U* Tottenham Court Road

Frith Street Gallery, 59-60 Frith Street, *T* 020 7494 1550, www.frithstreetgallery.co.uk. Shows painting, photography, sculpture and video works by British and international contemporary artists, including Cornelia Parker and Callum Innes. *U* Tottenham Court Road

Rebecca Hossack, 35 Windmill Street and 28 Charlotte Street, *T* 020 7436 4899, www.r-h-g.co.uk. Aboriginal and other non-Western art, contemporary Scottish painting, ceramics. *U* Goodge Street

October Gallery, 24 Old Gloucester Street, *T* 020 7242 7367, www.theoctobergallery.com. Contemporary art from cultures around the world, performances and readings. *U* Holborn, Russell Square

Spink & Son Ltd, 69 Southampton Row, *T* 020 7563 4000, www.spink.com. Dealers in stamps, coins, medals and books. *U* Russell Square, Holborn

eating and drinking

AT THE MUSEUMS

BRITISH MUSEUM
£ **Court Café**, on the floor of the Great Court. Sandwiches, salads, cakes and hot and cold drinks. The **Gallery Café**, next to Room 12, also offers light meals and may be less crowded. Both self-service.

££ **Court Restaurant**, *T* 020 7323 8990. On Level 3 above the Reading Room. Eclectic modern cooking, and coffee and tea, served 11.00-17.00 (last orders) till 21.00 Thur-Sat. Waiter service.

WALLACE COLLECTION
£ **Café Bagatelle**, *T* 020 7563 9505. Mediterranean-style food suits the museum's bright new covered courtyard. Also morning coffee and afternoon tea.

SURROUNDING AREA

£ **Fryer's Delight**, 19 Theobald's Road, *T* 020 7405 4114. Friendly and busy traditional chippie. *U* Holborn, Chancery Lane

Planet Organic, 22 Torrington Place, *T* 020 7436 1929. Airy café selling fresh juices, sandwiches, salads and other snacks, to take away or eat at outside tables. All organic produce. *U* Goodge Street

Ragam, 57 Cleveland Street, *T* 020 7636 9098. Friendly restaurant serving reliable South Indian food. *U* Goodge Street

Wagamama, 4a Streatham Street, *T* 020 7323 9223. Branch of the reliable chain of Japanese noodle bars. *U* Tottenham Court Road

££ **Abeno**, 47 Museum Street, *T* 020 7405 3211. Friendly and fun diner serving Japanese-style omelettes. *U* Tottenham Court Road

Cigala, 54 Lamb's Conduit Street, *T* 020 7405 1717. Popular Spanish restaurant with good set menus. Push further east to Moro in Exmouth Market for top-class Moorish food. *U* Russell Square

Ikkyu, 67A Tottenham Court Road, *T* 020 7636 9280. Great-value Japanese staple, recommended for its sushi and large portions. Closed weekends except for Sunday dinner. *U* Goodge Street

Malabar Junction, 107 Great Russell Street, *T* 020 7580 5230.

Cooking from Kerala: lots of choices for vegetarians and fish-lovers. Attractive conservatory at the back. *U* Tottenham Court Road

North Sea Fish, 7-8 Leigh Street, *T* 020 7387 5892. A bit out of your way, but worth it for simply cooked fresh fish at this established seaside-style café. *U* Russell Square

The Perseverance, 63 Lamb's Conduit Street, *T* 020 7405 8278. Modern British food and good Sunday roasts served upstairs, while remaining a smoky boozer downstairs. *U* Russell Square, Holborn

Pizza Express, 30 Coptic Street, *T* 020 7636 3232. Oldest branch of the extensive, and usually reliable, chain. It is housed in the attractive former Dairy Supply Company. *U* Tottenham Court Road

Villandry, 170 Great Portland Street, *T* 020 7631 3131. Rustic French cooking with authentic ingredients, an oasis on the way to the Wallace Collection. The more informal bar also serves food and there is a shop (see below). *U* Great Portland Street

£££ Elena's L'Etoile, 30 Charlotte Street, *T* 020 7636 7189. Old-established, comfortable restaurant serving traditional and modern French food under the eye of Elena herself. *U* Goodge Street

Hakkasan, 8 Hanway Place, *T* 020 7927 7000. Classy designer interpretation of Chinese food. Lunchtime dim-sum may be the best choice on a budget. *U* Tottenham Court Road

Passione, 10 Charlotte Street, *T* 020 7636 2833. Popular modern Italian food, served in a relaxed setting. *U* Goodge Street

Pied à Terre, 34 Charlotte Street, *T* 020 7636 1178. Expensive but very haute French cuisine and excellent wine list. *U* Goodge Street

Rasa Samudra, 5 Charlotte Street, *T* 020 7637 0222. Delicious vegetarian and fish dishes from South India, in a rambling Georgian house. Set meals are good value. *U* Goodge Street

LATE-NIGHT BARS

a.k.a., 18 West Central Street, *T* 020 7836 0110. Converted 19c building in a relaxed, minimal style. Downstairs bar and dance floor, dining above. Open Mon-Fri, Sun till 3.00, Sat till 7.00. *U* Tottenham Court Road

Ling Ling @ Hakkasan, 8 Hanway Place, *T* 020 7927 7000. Sexy designer bar attached to the fashionable Chinese restaurant (see above). Open Mon-Wed till 24.00, Thur-Sat till 3.00, Sun till 10.30. *U* Tottenham Court Road

Point 101, 101 New Oxford Street, *T* 020 7379 3112. Huge, glass-walled bar designed to complement Richard Seifert's iconic Centrepoint tower (1966). Open Mon-Thur till 2.00, Fri, Sat till 2.30, Sun till 23.30. *U* Tottenham Court Road

Long Bar at the Sanderson, 50 Berners Street, *T* 020 7300 1444. It's out of your way and expensive (£10 cocktails) but you might want to gawp at the makeover on this 60s office block, by Philippe Starck for Ian Schrager's hotel. The space-age lift interiors are recommended. Open Mon-Sat till 1.00, Sun till 10.30. *U* Tottenham Court Road

shopping

Bloomsbury is not a place for the fashionista, but it is only a short bus or Tube ride to the promised land of South Molton Street and Selfridges, via all the major department stores and fashion chains along Oxford Street. Covent Garden is just to the south and Marylebone High Street makes a chic detour on the way to the Wallace Collection. Tottenham Court Road is packed with competing electronics shops.

ACCESSORIES

James Smith & Sons, 53 New Oxford Street, *T* 020 7836 4731. Umbrella and stick-makers since 1830. The largest such store in Europe, it has an entertaining Victorian shopfront of 1857. *U* Tottenham Court Road

ANTIQUES & COLLECTABLES

Coincraft, 45 Great Russell Street, *T* 020 7636 1188. If your appetite for antiquities has been whetted, you will enjoy the selection of coins, medals, Roman lamps etc here. *U* Tottenham Court Road

BOOKS

Arthur Probsthain, 41 Great Russell Street, *T* 020 7636 1096. Books on Oriental and African art. *U* Tottenham Court Road

Cinema Bookshop, 13-14 Great Russell Street, *T* 020 7637 0206. Tiny shop devoted to new and hard-to-find books about film, with posters and stills. *U* Tottenham Court Road

Robert Frew, 106 Great Russell Street, *T* 020 7580 2311. Antique books, prints and maps in an attractive Victorian shop. *U* Tottenham Court Road

Forbidden Planet, 71-75 New Oxford Street, *T* 020 7836 4179. SF comics, figures, magazines, T-shirts, etc. *U* Tottenham Court Road

Gay's the Word, 66 Marchmont Street, *T* 020 7278 7654, www.gaystheword.co.uk. Britain's biggest gay and lesbian bookshop. *U* Russell Square

Gosh, 39 Great Russell Street, *T* 020 7636 1011. Comics and graphic novels, with original cartoons for sale downstairs. *U* Tottenham Court Road

Jarndyce, 46 Great Russell Street, *T* 020 7631 4220. 18c and 19c books, and a sideline in the bizarre (see their window display, with *The Art of Faking Exhibition Poultry* and *How to Abandon Ship*). *U* Tottenham Court Road

London Review Bookshop, 14 Bury Place, *T* 020 7269 9030. Newish booksellers linked with the famous publication and aiming to be 'the best small independent in London'. *U* Holborn

Museum Bookshop, 36 Great Russell Street, *T* 020 7580 4086. New and out-of-print books on archaeology, especially of Egypt, the Near East and Mediterranean, conservation and museology. *U* Tottenham Court Road

Ulysses, 40 Museum Street, *T* 020 7831 1600. For collectors of 20c first editions and rare children's books, and much more to browse besides. *U* Holborn, Tottenham Court Road

FLOWERS

Chivers Flowers, 43-45 Charlotte Street, *T* 020 7580 7595. Traditional service producing bouquets and arrangements. *U* Goodge Street

FOOD

Konditor and Cook, 46 Gray's Inn Road, *T* 020 7404 6300. Top pastries, cakes, breads and other goodies. *U* King's Cross, Russell Square

Villandry, 170 Great Portland Street, *T* 020 7631 3131, www.villandry.com. If not visiting the restaurant (see above), you can still sample fine Parisian groceries, organic meats and continental charcuterie, cheese and pastries. ***U*** Great Portland Street

HOMES

Habitat, 196 Tottenham Court Road, ***T*** 020 7631 3880, www.habitat.net. Large branch of the influential, inexpensive furnishing chain founded by designer Terence Conran in the 1960s. ***U*** Goodge Street

Heal's, 196 Tottenham Court Road, ***T*** 020 7636 1666, www.heals.co.uk. In the same fine building (1912-17) as Habitat, with more sophisticated (and pricier) designs. ***U*** Goodge Street

Mosaic Workshop, 1a Princeton Street, ***T*** 020 7831 0889, www.mosaicworkshop.com. Supplying materials - including a rainbow selection of glass and ceramic tiles - and books on making mosaics; commissions also undertaken. Open Tues-Fri. ***U*** Holborn

Purves and Purves, 220-224 Tottenham Court Road, ***T*** 020 7580 8223, www.purves.co.uk. Large store showcasing contemporary furniture, rugs, kitchen accessories and designer trinkets. ***U*** Goodge Street

MUSIC

Virgin Megastore, 14-16 Oxford Street, ***T*** 020 7631 1234, www.virgin.com. Internet café, games, DVD and video, T-shirts, books, and some music, too. ***U*** Tottenham Court Road

STATIONERY & ART SUPPLIES

L. Cornelissen & Son, 105 Great Russell Street, ***T*** 020 7636 1045. Beautiful shop supplying artist's materials, founded in 1856 and fitted out with wooden drawers and jars of pigment like sweets. ***U*** Tottenham Court Road

Paperchase, 213-15 Tottenham Court Road, ***T*** 020 7467 6200. Huge store selling colourful modern stationery, decorations, gifts, and a good range of papers and artist's materials on the top floor. ***U*** Goodge Street

BANKSIDE

Tate Modern

OPEN	Daily 10.00-18.00, Fri, Sat till 22.00
CLOSED	24-26/12
CHARGES	Admission free to galleries; charge for special exhibitions, lower rates for senior citizens, full-time students, unwaged and disabled visitors
TELEPHONE	**020 7887 8000** for information (minicom **020 7887 8687**); **020 7887 8888** for tickets to special exhibitions and events; **020 7401 5031** to book special tours
RECORDED INFO	**020 7887 8008**
WWW.	**tate.org.uk**
MAIN ENTRANCE	North Entrance on Bankside (between Blackfriars and Southwark Bridges); West Entrance on Holland Street
UNDERGROUND	Southwark, Blackfriars, London Bridge, Waterloo
RIVER BOAT	Tate to Tate services between Bankside and Millbank Millennium Piers via the London Eye, 10.00-16.40, journey time 18 minutes, buy tickets on board, from Tate ticket booths or website, or at London Eye customer services desk, schedules at www.thamesclippers.com
DISABLED ACCESS	North and Café Entrances offer the best access to wheelchairs and buggies. There are lifts to all floors. Wheelchairs and disabled parking spaces in Holland Street can be booked, **T 020 7887 8888**; other parking is very limited
GUIDED TOURS	Guided tours introduce highlights of each themed section (Nude/Action/Body at 11.00, History/Memory/Society at 12.00, Still Life/Object/Real Life at 14.00, Landscape/Matter/Environment at 15.00, daily, free). Audio tours include highlights, a children's tour and another for the visually impaired (£1). Radio receivers for use with hearing aids can be borrowed from the information desk for any talk or tour
SERVICES	Cloakroom and information desk on Level 1. Toilets and telephones on Levels 2, 3, 4, 5 and 7.
SHOPS	Largest shop on Level 1, with books on modern art, critical theory, film, photography, graphics and design, postcards, posters, and other souvenirs. There is another shop on Level 2. A smaller shop on Level 4 is linked to temporary exhibitions
EATING	Café/restaurants on Level 2 and Level 7; Espresso Bar on Level 4; kiosk outside main entrance on Level 2

Tate Modern presents regular special exhibitions on Level 4 (tickets from the desk in the Turbine Hall) as well as films, lectures and events.

Tate Modern Turbine Hall

Tate Modern is the new home for Britain's collection of international modern art from 1900 to the present day. It opened to much fanfare (largely deserved) in May 2000 and in its first year attracted 5 million visitors, confirming Britain's growing status as an international centre for contemporary art. The gallery has made public wonderful views along the river and the re-opening of the beautiful Millennium Bridge - after a wobbly start - has linked it with St Paul's Cathedral.

THE BUILDING

Bankside Power Station was originally designed by Sir Giles Gilbert Scott, who was also responsible for the less fortunate Battersea Power Station downriver. Its 4.2 million bricks are supported on a steel skeleton: at 99m high, the chimney was deliberately kept lower than the dome of St Paul's. It was built in two stages between 1947 and 1963 but rising oil prices meant it was used for only a few years and was empty when the Tate decided it had outgrown its Millbank building and began looking for a new home for its modern collections. The huge power station stood out as a candidate for conversion and became the focus for regenerating Southwark, the historic area of London in which it stands.

The Swiss architectural team of Jacques Herzog and Pierre de Meuron were chosen to oversee the transformation because they proposed to adapt the power station rather than rebuild it wholesale: 'using your enemy's energy for your own purposes'. They integrated seven storeys of new galleries and facilities with the existing turbine hall and chimney, retaining the industrial feel of bricks and girders, and the 'sexy' hum of the switching station (which will eventually be developed for new space). They added a two-storey 'light beam' on top to allow natural illumination of the uppermost galleries and house the restaurant, and co-designed the beacon at the chimney's summit with the artist Michael Craig-Martin.

HIGHLIGHTS

Works may appear under different themes at different times: check their location in the Information Room or with staff members.

Cubist still lifes and portraits of mistresses, *Weeping Woman*, *Woman in a Red Armchair*	Pablo Picasso
The Snail **and powerful sculptures of** *Backs*	Henri Matisse
Lobster Telephone **and Surrealist paintings**	Salvador Dalí
Jean Genet, **and fragile standing figures**	Alberto Giacometti
Seagram Paintings, **made for a restaurant**	Mark Rothko
Henry Moore, Barbara Hepworth, Richard Deacon, Antony Gormley and others	British sculpture
Equivalent VIII, **the 'bricks' at the centre of a media-manufactured furore in 1976**	Carl Andre
Concert for Anarchy **draws the crowds**	Rebecca Horn

The new building is on seven levels, linked by escalators, stairs and lifts. **Level 1** is the floor of the Turbine Hall, with the main shop and the Information Room. The ground-level entrances are on **Level 2**, where there is a smaller shop, auditorium and a café overlooking the gardens. The art starts on **Level 3**, with suites of galleries on the themes of Landscape/Matter/Environment and Still Life/Object/Real Life. The main temporary exhibitions are on **Level 4**. Displays called History/Memory/Society and Nude/Action/Body are on **Level 5**. Lifts and stairs go up to the restaurant and bar on **Level 7**.

MILLENNIUM BRIDGE

A short walk across the Millennium Bridge offers the most dramatic approach to Tate Modern. The first new bridge over the Thames in central London for over a century, it was proposed by architects Foster and Partners, engineers Arup, and the distinguished British sculptor Sir Anthony Caro. The 325m span is supported by cables that sag at mid-point to give uninterrupted views up and down the river. The bridge was so popular at its opening in June 2000 that the sway it developed when people walked on it in unison was soon apparent: it was closed after two days and tests and modifications began. The bridge, now steady as a rock, reopened in 2002. (To learn more about 'synchronous lateral excitation' and how it was solved, see www.arup.com/millenniumbridge.)

The bridge has lighting at deck level which creates a 'blade of light' effect that looks magical if you are crossing an adjacent bridge at night, or are viewing it from the **gardens** of Tate Modern, planted with rows of birches. The chimney of the power station looms above. Below it, with level access from the gardens, is the **North Entrance**.

LEVEL 1

TURBINE HALL The best way to appreciate the scale of the Turbine Hall is to enter the building from the **West Entrance**, off Holland Street, and walk down the ramp. The enormous space you now see - 35m high,155m long and 23m wide - was created by excavating the original basement, giving even greater height. Herzog and De Meuron used only half the space for the galleries, which protrude in a series of jutting boxes from the interior wall to your left. High above hangs a crane, testifying to the building's past; and you can hear the hum of the remaining electricity sub-station.

At the bottom of the slope are the **ticket desks**, where you can also hire **audio tours** (£1) round selected works in the collection, with commentaries by contemporary artists. The far end of the hall beyond the desks is used for temporary displays of sculpture, performance works and other events. Until 2004 the Turbine Hall will also be the site of specially commissioned sculpture projects by internationally acclaimed artists: so far Anish Kapoor's vast

TATE MODERN

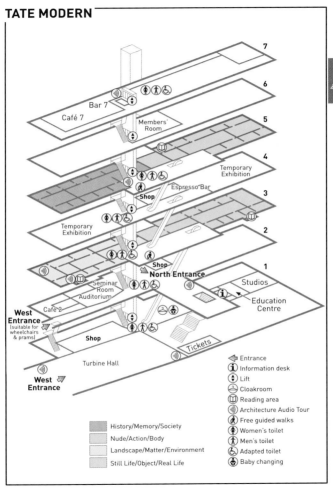

7

6

Bar 7

Café 7

Members'
Room

5

4

Temporary
Exhibition

Espresso Bar

Shop

3

Temporary
Exhibition

2

Shop
North Entrance

1

Studios

Seminar
Room
Auditorium

Education
Centre

Café 2

West
Entrance
(suitable for
wheelchairs
& prams)

Shop

Tickets

Turbine Hall

West
Entrance

◁ Entrance
ⓘ Information desk
🛗 Lift
Cloakroom
📖 Reading area
))) Architecture Audio Tour
Free guided walks
Women's toilet
Men's toilet
Adapted toilet
Baby changing

History/Memory/Society
Nude/Action/Body
Landscape/Matter/Environment
Still Life/Object/Real Life

Marsyas (2002), a membrane of red plastic stretched over three massive steel rings, has been the most successful at imposing its own identity on the vast space. Olafur Eliasson will attempt to do the same in 2003/4.

The enormous **shop** is accessible from the glass-walled atrium that also houses the cloakroom and the **Information Room**, which has a small library of reference books, art magazines, videos, audio tapes and press cuttings, and terminals where you can access the collection online; large-print guides and raised-line plans can also be found here. Outside this room and around the building are wooden posts carrying captive **audio guides** to 20c art movements and the conversion of the power station.

An escalator in the middle of the atrium goes straight to Level 3; lifts and stairs are at the end near the shop and give access to Level 2.

LEVEL 2

Basically a service level, this has the café at one end, an auditorium and another shop, often used for sales. A bridge allows views down to the floor of the Turbine Hall.

LEVEL 3

CONCOURSE A **free guided tour** to either of the themed collections on this level starts from the concourse: Still Life/Object/Real Life leaves at 14.00 daily, Landscape/Matter/Environment at 15.00 daily. **Audio guides** can be hired here and you can pick up foldable stools from racks near the stairs to provide some support on the art odyssey you are about to undertake. (There are more on Levels 4 and 5.)

The choice of this particular building for Tate Modern, and the manner of its conversion, meant that the art collection had to be hung in a new way. Suites of different-sized rooms on different floors did not lend themselves to the usual chronological tour. The curators therefore devised four exhibitions - based on the familiar academic themes of the nude, still life, landscape and history painting - each of which could provide an overview of 20c and 21c art practice. Works from different periods and places now hang together to illustrate new histories; some rooms may be devoted to single artists or groups. The content of these exhibitions also evolves constantly: rooms are rearranged every few months, raising new topics for exploration and allowing more works to be seen regularly.

This is certainly of benefit to those who can visit Tate Modern often: startling juxtapositions and interesting new interpretations are always to be found. But visitors with only one chance to 'do' the collection may feel frustrated if particular works are not on view, and pieces by one artist are scattered throughout the building. It is possible to check what is on display on the Tate's website, and staff may be able to locate works for you. The following descriptions are based on recent displays and try to suggest the topics covered and the breadth of work on show. Any one or two of the themed suites explored in depth would make a good day's visit.

STILL LIFE/OBJECT/REAL LIFE Still life - the depiction of objects alone - was traditionally one of the most modest artistic pursuits. But in the 20c, as scientific discoveries undermined belief in the stability of 'reality', artists used still life to explore subjectivity and flux, our relationship to new technologies and consumerism. Claes Oldenburg's *Giant 3-Way Plug Scale 2/3* (1970) dangling outside the entrance vividly illustrates how mass-produced objects loom large in modern lives.

Paul Cézanne was one of the first artists to question how we actually see reality, abandoning consistent viewpoints and perspective and interpreting images such as *Still Life with Water Jug* (1892-3) as discrete patches of colour. The equally single-minded Giorgio Morandi explored subtle relationships of colour and shape by painting the same cast of humble bottles and bowls, seen in the contemplative *Still Life* (1946).

From the turn of the 20c, artists everywhere were appropriating everyday products in their art, either as subject, as in Natalya Goncharova's *Linen* (1913), a tangle of male and female laundry, or as actual material. From about 1912 Pablo Picasso and **Georges Braque** developed Cézanne's experiments and fragmented mundane imagery in Cubist collages and paintings: Picasso's *Bottle of Vieux Marc, Glass, Guitar and Newspaper* (1913) incorporates a yellowing scrap from a real copy of *Le Figaro*.

Another collagist, Kurt Schwitters, made poignant combinations of old tickets, magazine advertisements and found objects, which he called *Merz*; Daniel Spoerri's *Prose Poems* (1959-60) traps the remains of a meal on a board that is hung like a painting. The British artist **Eduardo Paolozzi** has described his own work as the 'metamorphosis of rubbish'. He uses an even broader range of materials - cheap toys, machine parts, film star photos - to inspire sculptures and prints such as the series *As Is When* (1964-5), in which Wittgenstein meets Mickey Mouse.

Paolozzi was influenced by the Surrealists, who were some of the most famous manipulators of the rules of still life in the 20c. They made provocative objects that were intended to collide the subconscious and the conscious, the most famous probably Salvador Dalí's *Lobster Telephone* (1936), with the crustacean's tail over the mouthpiece. These works often have a sinister and erotic edge, as in Dorothea Tanning's blush-pink *Nue Couchée* (1969-70) and especially *The Doll* (1934, replica 1965) by Hans Bellmer. More recent artists have used similar techniques to comment on consumerism - Piero Manzoni's neatly labelled tin of *Artist's Shit* (1961), for example - and sexual politics. In Rosemarie Trockel's *Balaklava Box* (1986-90), the cosy knitted headgear has disturbing patterns of swastikas and bunny girl logos, and no holes to breathe through.

In the 20c photography offered an easy means to capture visual reality, so artists experimented with different forms of representation, often calling attention to their choices. Patrick Caulfield combines a 'photographic' realism with a flat graphic style in *After Lunch* (1975); **Roy Lichtenstein**'s appropriation of comic-book printing textures is instantly recognizable in *Interior with Waterlilies* (1991), which is so big as to invite you inside.

This use of the mass-produced is founded on a belief promoted by **Marcel Duchamp**, that an artist can make art out of anything: the idea is the important thing. The most notorious example is the urinal he simply retitled *Fountain* (1917, replica 1964). Duchamp's 'readymades' had a major influence on the work of subsequent artists, who looked at all objects for inspiration. Julian Opie's *H* (1987) entertainingly reverses the procedure, being a meticulously accurate but useless representation of an air vent, and relates to the wooden *Brillo* (1964) boxes made by **Andy Warhol**.

Some artists tried to erase their identity as makers, leaving the sculpture or painting as an 'autonomous object' needing no interpretation. The stripes on **Frank Stella**'s *Six Mile Bottom* (1960) were sized according to the width of a house-painter's brush and followed the shaped canvas. Sol Lewitt had assistants make his *Five Open Geometric Structures* (1979), which yet have the presence of three-dimensional hieroglyphs. **Richard Deacon**, on the other hand, calls attention to the engineering skills that fashion his sculptures, which seem inspired by natural forms. *After* (1998) is a segmental, twisting loop of wood, glue and aluminium; *Struck Dumb* (1988), a hollow, fossil-like lump with its 'mouth' closed by a featureless plate of steel.

One room is often used as a small cinema, where you might see Lázsló Moholy-Nagy's experimental film (1930) of the play of light on a mobile made at the Bauhaus. More kinetic art includes Heinz Mack's gleaming silvery *Light Dynamo* (1963), and headache-inducing optical effects are explored in Jésus Rafael Soto's *Cardinal* (1965). Cornelia Parker tried to freeze rather than animate her material in *Cold Dark Matter* (1991): she filled a garden shed with discarded objects and had the British Army blow it up, then suspended the resulting bits and pieces in a room-sized installation.

The very old genre of *vanitas* or *memento mori* ('Remember you must die'), in which natural and manmade objects are used to stress the brevity of life and its material comforts, survives into the 21c. Picasso used it to express post-war political fears in the grey, fragmented *Goat's skull, bottle and candle* (1952). In *Forms without life* (1991), exotic seashells in a clinical cabinet, **Damien Hirst** questions the way we kill beauty to acquire knowledge.

Hirst's pseudo-scientific presentation also comments on our need to collect and order. Similarly Mark Dion's *Tate Thames Dig* (1999), commissioned when the Tate split its collections, presents a cabinet of finds from Bankside and Millbank that deliberately fails to distinguish the archaeologically valuable from everyday rubbish.

A snug **reading room** near the end of the first chain of galleries has a view down to the Turbine Hall, and catalogues and guide books to the art on display (there is another on this level in the other suite).

LANDSCAPE/MATTER/ENVIRONMENT This theme not only encompasses depictions of nature, but also artists' responses to the urban environment and even their imagining of 'inner space'.

At the turn of the 20c, **Claude Monet** was engaged in influential experiments with the depiction of nature. His large *Water Lilies* (after 1916) is a close-up on the surface of the water, drawing the viewer into the image rather than setting up pictorial boundaries. It might be reflected in the work of Colour Field painters such as Jules Olitski, whose *Instant Loveland* (1968) is a filmy, almost iridescent expanse of paint dots. Or it might be contrasted with the work of **Richard Long**, who brings nature into the galleries as stone circles or wall paintings of mud, and makes art of his experiences in nature by displaying accounts of cross-country walks. Other Land Art on display might be Robert Smithson's film of the building of his *Spiral Jetty* (1970).

The matter from which art is made has been a continual preoccupation but in the 1950s and 1960s some artists reduced it to single colours, shapes and voids. Yves Klein's *IKB 79* (1959) is simply an intense slab of the shade of blue he patented, representing nothing but itself. **Lucio Fontana**, meanwhile, was destroying the illusion of the painted surface by presenting bare canvas slashed with a razor to reveal the space beyond, as in *Spatial Concept 'Waiting'* (1960). Spare a thought for Shozo Shimamoto, who had been blurring the creative and destructive acts in a similar way, as in *Holes* (1954): he gave up for fear of being thought a copyist of the better-known Fontana.

Meanwhile others attempted to evoke natural forms by abstract means. Nowadays microphotography and physics lead us to expect certain laws defining natural structures: **Henri Matisse** just held a snail shell in his hand before producing *The Snail* (1953), a spiral of cut and coloured paper. In *Corinthos* (1954-5), a satisfying chunk of polished hardwood, **Barbara Hepworth** carved a spiral tunnel suggestive of the internal structures of a shell. And Alexander Calder's delicate mobile, *Antennae with red and blue dots* (1960) makes explicit its debt to insect fragility and balance. Ellsworth Kelly's more enigmatic *White Curve* (1974), an aluminium panel seeming to detach itself from the wall, refers to a hill near his home.

At the far end of this suite of rooms there is a grand, double-height gallery for major installations. Currently it is showing Joseph Beuys' towering *Lightning with Stag in its Glare* (1958-85).

The Surrealists used landscapes as a metaphor for inner space: in Giorgio di Chirico's *The Uncertainty of the Poet* (1913), a deserted, shadowy city; in Max Ernst's *Forest and Dove* (1927), a towering mass of timber rendered in an innovative scraping technique. You will probably also see paintings by **Salvador Dali**: *Metamorphosis of Narcissus* (1937) and *Autumn Cannibalism* (1936), a comment on the Spanish Civil War in which a monstrous couple seem to devour each other in a dry landscape. The Surrealist Movement included a number of women artists, among whom Leonor Fini and Dorothea Tanning might be represented: their paintings *Little Hermit Sphinx* (1948) and *Eine Kleine Nachtmusik* (1943) are no less disturbing for their small size.

The self - and its intuitive movements and decisions - was also the focus of the Action Painters, among whom **Jackson Pollock** said 'I am nature'. His *Summertime Number 9A* (1948) is probably one of the Tate's most famous images, a dripped, poured and dabbed scroll of rhythmic lines with accents of yellow, blue and red, an attempt to be entirely instinctive rather than imitative. The bulging, biomorphic forms and blended colours of Arshile Gorky's *Waterfall* (1943) refer more recognizably to his experience of nature.

A more traditional approach to painting nature is seen in Cy Twombly's *Quattro Stagione* ('Four Seasons', 1993-4), where colours refer to natural cycles and fragments of poetry to his home in the Mediterranean. **Anselm Keifer** uses the German landscape - and the horrors inflicted on it by war and industrialization - to explore national identity, as in his book of woodcuts *The Rhine* (1981).

At the centre of this suite of rooms is one devoted to the *Seagram Paintings* (1958-9) by **Mark Rothko**, large 'murals' originally commissioned for the Four Seasons restaurant in New York. Rothko donated them to the Tate in 1968 (ironically, swayed by the thought that his work would be in the same building as Turner's) and at the same time conceived their setting, down to the wall colour and low light levels. The sombre palette of maroon and grey requires you to look for some time before the subtleties of colour emerge from the murk; the intended mood of contemplation is somewhat undermined by the room's usefulness as a thoroughfare across the suite.

LEVEL 4

Travel up to the next floor to see temporary exhibitions in the suites of rooms either side of a **shop** and **espresso bar**, leading to a balcony.

LEVEL 5

CONCOURSE A **free guided tour** to either of the themed collections on this level starts from the concourse: Nude/Action/Body leaves at 11.00 daily, History/Memory/Society at 12.00 daily.

NUDE/ACTION/BODY In the 20c, art's relationship to the human body was pushed far beyond the academic convention of the nude. Many artists rejected the voyeuristic role and used their own bodies to reflect on individuality, mortality and gender stereotypes, and some even used the viewer's body to complete a work.

The suite may begin with a variety of 20c paintings of nudes. Euan Uglow's *Nude* (1962-3) typifies his analytical approach, making painstaking measurements and marks over many months. Contrast the passion of Picasso in *Nude Woman in a Red Armchair* (1932), in which every line is curvaceous and even the chair embraces the model. Female subjects far outnumber the men, though roles were reversed by Alice Neel, who generously gave *Joe Gould* (1933) five penises: he looks suitably pleased. **Stanley Spencer**'s *Double Nude Portrait. The Artist and his Second Wife* (1937) is a fiercely honest look at marital misery. John Coplan's huge photographs use his own naked body to express a common humanity, as in *Self-Portrait (Frieze No.2 Four Panels)* (1994).

In the early 20c artists became excited by the African tribal art and other 'primitive' work that was entering Europe. It seemed to suggest a physical freedom at odds with their own civilization. (They did not pay too much attention to the cultural context of the carvings or the colonialism that made them available.) Some collected the art and allowed it to influence their own vision of the body: there is a case of ethnographic material, including a Baga figure from Guinea that belonged to Jacob Epstein, who carved *Female Figure in Flenite* (1913). You may see African-inspired paintings and sculptures by Picasso; **Amadeo Modigliani**'s enigmatic *Head* (c 1911-12), exuding a calm spirituality; Matisse's massive, progressively reductive sculptures, *Back I* (c 1909-10) and *Back II* (c 1913-14), from a series of four; and Ernst Ludwig Kirchner's loud paean to mixed skinny-dipping, *Bathers at Moritzburg* (1909/26).

Meanwhile, the depiction of women - so often portrayed as mere bodies - was developing to reflect their changing roles. John Singer Sargent's bold brushwork shows *Hylda Wertheimer* (1901) as a woman of fashion, but she insisted on keeping her *pince nez*.

Clothes projected social attitudes as well as status. Gustav Klimt's *Hermine Gallia* (1904) wore an avant-garde, filmy chiffon dress, perhaps designed by him, while Epstein's thoroughly modern *Iris Beerbohm Tree* (1915) has a helmet of burnished hair.

During and after the Second World War, some art used the vulnerable and suffering body to reflect on recent events - see the scarred, pitted *Head of a Hostage* (1943-4) by Jean Fautrier. Francis Bacon's *Figure in a Landscape* (1945), spewing blackness, derived from photographs of Nazi dictators. Some of the most powerful renderings of human form and personality were achieved by the most apparently fragile means in the work of **Alberto Giacometti**: his slender figures are isolated but stand firm while his portrait of *Jean Genet* (1954 or 55) catches a character in a web of spidery lines.

Marcel Duchamp's iconic *Large Glass (The Bride Stripped Bare by her Bachelors, Even)* (1915-23), re-created by the British artist Richard Hamilton (1965-6), treats the relations between the sexes as a comedy of frustrated machinery. The pink bride floats in the upper half, while her admirers crank away fruitlessly below. A miniature version is seen in the *Box in a Valise* (c 1943), a tiny museum of Duchamp's most famous works.

In some performance art the artist's own body is tested. A video of Paul McCarthy's very physical *Rocky* (1976) is meant to convey the absurdity of the human condition but it is not for young children - there will be warnings. **Cindy Sherman**'s photographs of *Bus Riders* (1976/2000) involve her transformation into people of all ages, races and both sexes. Other artists using film include Bruce Nauman, who confronts us with people locked in cycles of physical or emotional violence, as in *Good Boy Bad Boy* (1985); while **Bill Viola**'s ambitious *Five Angels for the Millennium* (2001) creates a disorientating environment of ungraspable sounds and slow-motion watery floating images.

Carl Andre's *Equivalent VIII* (1966) also involves the viewer by demanding attention to the space in which the artwork is experienced, in this case the floor. **Richard Serra**'s massive

Trip Hammer (1988) invites contemplation about our relation to the work were it ever to fall over.

As you leave this suite there is a **reading room** with comfy sofas and catalogues, and a picture window overlooking the Thames, a beautiful tapestry of London in surprisingly warm browns and greys. Video works play in niches off both reading rooms on this floor.

HISTORY/MEMORY/SOCIETY Traditional history painting recorded and often celebrated major events of the past, but in the 20c art sought to bring the impact of political decisions and social upheavals closer to home. In this display, artists are shown responding to the movements of history, sometimes even believing they could alter its course (as in the manifestos of the Vorticists and Futurists): others depicting their individual victimhood. In *Weeping Woman* (1937) by **Pablo Picasso**, his mistress Dora Maar stands for Spain suffering under the Civil War, in a painting which manages to convey intense anxiety while remaining unequivocally pretty. The distorted but robust, striding figure in *Unique Forms of Continuity in Space* (1913) by **Umberto Boccioni** illustrates the Futurists' confidence and fascination with speed. You might see a collection of Soviet poster art, exhorting handsome factory workers and peasants to overthrow the capitalist oppressor: these 'realistic' styles were favoured by Stalin, who soon got rid of anyone working in a more progressive, modernist photomontage technique.

Umberto Boccioni *Unique Forms of Continuity in Space* (1913)

Naum Gabo left Russia in 1922. A room is devoted to his work, and *Head No. 2* (1916) stands outside these galleries. His utopian Contructivist ideas, with form reduced to essentials and suggested by planes rather than mass, are visible in delicate maquettes using futuristic materials like perspex, which also allowed for multiple viewpoints. An example is *Spheric Theme (Penetrated Variation)* (c 1937-40) where a sphere is defined by its internal movements. **Dan Flavin** admired the Constructivists and used equally mundane fluorescent strip lights to subtly alter the spaces around them, as in *Untitled (Monument for V Tatlin)* (1969).

Another group of idealists, the artists of De Stijl, sought universal laws of artistic harmony by imposing strict limits on their use of line and colour, favouring grids of horizontals and verticals. The most famous is **Piet Mondrian**, whose beliefs found their purest expression in works like *Composition with Red and Blue* (1935). He fell out with another De Stijl member, Theo van Doesburg, who allowed himself to use diagonal lines, as in *Counter Composition VI* (1925).

Other artists wanted much more direct communication with their audience and with history. Andre Fougeron, a French Communist who came to prominence in the 1930s, brought realism to the service of politics, as in the whopping *Atlantic Civilisation* (1953), a cartoon-like protest against American capitalism and the Algerian war. Boris Taslitsky's *Riposte* (1951) - a dockside riot against war in Indo-China - has more energy. Film was also brought to the service of politics and you might see Jean Vigo's attack on French bourgeois society, *A Propos de Nice* ('Concerning Nice', 1929).

Intense emotional or psychological states brought about by events are conjured in Rebecca Horn's *Concert for Anarchy* (1990), a grand piano suspended upside down from the ceiling and periodically eviscerating itself. It usually makes its presence felt throughout the gallery, drawing people by the noise it makes. Cathy de Monchaux's *Wandering about in the future, looking forward to the past* (1994) uses her characteristically menacing combination of soft velvet, ribbon and pierced metal to explore memory. Josef Beuys's *Felt Suit* (1970) carries with it the artist's experience of being shot down in an aeroplane in the Second World War and being saved by Tartars, who wrapped him in felt and fat. Nastier memories might be summoned by Louise Bourgeois' *Cell (Eyes and Mirrors)* (1989-93), a cage of metal mesh and glass panes that evokes her traumatic childhood circumstances. It is dominated by a pair of giant marble eyeballs.

The potential of new kinds of social relationship using modern communications was also embraced by 20c artists. Postal art of the 1960s, collected by the American artist Ray Johnson, consists of postcards, photocopies and handmade items mailed all over the world. Participants included On Kawara, who sent daily postcards to Barbarba Reise telling her what time he got up each morning; Gilbert and George; Fluxus; and Yoko Ono and John Lennon.

Saatchi Gallery

OPEN	Daily 10.00-18.00, Fri, Sat till 22.00
CLOSED	Check website or telephone for details
CHARGES	£8.50, concessions £6.50, family ticket £25
TELEPHONE	020 7823 2363
WWW.	saatchi-gallery.co.uk
MAIN ENTRANCE	County Hall, South Bank
UNDERGROUND	Waterloo, Westminster
DISABLED ACCESS	Wheelchair access from Belvedere Road entrance

The imposing County Hall (1912-33) became redundant with the abolition of the Greater London Council in 1986. Since then it has been carved up between various tourist attractions (see below), hotels and eateries. The newest of these is the Saatchi Gallery, which moved here in 2003 from its previous home in north London. Now the wood-panelled rooms exhibit the collection of

Saatchi Gallery
Central exhibition room

contemporary art amassed by Charles Saatchi, a key player in the rise of the Young British Artists of the 1990s. The works here - by Damien Hirst, Tracey Emin, Chris Ofili, Sarah Lucas, Gary Hume, Jenny Savile, Marc Quinn, Jake and Dinos Chapman, and other British and international artists - have become instantly recognizable through constant media exposure (Saatchi did not make a fortune in advertising for nothing). But in these surroundings, very different from the conventional 'white cube' environment, the paintings, sculptures and installations have a new immediacy as made objects, and a pleasantly light touch with supervision means you can inspect them at very close quarters. The setting does not suit everything, but the sad fate of the building adds an appropriate poignancy to others, such as Duane Hanson's bewildered *Tourists*. After its opening Damien Hirst retrospective, the Saatchi is promising to exhibit unknown British and other contemporary artists and to host shows from other museums and collections.

Next door to the Saatchi Gallery, the County Hall Gallery hosts **Dalí Universe**, an exhibition of Surrealist sculptures, drawings and prints, and other temporary shows (entrance charge, daily 10.00-17.30, July, Aug till 18.30, *T* 020 7620 2720, www.daliuniverse.com). The **London Aquarium** has huge seawater tanks and petting pools (entrance charge, daily 10.00-18.00, *T* 020 7967 8000, www.londonaquarium.co.uk).

on route

Bishop of Winchester's Palace, Clink Street. Not a whole palace but part of the great hall, with an early 14c rose window in unexpected juxtaposition to 19c warehouses and 20c offices. *U* London Bridge

City Hall, Queen's Walk, Mon-Fri 8.00-20.00 and some weekends, *T* 020 7983 4000, www.london.gov.uk/gla/city_hall. Helmet-like new home for the Mayor and Assembly, designed by Norman Foster. Limited public access to the spiral ramp, but new public spaces include the Scoop amphitheatre outside. *U* London Bridge

Design Museum, 28 Shad Thames, entrance charge, daily 10.00-17.45, Fri till 21.00, *T* 020 7940 8790, www.designmuseum.org. Terence Conran's brainchild (opened 1989) was the first in the world devoted to the design and production of consumer products from cars to baked bean cans, demonstrated through colourful and popular exhibitions. *U* London Bridge, Tower Hill

Fashion and Textile Museum, 83 Bermondsey Street, entrance charge, Tues-Sun 11.00-17.45, *T* 020 7403 0222, www.ftmlondon.com. New museum, the creation of fashion designer Zandra Rhodes, in a pink-and-orange building by Ricardo Legoretta. *U* London Bridge

Golden Hinde, St Mary Overie Dock, entrance charge, daily 10.00-17.00, *T* 020 7403 0123, www.goldenhinde.co.uk. Replica of the ship in which Drake circumnavigated the world in 1577-80. *U* London Bridge

Jerwood Space, 171 Union Street, Mon-Fri 9.00-18.00, Sat, Sun 10.00-18.00 (exhibition times vary), *T* 020 7654 0171, www.jerwoodspace.co.uk. New centre for performance art and gallery showing young artists and winners of the Jerwood Foundation's awards and sponsorships in painting, drawing and sculpture. *U* Southwark

London Dungeon, 28 Tooley Street, entrance charge, daily 10.00-17.30, *T* 020 7403 7221, www.thedungeons.com. Celebration of gruesomeness - Jack the Ripper, famous murders, etc - built into the arches of London Bridge station. *U* London Bridge

London Eye, Jubilee Gardens, entrance charge, daily 9.30-20.00 or later, closed most of Jan, *T* 0870 5000 600, disabled bookings *T* 0870 990 8885, www.londoneye.com. A consistently popular attraction, the world's tallest observation wheel is 135m tall, giving passengers a 25 mile view from the suspended capsules. *U* Waterloo, Westminster

London Eye

Millennium Bridge, Bankside to St Paul's Cathedral. Stunning new bridge linking Tate Modern to St Paul's Cathedral. Designed by Norman Foster, it lives up to his intention to create a 'blade of light' across the river. Try to see it at night. *U* Southwark, London Bridge, St Paul's

Rose Theatre, 56 Park Street, entrance charge, daily 10.00-17.00 summer, 12.00-17.00 winter, *T* 020 7593 0026, www.rosetheatre.org.uk. A sound-and-light show illuminates the remains of the earliest Bankside theatre, where Shakespeare once acted. *U* London Bridge

St Paul's Cathedral, entrance charge, Mon-Sat 8.30-16.00, Sun between services, *T* 020 7236 4128, www.stpauls.co.uk. If you've been tantalized by the sight of Christopher Wren's masterpiece across the river from the Tate, it is only a short walk away across the Millennium Bridge. *U* St Paul's

Shakespeare's Globe

Shakespeare's Globe, Bankside, entrance charge, exhibition and tours hourly Oct-April 10.00-17.00, May-Sept 10.00-12.00 (plays in afternoon), *T* 020 7902 1500, box office 020 7401 9919, www.shakespeares-globe.org. Loving re-creation of the original theatre inspired by the American actor Sam Wanamaker, now staging award-winning productions of plays by WS and his contemporaries. *U* Southwark, London Bridge

South Bank Centre, between Hungerford and Waterloo Bridges, box office *T* 020 7960 4201, www.rfh.org.uk. The Royal Festival Hall, one of London's premier music venues, was a legacy of 1951's Festival of Britain and is soon to be refurbished. The already revamped Hayward Gallery (www.hayward.org.uk) holds major art exhibitions. Beyond Waterloo Bridge are the National Film Theatre and Royal National Theatre. *U* Waterloo, Embankment, Southwark, London Bridge

Southwark Cathedral, Montague Court, daily 8.00-18.00, refectory 10.00-17.00, *T* 020 7367 6700, www.dswark.org.uk. Incorporating the 13c remains of the earliest Gothic church in London. Wenceslaus Hollar made a panoramic drawing of London from the tower in 1638; a new exhibition updates it for the 21c. *U* London Bridge

Southwark Underground station, Blackfriars Road. Like all the new stations on the Jubilee Line extension (opened 1999), this was designed by a leading architect, Richard MacCormac. It offers intriguing vistas up escalator tunnels to Alexander Beleschenko's wall of blue glass on the lower concourse. *U* Southwark

Vinopolis, 1 Bank End, admission charge, Tues-Fri, Sun 11.00-18.00, Sat, Mon 11.00-20.00, *T* 0870 4444 777, www.vinopolis.co.uk. A museum of wine which takes you on a tour of the world's vineyards, and includes free tastings in the ticket price. *U* London Bridge

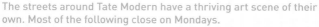

commercial galleries

The streets around Tate Modern have a thriving art scene of their own. Most of the following close on Mondays.

Bankside Gallery, 48 Hopton Street (entrance from Thames footpath), *T* 020 7928 7521, www.banksidegallery.com. One-person, group and themed shows of work by members of the Royal Watercolour Society and the Royal Society of Painter-Printmakers, and practical art books and materials to feed your enthusiasm. *U* Blackfriars, Southwark

Llewellyn Alexander Gallery, 124-126 The Cut, *T* 020 7620 1322, www.llewellynalexander.com. Oils, watercolours and pastels by living artists, plus the annual 'Not the Royal Academy' show for Summer Exhibition rejects. *U* Waterloo

Purdy Hicks Gallery, 65 Hopton Street, *T* 020 7401 9229, www.purdyhicks.com. Contemporary international painters and photographers represented in one-person shows throughout the year. *U* Blackfriars, Southwark

Skylark 2, 1.09 Oxo Tower Wharf, *T* 020 7401 9666, www.skylarkgallery.com. Artists' collective showing affordable paintings, prints, sculptures and ceramics in monthly shows. Skylark 1 is at Gabriel's Wharf. *U* Southwark, Waterloo

Southbank Printmaker's Gallery, 11 Gabriel's Wharf, *T* 020 7928 8184. Artist-run gallery selling etchings, screenprints and woodcuts. *U* Southwark, Waterloo

Studio Fusion Gallery, 1.06 Oxo Tower Wharf, *T* 020 7928 3600, www.studiofusiongallery.co.uk. Britain's first gallery devoted to work in enamels (glass fused to metal), showing and selling jewellery and larger item. *U* Southwark, Waterloo

eating and drinking

AT THE MUSEUM

£ **Espresso Bar** on Level 4 serves drinks, sandwiches and snacks, and has riverside balconies for the nicotine-deprived. Self-service.

££ **Café 2**. Light and more substantial meals, snacks, tea and coffee. Overlooks the garden. Waiter service.

Café 7, *T* 020 7402 5020. Serves a similar menu, enhanced by spectacular views over the river. You can now secure these, and avoid the queue, by booking. Waiter service.

SURROUNDING AREA

£ **The Anchor**, 34 Park Street, *T* 020 7407 1577. This historic pub, recently extended with massive insensitivity, still has parts of its cosy, labyrinthine interior. An outside area with tables overlooks the Thames. Beer and food are average. *U* London Bridge

Café Brood, 1-6 Green Dragon Court, *T* 020 7357 8484. Well-positioned for an assault on Borough Food Market, with tables overlooking Southwark Cathedral. *U* London Bridge

Design Museum Café, 28 Shad Thames. Candy-coloured furniture, a riverside terrace and cakes by Konditor & Cook make this a pleasant place for a mid-museum snack. *U* London Bridge, Tower Hill

Eat., Barge House Street, *T* 020 7928 8179. Fresh sandwiches (bagels, baguettes, toasties), soups, salads and tempting breakfast options make this a popular chain. No credit cards. *U* Southwark, Waterloo

Founder's Arms, 52 Hopton Street, *T* 020 7928 1899. Well-located to draw in tourists staggering from Tate Modern, this modern riverside pub serves decent if unspectacular lunches, and has a coffee bar and riverside terrace. *U* Southwark, Blackfriars

Fusebox, 12 Stoney Street, *T* 020 7407 9888. Deli meals with an Eastern/Pacific Rim edge, to eat in or take away. *U* London Bridge

George Inn, 77 Borough High Street, *T* 020 7407 2056. This is what remains of London's last surviving galleried coaching inn (1676). Recommended more for its literary associations than its reasonable beer or pub grub. *U* Southwark

Konditor & Cook, 10 Stoney Street, *T* 020 7407 5100. Very small café (offshoot of the original at 60 The Cut, by the Young Vic theatre) famous for delicious cakes and pastries but also serving breakfast and light savouries. *U* London Bridge

Mesón don Felipe, 53 The Cut, *T* 020 7928 3237. Very popular tapas bar with a good atmosphere, very fresh food and sometimes less warmly received live guitar music. *U* Southwark, Waterloo

Studio 6, Gabriel's Wharf, Upper Ground, *T* 020 7928 6243. Shed-like bar and restaurant with plentiful outdoor tables serving good pub grub. Best in summer. *U* Southwark, Waterloo

££ **Bankside**, 32 Southwark Bridge Road, *T* 020 7633 0011. Friendly basement restaurant offering unassuming bistro food in large quantities. *U* London Bridge

Café 171, Jerwood Space, 171 Union Street, *T* 020 7654 0100. Especially good soup, sandwiches and modern canteen-style food served in the gallery complex. Recently extended into a garden restaurant. *U* Southwark

Delfina Studio Café, 50 Bermondsey Street, *T* 020 7357 0244. Some way from Tate Modern but recommended for its setting in a local artist-run gallery and its innovative cuisine. Lunch only. *U* London Bridge

Feng Sushi, 13 Stoney Street, *T* 020 7407 8744. Informal Japanese restaurant, with good sushi fairly priced. *U* London Bridge

Fish!, Cathedral Street, *T* 020 7407 3803. This branch in a chain of diners, almost in the precincts of Southwark Cathedral, offers a choice of fresh fish and sauces, simply prepared. *U* London Bridge

George & Vulture, 3 Castle Court, *T* 020 7626 9710. A fair walk from Tate (via London Bridge), but you'll need to burn off the traditional grub served here to old-style City gents (jacket and tie required). Most often described as 'Dickensian'. *U* Monument

Laughing Gravy, 154 Blackfriars Road, *T* 020 7721 7055. The environs may not be very appealing but this is a friendly wine bar serving imaginative, reliable food. *U* Southwark

Tas, 33 The Cut, *T* 020 7928 2111. Tasty, good-value Turkish food including excellent mezze. Often packed so try to book an upstairs table. There is another branch at 22 New Globe Walk. *U* Waterloo

Wine Wharf, Stoney Street, *T* 020 7940 8335. The other eatery at Vinopolis, and perhaps better value than the Cantina (see below),

offering lighter meals and over 50 wines by the glass.
U London Bridge

£££ Baltic, 74 Blackfriars Road, **T** 020 7928 1111. This stark modern conversion of a wonky 19c building is a great space in which to eat good Eastern European food, washed down with an array of vodkas. Set pre-theatre menus. **U** Southwark

Blueprint Café, 28 Shad Thames, **T** 020 7378 7031. Great views of Tower Bridge from this modern Mediterranean restaurant in the Design Museum. **U** London Bridge

Cantina Vinopolis, 1 Bank End, **T** 020 7940 8333. Restaurant under the railway arches, with a memorable choice of drink (unsurprisingly, given that it is attached to the wine museum), serving Mediterranean-style food. **U** London Bridge

Livebait, 41-45 The Cut, **T** 020 7928 7211. Big, black-and-white-tiled branch of fresh fish and seafood chain, which can be excellent if pricey: the set menu may offer best value. **U** Waterloo

Oxo Tower, Barge House Street, **T** 020 7803 3888. Euro-Oriental food and spectacular eighth-floor views, with sky-high prices to match. **U** Southwark, Waterloo

People's Palace, Royal Festival Hall, South Bank, **T** 020 7928 9999. River views, especially dramatic at night, and modern international cuisine, with a lively bar. **U** Waterloo, Embankment

River Walk, Oxo Tower, Barge House Street, **T** 020 7928 2864. This Modern European brasserie and larger restaurant on the second floor offer probably the best-value eating in this landmark building. **U** Southwark, Waterloo

RSJ, 13a Coin Street, **T** 020 7928 4554. The décor in this established restaurant may not be up to much but the Anglo-French food is great value and the list of Loire wines said to be the best in the country and reasonably priced. **U** Waterloo

Shakespeare's Globe, New Globe Walk, **T** 020 7928 9444. River views and the chance to see the Globe's actors stoke up between rehearsals are a bigger draw than the limited menu. Traditional cream teas are good. Cheaper café on floor below. **U** London Bridge, Southwark

Sweetings, 39 Queen Victoria Street, **T** 020 7248 3062. You'll have to cross the Thames to reach this City gents' favourite, serving good, simple fish and seafood. Lunch only and closed weekends. **U** Mansion House

LATE-NIGHT BARS

Baltic, 74 Blackfriars Road, *T* 020 7928 1111. Part of the newly opened and popular Eastern European restaurant (see above), this has a relaxed ambience, an award-winning cocktail bartender and lots of vodka. Open Mon-Sat till 23.00, Sun till 10.30. *U* Southwark

shopping

Borough Market

The South Bank is becoming a centre for designer-makers, especially of jewellery and homewares. This list gives a flavour of what you can see at the Oxo Tower studios and at Gabriel's Wharf, along the pleasant riverside walk. The most fun to be had, however, is at the superlative Borough Food Market on Fridays and Saturdays.

ACCESSORIES

Heads Rule Hearts, 8 Gabriel's Wharf, Upper Ground, *T* 020 7928 1122. Hats from mother-of-the-bride straws to furry winter warmers for kids, plus some bags and scarves. *U* Waterloo

BOOKS

Calder Bookshop, 51 The Cut, *T* 020 7620 2900, www.calderpublications.com. Outlet for a groundbreaking, often controversial and now venerable publisher (of Samuel Becket and William Burroughs, among others). Plays, poetry and foreign titles stock the shelves. *U* Waterloo

Marcus Campbell Art Books, 43 Holland Street, *T* 020 7621 0111, www.marcuscampbell.demon.co.uk. Out of print, second-hand and rare books on 20c art, including artist's books. Closed Sat, Sun. *U* Southwark, Blackfriars

CLOTHES

For Design Sake, 1.19 Oxo Tower Wharf, *T* 020 7928 2021. Trendy tops, bikinis and other clothes inspired by vintage pop. *U* Southwark, Waterloo

Lauren Shanley, 4 Gabriel's Wharf, *T* 020 7928 5728. Hand-dyed and embroidered clothes, also intricate bead jewellery. *U* Southwark, Waterloo

Michèle Oberdieck, 1.04 Oxo Tower Wharf, *T* 020 7261 1414. This designer prints textiles with delicate natural forms to produce a small collection of clothes, wall hangings and window coverings. *U* Southwark, Waterloo

FLOWERS

Flower Store, g3/10 Oxo Tower Wharf, *T* 020 7928 7400, www.flowerstore.co.uk. Hand-tied bouquets, exotics (orchids, potted palms) and bright containers. *U* Southwark, Waterloo

Phlox, 2 Coin Street, *T* 020 7401 8244. Eclectic array of growing plants, containers and accessories (ostrich eggs, scented candles) as well as cut flowers. *U* Waterloo

FOOD

Borough Food Market, Southwark Street (by the Cathedral), *T* 020 7407 1002, www.boroughmarket.org.uk. Foodie heaven: stalls sell traditionally produced, often organic fruit and veg, meat and cheese, fresh seafood and fish, breads, honey, exotic oils, cakes and puds, Spanish jamon and West Indian hot sauces. Plenty of opportunities to taste or take away. Open Fri 11.00-18.00, Sat 9.00-16.00. *U* London Bridge

Bedales, 5 Bedale Street, *T* 020 7403 8853, www.bedalestreet.com. Hampers of Italian and French goodies and wines. *U* London Bridge

Neal's Yard Dairy, 6-8 Park Street, *T* 020 7378 8195. Join the queue for fine British and Irish cheeses, pain Poilâne, etc. *U* London Bridge

Saffron, 2 Bedale Street, *T* 020 7403 0356. Middle Eastern deli, with a tempting window of baklava and Turkish delight. *U* London Bridge

HOMES

Archipelago Textiles, 1.07 Oxo Tower Wharf, *T* 020 7922 1121, www.archipelagotextiles.co.uk. Unique textiles for the home, also fine shawls for you. *U* Southwark, Waterloo

Bodo Sperlein, 1.05 Oxo Tower Wharf, *T* 020 7633 9413, www.bodosperlein.com. Homewares in bone china, stone and leather include dishes with an oriental inflexion. *U* Southwark, Waterloo

Caterina Fadda, 1.08 Oxo Tower Wharf, *T* 020 7928 0024, www.caterinafadda.com. Cutting-edge designs for stackable storage, furniture, lighting, cutlery and tableware. *U* Southwark, Waterloo

Furniture Union, Bankside Lofts, 65a Hopton Street, *T* 020 7928 5155. Contemporary designer furniture and accessories by the likes of Philippe Starck and Kenzo. *U* Blackfriars, Southwark

Fusion Design, 2.02 Oxo Tower Wharf, *T* 020 7928 4838, www. studiofusion.com. A wide range of quirky but functional products like the mittscarf and magnetic teatowel. *U* Southwark, Waterloo

Ganesha, 3 Gabriel's Wharf, Upper Ground, *T* 020 7928 3444, www.ganesha.co.uk. Furnishings and accessories from India with a fair-trade angle include silk cushion covers and hip printed bags. *U* Southwark, Waterloo

Joseph Joseph, 1.21 Oxo Tower Wharf, *T* 020 7261 1800, www.theglasscompany.co.uk. Funky, retro-styled kitchen wares, mostly of colourful printed glass. *U* Southwark, Waterloo

Salt., 1.17 Oxo Tower Wharf, *T* 020 7593 0007. See weaving in progress, making bespoke blinds from textured textiles. *U* Southwark, Waterloo

Shelley Thomas, 13 Gabriel's Wharf, Upper Ground, *T* 020 8569 7386. Loopy ornamental ironwork: gates, fireplaces, beds. *U* Southwark, Waterloo

Viviene Legg, 16 Gabriel's Wharf, Upper Ground, *T* 020 7401 2240. Ceramics with ethereal decoration and organic forms, can be made to order. *U* Southwark, Waterloo

JEWELLERY

D'Argent Gallery, 1.01 Oxo Tower Wharf, *T* 020 7401 8454. Bespoke wedding and engagement rings and other jewellery by young designers. *U* Southwark, Waterloo

David Ashton, 6 Gabriel's Wharf, Upper Ground, *T* 020 7401 2405, www.davidashton.co.uk. Restrained, chunky jewellery with matt finishes and combinations of gold and other metals. *U* Southwark, Waterloo

Miranda Watkins, 2.11 Oxo Tower Wharf, *T* 020 7620 0330. Minimalist jewellery and some 'interior accessories'. *U* Southwark, Waterloo

KIDS

Bunny London, 1.22 Oxo Tower Wharf, *T* 020 7928 6269, www.bunnylondon.com. Eccentric children's clothes in antique fabrics. Designer Debbie Bunn's work is already in the Victoria and Albert Museum. *U* Southwark, Waterloo

Little Badger, 2.06 Oxo Tower Wharf. Handmade children's clothes, especially knits in natural fibres. *U* Southwark, Waterloo

MUSIC

Holywell, 58 Hopton Street, *T* 020 7928 8451. A strange setting for a shop devoted to harps. *U* Southwark

WESTMINSTER

Tate Britain

OPEN	Daily 10.00-17.50; Prints and Drawings Study Room Mon-Fri 10.30-13.00 and 14.00-16.30
CLOSED	24-26/12
CHARGES	Admission free to galleries; charge for special exhibitions, lower rates for senior citizens, full-time students, unwaged and disabled visitors
TELEPHONE	**020 7887 8000** for information (minicom **020 7887 8687**); **020 7887 8888** for tickets to special exhibitions and events or to reserve a disabled parking space or wheelchair; **020 7887 8042** for appointments to use Prints and Drawings Study Room
RECORDED INFO	**020 7887 8008**
WWW	**tate.org.uk**
MAIN ENTRANCE	Millbank; level access at the Manton Entrance on Atterbury Street and via the Clore Galleries
UNDERGROUND	Pimlico
RIVER BOAT	Tate to Tate services between Millbank Millennium and Bankside Piers via the London Eye, 10.20-17.00, journey time 18 minutes, buy tickets on board, from Tate ticket booths or website, or at London Eye customer services desk, schedules at www.thamesclippers.com
DISABLED ACCESS	Tapes with directions to the Tate and other information are available on request and wheelchairs can be supplied. The Manton and Clore entrances offer the best access to wheelchairs and buggies. There are lifts to all floors. Disabled parking spaces in the staff car park off John Islip Street can be booked and there are two spaces for Orange Badge holders at the front of the building
GUIDED TOURS	Guided tours Mon-Fri at 11.00, 12.00, 14.00 and 15.00; Sat, Sun 12.00 and 15.00 only; talks on the Painting of the Month on Mon at 13.15 and Sat at 14.30 and other lunchtime gallery talks most Wed-Fri; slide lectures in the Clore Auditorium Sat at 13.00 and Sun at 14.30 (all free). Audio tours, including one for families, introduce highlights (£3) and are available from the desks in the Rotunda and Manton Entrance, as are audio guides with induction loops
SERVICES	Cloakroom and toilets at the Manton Entrance; toilets in the Clore. Information desks at the Manton, Millbank and Clore entrances
SHOPS	Largest shop on Level 2 near the Millbank Entrance sells books, posters and other souvenirs inspired by the collection,

and has a special section for postcards and greeting cards; smaller shop by the Manton Entrance

EATING   Restaurant, café and espresso bar all on Level 1

Tate Britain presents regular special exhibitions on Levels 1 and 2 (tickets from the desks in the Rotunda and Manton Entrance) as well as lectures and events.

Tate Britain is one result of the old Tate Gallery's decision in the 1990s to split between two venues its collections of British and international modern art – the other being Tate Modern. With this move the original conception of Sir Henry Tate in the 19c, of a gallery devoted to the national school, has been revived. Tate offered his private collection to form the nucleus of the Gallery,

Tate Britain Sculpture Hall

which opened in 1897; in 1917 it was made responsible for developing a collection of international modern art. Tate Britain was launched in 2000. The removal of artworks to Tate Modern and the opening of the Centenary Development in 2001 provided a third more space in which to present the collection and special exhibitions, and improved visitor and educational facilities. Tate Britain remains the home of the now notorious Turner Prize, and hosts an annual exhibition by the shortlisted artists.

THE BUILDING

Sir Henry Tate offered to build a home for the new collection provided the government undertook to supply the land and administration. Eventually the site of Millbank Penitentiary was chosen, and the building designed by Sidney Smith. To cope with the expanding collections more galleries were added in 1899, 1909, 1926 and 1937 (when it acquired the characteristic dome), the last three phases paid for by the connoisseur Joseph Duveen and his family. In 1984 the Clore Galleries, designed by James Stirling, finally gave J.M.W. Turner's work the home he had stipulated in his bequest to the nation. The Centenary Development, which involved excavating under the western side of the building to install new rooms, was designed by John Miller + Partners and the surrounding spaces were re-landscaped. In 2003 an angular new pier, designed by Marks Barfield, opened to allow a ferry service between Tate Britain and Tate Modern.

HIGHLIGHTS

Works may appear in different rooms at different times: check their location on the website or with staff members.

Man in a Black Cap, the Tate's oldest work	John Bettes
Lavish Stuart portraits	Antony van Dyck
Portraits and 'modern moral subjects'	William Hogarth
Drawings, prints and books	William Blake
Major paintings such as *Flatford Mill*, sketch books and delightful studies of sea and clouds	John Constable
Vast bequest of paintings and drawings	J.M.W. Turner
Ophelia and other Pre-Raphaelite favourites	J.E. Millais
The eerie *Merry-go-Round*	Mark Gertler
Family Group sculpture and *Shelter Drawings*	Henry Moore
Girl with a White Dog and *Standing by the Rags*	Lucian Freud

The curators of Tate Britain have used the recent developments to institute a new way of showing the collection that, as at Tate Modern, involves altering the hang regularly so there is always something new to see. The displays of work made after the Second World War, for example, are rotated every nine months. The following descriptions are based on recent displays.

The works are divided between those made in the period 1500 to

1900 (Rooms 1-17) and those made since 1900 (Rooms 18-31): within this framework, the art is arranged along broadly chronological lines but some rooms are devoted to a single artist while others explore specific themes. The Duveen Galleries run on an axis from the Millbank Entrance and link the two halves of the display; they often show larger sculptural work and are the venue for the Turner Prize show. With the exception of Rooms 44 and 45 in the Clore Galleries, all the permanent displays are on **Level 2**, as is space for temporary exhibitions. Special shows are also presented in rooms on **Level 1** off the Manton Entrance, where the main visitor facilities are also located.

BRITISH ART FROM 1500 TO 1900: ROOMS 1-17

ENTRANCE To tackle the collection chronologically, begin at the **Manton Entrance**, part of the Centenary Development on Atterbury Street. Opened in 2001, it is all very sleek, calm or bland depending on your temper. Up some steps or a ramp to the right are the cloakroom, toilets, café and restaurant and on the left a desk that hires audio guides, the entrance to special exhibitions, and stairs and lifts up to the main collection displays.

At the top of the stairs there are a seating area, where you may see sculptures, and two more galleries for temporary exhibitions, including the **Art Now** space, where new work is regularly shown.

RENAISSANCE PORTRAITS Turn left to see the earliest works in the collection, from the time of the English Renaissance in the 16c and 17c. Britain was opening up to new ideas from the Continent and at the same time received many foreign artists, either invited by monarchs, such as Hans Holbein or Pietro Torrigiano, or as Protestant refugees from religious strife, among whom were Hans Eworth or Marcus Gheeraerts.

The portrait was clearly the most popular genre. The **Tudors** wanted to assert their status, show off their wealth in jewels and fine costumes, and indicate their learning by toying with symbolic props - a book, a shepherd's staff, a cameo on a ribbon - or making telling gestures. The oldest painting in the Tate, however, is more

TATE BRITAIN

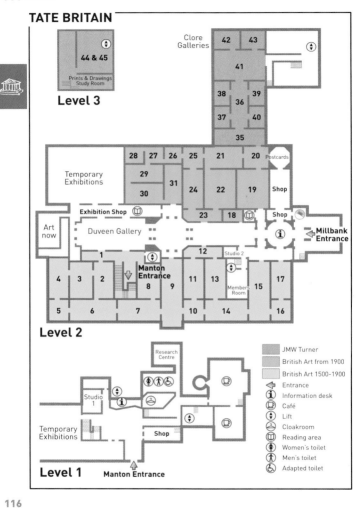

Level 3

44 & 45
Prints & Drawings Study Room

Clore Galleries
42 43
41
38 39
36
37 40
35

Level 2

Temporary Exhibitions

28 27 26 25 21 20 Postcards
29
31 24 22 19 Shop
30
23 18 Shop

Exhibition Shop

Art now

Duveen Gallery

Millbank Entrance

1
Manton Entrance
12 Studio 2

4 3 2 8 9 11 13 Members Room 15 17

5 6 7 10 14 16

Level 1

Research Centre

Studio 1

Temporary Exhibitions
Shop

Manton Entrance

JMW Turner
British Art from 1900
British Art 1500–1900
Entrance
Information desk
Café
Lift
Cloakroom
Reading area
Women's toilet
Men's toilet
Adapted toilet

subdued. The dour, faraway look in the portrait of a *Man in a Black Cap* (1545) convinces us of its psychological accuracy. (The artist John Bettes may have worked with Holbein; the blue background that would emphasize the resemblance to Holbein's work has faded to brown.) On the other hand **Nicholas Hilliard**'s portrait of *Elizabeth I* (c 1575) - with intricate details of gold thread and pearls but a flat, mask-like face - shows how she turned her own image into an icon of monarchy. The love of allusions, puzzles and pattern is embodied in Gheeraert's *Unknown Lady* (c 1593), who seems encrusted with chaste pearls: her rare smile and the clear indication of her pregnancy warm the painting up. An apparently simpler portrait by an unknown artist, the *Cholmondely Ladies* (c 1600-10), shows that dynastic concerns were still important beyond the court: it records relatives who were allegedly born, married and gave birth on the same day.

The **Stuarts** were no less susceptible to portraiture: a painting of *James Hamilton* (1623) by Daniel Mytens the Elder shows him in black silk with dashing vermilion stockings. Hamilton shared Charles I's interest in the arts, and his later fate on the block. The king appointed **Antony van Dyck** as his Principal Painter in 1632: you might see his demure *Lady of the Spencer Family* (c 1633-8) and the very undemure *Rachel de Ruvigny, Countess of Southampton* (c 1638-40), with an extravagant sunburst and swirling blue draperies. She is depicted as Fortune, but the skull at her feet foretells her early death. William Dobson's ruddy-faced *Endymion Porter* (c 1642-5) is surrounded by the attributes of the English country gent: slaughtered game and the classical sculptures befitting the tastes of a connoisseur.

The increasingly glamorous court of Charles II was well served by **Peter Lely**, who painted cherry-lipped *Elizabeth, Countess of Kildare* (c 1679). Lely's portraits, which show the influence of Van Dyck, were so much in demand that assistants probably painted many of the draperies and backgrounds. Beyond London, more sober-minded clients might choose to be immortalized by John Michael Wright. In *Mrs Salisbury with her Grandchildren* (1675-6), he shows the dynasty before a chunk of country estate, Mrs S in black widow's weeds and an extraordinary hat.

COUNTRY AND CITY: THE 18C In the 17c, a new subject for painting developed, as landowners ordered records of their properties, gardens and houses. Back in town, the emerging middle classes could now afford to have their own daily lives painted, as in *An English Family at Tea* (c 1720) by Joseph van Aken.

Art was no longer the sole preserve of the aristocracy and this democratization is exemplified in the career of **William Hogarth**. The study of the *Heads of Six of Hogarth's Servants* (c 1750-5) was a unique choice of sitter for its time and the plainly but sympathetically depicted faces are touching. In *The Painter with his Pug* (1745), Hogarth declares the influence of Shakespeare, Milton and Swift in the titles of the books on which he rests, and his own art theories in the 'line of beauty' on his palette. He was fascinated by the theatre and the life of the modern city, and involved himself in philanthropic ventures as much as in the promotion of British art. His artistic allies included Joseph Highmore, who wonderfully depicts the gruffly convivial *Mr Oldham and his Guests* (c 1735-45) and also produced the kind of 'modern moral subjects' favoured by Hogarth, including scenes from Samuel Richardson's moralizing novel, *Pamela*.

Room 5 has frequently changing displays that focus on specific features or artists of the period. Recently it has shown works by **George Stubbs**, Britain's greatest painter of horses. He earned his living immortalizing racehorses for their owners, such as *Otho, with John Larkin up* (1768), but elevated the subject in idealized compositions such as *Mares and Foals in a River Landscape* (c 1763-8).

THE INFLUENCE OF ITALY While Hogarth focused on modern realities close to home, others were being drawn to Italy as the source of superior culture. Artists and aristocrats travelling south were influenced by both classical remains and natural landscapes. Joseph Wright of Derby painted several dramatic versions of *Vesuvius in Eruption* (c 1776), the dark clouds and fiery lava no less effectively evoked because he did not see the event. **Joshua Reynolds** showed he had studied Titian's compositions in his *Holy Family with the Infant St John* (1788-9) and even Thomas

Gainsborough produced a large-scale nude, of the nymph *Musidora* (c 1780-8), based at second-hand on a classical sculpture. Richard Wilson's views of Rome were made for English patrons in Italy. Back at home, he rearranged local scenes like the *Thames near Marble Hill, Twickenham* (c 1762) to conform to a classical ideal.

On his return to Britain Reynolds and other founder members of the **Royal Academy** strove to elevate British art to the 'great style' seen abroad, by producing history paintings with mythological or classical subjects. Their patrons were not always convinced and the demand for portraits was still high. Reynolds had to compromise, with results such as *Three Ladies adoring a Term of Hymen* (1773), in which healthy-looking English girls strike poses from Poussin. One of Reynolds' allies was **Angelica Kauffmann** - you may see her *Portrait of a Lady* (c 1775) as a Roman matron; she was one of only two women Academicians until the 20c.

LANDSCAPE AT HOME AND ABROAD Meanwhile, landscape painting was acquiring a more political edge, although the urban audience was still protected from the realities of rural poverty. Artists were understandably attracted to the picturesque qualities of country life: Stubbs' *Reapers* and *Haymakers* (both 1785) seem too elegantly posed for real peasants and even Wright of Derby bathed industrial scenes in a cosy glow in *An Iron Forge* (1772). Later, more sentimental genre paintings such as David Wilkie's *Blind Fiddler* (1806) were popular at exhibitions.

The Tate has a quite extensive collection relating to **John Constable**, including a number of family letters and his pencil *Self-Portrait* (1806), as well as some of his more famous paintings and prints. Constable sketched and painted in the open air, despite the difficulties of handling pre-tube oil paints. This 'natural painture' had been developed by others around 1800, and you might see John Linnell's beautiful studies of crumbling buildings and reflections in rivers and canals, and less 'picturesque' subjects such as *Kensington Gravel Pits* (1811-12). Other artists sketched outdoors but finished the paintings back in the studio: Constable could produce even medium-sized paintings out in the open, like the *View in a Garden at Hampstead* (c 1821), the laundry hanging out despite an impending storm. Hampstead was one of his favourite spots for making cloud studies, breezy but meticulously annotated with date, time and weather conditions.

Landscape painting could be used to consolidate the image of the home country but also to explore the growing **British Empire**. In India, the brothers William and Thomas Daniell recorded some of the sub-continent's great buildings, including *Sher Shah's Mausoleum, Sasaram* (1810). After the Napoleonic Wars, Britons artistic and otherwise could travel again to the **Near East**: some wanted a taste of *Arabian Nights* exoticism, others to research authentic backdrops for religious scenes to be painted in Britain. John Frederick Lewis stayed 10 years in the region before returning to win acclaim for highly detailed paintings of camel trains, bazaars and scenes like *Edfu, Upper Egypt* (1860), while David Roberts' records of sites such as the *Ruins of the Temple of the Sun at Baalbec* (1842) were very popular. Finally, you might see St Paul's Cathedral as you never have before, in William Marlow's *Capriccio: St Paul's and a Venetian Canal* (c 1795).

VISIONARIES   Drawings, paintings, books and coloured prints by the poet and artist **William Blake** may get a room to themselves: you might see his illustrations to Dante's *Divine Comedy* (1824-7) and the tiny but menacing *Ghost of a Flea* (c 1819-20), inhabited by the soul of a human bloodsucker. Blake's almost abstract, swirling clouds and attenuated figures hint at his feel for Gothic. Blake's followers, who called themselves 'The Antients', included **Samuel Palmer**, who made visionary pen-and-ink drawings and jewel-like coloured works, such as *Coming from Evening Church* (1830).

HISTORY PAINTING   This had been considered the highest form of visual art for centuries: in 19c Britain the subjects were often not biblical or classical but taken from English literature from Chaucer to Walter Scott. William Holman Hunt, for example, produced *Claudio and Isabella* (1850), from Shakespeare's *Measure for Measure*, and fellow Pre-Raphaelite **Edward**

Burne-Jones the Chaucerian *Love and the Pilgrim* (1896-7).

Scenes from the contemporary theatre and portraits of famous actors were also popular, as were anecdotes from history, especially from the defining Civil War period. Many of these are still burned on the British imagination: **John Everett Millais** was responsible for quite a few, including *Ophelia* (1851-2) and the *Boyhood of Ralegh* (1870), and you may also see Henry Wallis' *Chatterton* (1856), showing the 17-year-old poet's suicide in a garret. Recent military victories also went down well: J.M.W. Turner imagined the *Battle of Trafalgar* (1806-8) from amidst a chaos of masts.

SEASCAPES This genre developed out of the Dutch school of the 17c, when Willem van de Velde the Elder and Younger had worked for Charles II; as Britain's maritime power grew in the 18c it became ever more popular. Later, political upheavals and Romantic notions of nature's power to crush frail mankind created a vogue for shipwreck scenes. In Turner's *Shipwreck* (exhibited 1805), walls of white-flecked water threaten to overwhelm the lifeboats while their capsized vessel sinks in the distance. But marine painting was not all death and disaster. Turner also showed seaside recreations at the Cowes regatta (1827) and in *New Moon, Margate* (exhibited 1840), with children squabbling on the beach.

THE SUBLIME The idea of nature's power that inspired Turner's shipwreck found expression in the work of other 19c artists. **John Martin** and Francis Danby wanted to instil awe in their audiences as they imagined great biblical disasters. Martin reduced human figures to helpless specks against fiery apocalyptic backdrops in *The Great Day of his Wrath*, from his 'Judgement' series (1851-3). These three showstopping paintings, though rejected as vulgar by the Royal Academy, continued to be exhibited to packed houses for 20 years after Martin's death. His vision of a beautiful alpine heaven also says a great deal about artists' attitudes to mountain scenery in this Romantic age.

A different interpretation of sublimity was made by Frederic Leighton and **G.F. Watts**, who, influenced by Michelangelo's heroic figures in the Sistine Chapel, saw it in the human form. Watts in particular made an ambitious series of spiritual paintings, including the wan *Hope* (1886), trying to play a lyre with a single remaining string.

VICTORIAN ART AND SOCIETY Victorian art is among the most popular in the Tate, and includes many Pre-Raphaelite favourites. Fascination with material detail and with stories reinforcing social conventions - class, the importance of hard work, family life and female purity - characterize many of the works, a response to the expectations of the confident entrepreneurs who were art's new patrons. *Derby Day* (1856-8) by **William Powell Frith** is as much a draw now as when first exhibited, its incident-packed panorama of the Victorian crowd - rich, poor, thieves, the hungry, the complacent, the gullible - minutely detailed and demanding attention, its multiple narratives suggesting the same teeming life as the great novels of the century. Augustus Leopold Egg's *Past and Present* (1858) is a more single-minded, triple-decker melodrama of wifely infidelity and the disasters that ensue for all involved, but Holman Hunt's *Awakening Conscience* (1853) holds out some hope for the errant female. In both, every detail is a carefully placed clue to reading the picture.

The Pre-Raphaelites' challenge to prevailing artistic and social values was less well-received when they ventured into biblical territory. **Dante Gabriel Rossetti**'s *Annunciation* (1849-50) - to a pinched and unenthusiastic Virgin - and Millais' *Christ in the House of his Parents* (1849-50) were early works that appalled onlookers with what was seen as a squalid realism inappropriate to the holy family.

James Tissot was also criticized for paying more attention to the lovingly detailed ruffled costumes of the young women at a *Ball on Shipboard* (c 1874) than to promoting a clear moral. Rossetti's *Monna Vanna* (1866) is another sensuous, glowing portrait (of Alexa Wilding) celebrating female beauty.

But the Victorian consciousness was being expanded by new knowledge - geological and astronomical discoveries and Darwinian theories. These are hinted at in *Pegwell Bay, Kent - a Recollection of October 5 1858* (1858-60) by William Dyce: the figures, who have the look of an old photograph, are collecting seashells beneath the ancient cliffs, and a comet crosses the sky above.

FOREIGN INFLUENCES Another small room with a mosaic floor has themed displays, recently on the Decadent artists of the 1890s, especially the illustrator Aubrey Beardsley.

In the late 19c, **French painting** began to have an increasingly direct effect on British artists. Painters on both sides of the Channel rebelled against the Academy and tried technical innovations, working out of doors or borrowing compositional formats from the Japanese as the Impressionist did. Scotland had a whole school of Colourists including J.D. Ferguson and Francis Cadell. In Bloomsbury, Vanessa Bell used an abstract background and a green stripe down the face of her subject - *Mrs St John Hutchinson* (1915) - that is reminiscent of Matisse. In Paris, **Gwen John** produced delicately penetrating portraits such as that of *Chloë Boughton-Leigh* (1904-8).

BRITISH ART FROM 1900: ROOMS 18-30

Cross to the other side of the building for the 20c displays, passing another little reading room. Beside this, entered from the Duveen Gallery, Room 18 presents small themed displays.

LONDON LIFE James Whistler saw elegant harmonies in Thames scenes such as *Nocturne: Blue and Gold - Old Battersea Bridge* (c 1872-5). Later urban painters looked to the bright colours and broken brushwork of the Fauves, bathing Camden Town in a purple Mediterranean light, as in Spencer Gore's *Fig Tree* (1912). By the turn of the 20c London had greatly expanded, and the crowded, accelerated lifestyles of its inhabitants presented artists with new scenes, such as Charles Ginner's *Piccadilly Circus* (1912), in which bright motor vehicles crowd the picture surface.

British life inside the home or boarding house might be celebrated for its cosy intimacy or depicted as an existence of tension and boredom. In *Ennui* (c 1914) by **Walter Sickert**, two uncommunicating figures are trapped in the corner of a room like the stuffed birds in their glass dome. Sickert also painted London's entertainments, including the music hall: *Minnie Cunningham at the Old Bedford* (1892) has the unconventional angles and colouring of a Degas (in fact the two artists were friends).

FIRST WORLD WAR Artists reacted in different ways to the Great War. Some still worked in the innovative manner of the pre-war years. C.W.R. Nevinson's *La Mitrailleuse* (1914) used a Futurist style to show technology turning on humanity; **Jacob Epstein** altered his original concept of the *Rock Drill* (1913-14) to leave an impotent torso with something organic exposed at its core. There seems to have been little direct commentary, as if the horror was beyond expression: an exception is the angry, anonymous bronze relief of *No Man's Land* (1919-20), a tangle of corpses in barbed wire. Other art seems mute, like the empty landscapes of **Paul Nash**, Sickert's *Brighton Pierrots* (1915), performing to a near-empty house under sickly artificial lights, or the hysterical riders on **Mark Gertler**'s haunting *Merry-go-Round* (1916).

Ahead as you enter Room 20 is the entrance to the Turner displays in the Clore Galleries, and to the right access to the main Tate shop. The displays in Room 20 change regularly: recently they have looked at the work of the Vorticist Wyndham Lewis, the precocious and short-lived Henri Gaudier Brzeska, and the dignified wooden sculptures of the Jamaican-born Ronald Moody.

TRADITION AND EXPERIMENT In the aftermath of the First World War, many British artists rejected machine-age optimism for a more traditional approach, including old crafts such as woodcut printing. The sculptor **Eric Gill** looked to medieval stone carving for inspiration. David Jones recalled Arthurian legend in his mystical, transparent drawings and there is a magical feel to Cecil Collins' *Artist and his Wife* (1939), showing the couple in their personal Eden, each protectively clutching an ankh, an Egyptian symbol of life. Henry Moore turned the human form into an element of the landscape, his *Recumbent Figure* (1938) like a sea-worn rock.

Meanwhile, other British artists were engaging with more extreme kinds of abstraction from Europe, where groups like the

Constructivists were experimenting with pure forms that had no root in observable reality. *Ball, Plane and Hole* (1936) by **Barbara Hepworth** has an engaging simplicity offset by the warmth of wood, while the marble *Three Forms* (1935) excludes colour, too. Her sometime husband Ben Nicholson also manipulated shape and space in shallow reliefs, and made paintings following Mondrian's experiments with planes of colour. Despite his intellectual aspirations - Constructivists saw science, art and society combining to create utopia - these were meant to look handmade, not mechanistic. Naum Gabo had brought some of these ideas to Britain and examples of his delicate perspex models are here.

SECOND WORLD WAR **Henry Moore** made drawings of Londoners sheltering from the Blitz in the tunnels of the Underground. The undifferentiated and faceless, yet human and vulnerable, figures in these *Shelter Drawings* (1940-1) are rendered in watercolour, crayon, pen and pencil that somehow suggest the squalid conditions that angered Moore. The experience cemented his belief in communal, fundamental values, as represented in the bronze *Family Group* (1949), an extension of his studies of natural forms.

Graham Sutherland also transformed motifs sketched from nature in the expressive, semi-abstract paintings that are his best-known works, showing the influence of Picasso and the Surrealists. The roots, branches and thorns he faithfully recorded in notebooks take on a menacing aspect, as in *Green Tree Form: Interior of Woods* (1940). In a similar way, **Francis Bacon** distorted the human body to express his view of the war-torn world: *Three Studies for Figures at the Base of a Crucifixion* (c 1944) is one of his most famous works.

Francis Bacon *Three Studies for Figures at the Base of a Crucifixion* (c 1944; one of three panels)

MYTH AND REALITY Again, mythology intrigued some post-war British artists like Lynn Chadwick, whose sculpted *Winged Figures* (1955) are part man, part animal. Alan Davie's entirely abstract *Entrance for a Red Temple No.1* (1960) still hints at the spiritual in its shapes and stained-glass colours.

A different group of artists was preoccupied with everyday realities. Josef Herman painted mining communities in Wales, as in *Evening, Ystradgynlais* (1948), while Carel Weight's images are of the urban working class. Some artists were labelled the **Kitchen Sink** school: John Bratby's *Still Life with Chip Frier* (1954) would seem to fit the bill.

THE LATE 20C The final suite of rooms covers the most recent works in the Tate's collection. Here you might see British **Pop Artists** including Peter Blake, with his iconic *Self-Portrait with Badges* (1961); prints by David Hockney or his portrait of *Mr and Mrs Clarke and Percy* (1970-1); wildly different types of figurative painting by Patrick Caulfield and **Howard Hodgkin**; and early video work of the 1960s and 1970s or more recent pieces by Douglas Gordon. British sculptors of the 1980s currently on show include **Tony Cragg**, whose *Britain Seen from the North* (1981) - and its observer - are composed of brightly coloured plastic scraps that reflect the industrial age. Other artists make rather than find objects, either using their own bodies, as in Antony Gormley's mute body casts, or Edward Allington's *Ideal Standard Forms* (1980), like mesmerizing chess pieces. Anish Kapoor's *Three* (1982), which of course has four components, suggests mysterious fruits but avoids too specific associations.

Of works by British painters of the 1990s you might see **Chris Ofili**'s *No Woman No Cry* (1995), in which tiny dots of paint, pinheads and beautiful translucent layers of resin enclose photographs of the murdered Stephen Lawrence. In Richard Patterson's *Painted Minotaur* (1996-7) scale and shape are blurred and distorted to powerful effect, while Gary Hume's *Water Painting* (1999) layers spidery drawings of nudes on a ground of flat household paint.

J.M.W. TURNER: ROOMS 35-45

ENTRANCE The **Clore Galleries** can be reached via Room 20 in the main building or through the separate entrance to the right of the steps, beyond a sculpture garden with a pool. Take the stairs or lift to the galleries.

BIOGRAPHY Room 35 introduces the life and times of Joseph Mallord William Turner (1775-1851). Around the walls runs a timeline linking his biography to national and world events, and the lives of his peers, including his exact contemporary William Wordsworth. Turner was the son of a Covent Garden barber and yet was elected a Royal Academician at the age of 27. At first the Napoleonic Wars kept him at home painting British subjects, often patriotic scenes such as the *Battle of Trafalgar* (1806-8). When he was able to travel across Europe he discovered the grand 17c history paintings of Poussin and the golden landscapes of Claude, his favourite Old Master. Their influences infuse such scenes as the *Decline of the Carthaginian Empire* (1817). He was concerned with the conditions for framing and presenting his work - a touch-screen display in one corner has a virtual reconstruction of his own West End gallery - and sought to safeguard his posthumous reputation, too. In 1856, nearly five years after his death, all the works by him found in his studio were accepted by the nation as the **'Turner Bequest'**. This comprises nearly 300 oil paintings and around 30,000 sketches and watercolours (including 300 sketchbooks). Also found were a metal box in which he kept paints and pigments, and a late palette with brushes. Two Turners, famously stolen while on loan in 1994, were recovered in 2003 and are back on display here. *Shade and Darkness* and *Light and Colour* (exhibited 1843) are both late, experimental works.

J.M.W. Turner *Norham Castle, Sunrise* (c 1845)

CLASSICAL MYTHOLOGY Turner was fascinated by legend, as in *The Golden Bough* (exhibited 1834). Depicting the clash of good and evil suited his technical experiments, while stories of the gods seemed to be borne out by his observations of nature's power. Turner's response to **nature** was often one of awe, which he communicates in pictures of storm-lashed mountains, avalanches and floods. In *Snow Storm: Hannibal and his Army crossing the Alps* (exhibited 1812), a wave-like cloud seems about to crash down on the puny humans below, in a reference not only to Hannibal but possibly to Napoleon, too.

VIEWS OF BRITAIN Nearer to home, Turner painted the places in Britain that attracted tourists, at first in watercolours such as *Tintern Abbey* (1794), which beautifully convey texture, light and shade. His sketchbooks show his precise, measuring eye. Later he made oil paintings of beauty spots including *London from Greenwich Park* (exhibited 1809) and idealized landscapes influenced by Claude, such as *England: Richmond Hill, on the Prince Regent's birthday* (exhibited 1819). England becomes Arcadia under the soft, pliant trees, although in some of his work such scenes were undercut by pessimistic verses.

The sublime angle he put on his landscapes is also seen in his response to the **industrial age**, from the almost abstract watercolour *Colour study: An Industrial Town at Sunset, Dudley* (c 1830-2) to *Snow Storm - Steam Boat at a Harbour's Mouth* (exhibited 1842). Many of his scenes were engraved as *Picturesque Views* ....

TURNER THE TOURIST While travelling in France, Switzerland, Germany and Italy Turner filled **sketchbooks** with coloured studies to be used as the basis for paintings to made on his return. Among these is *Venice - Maria della Salute* (exhibited 1844), its accurate topography dissolved in a pearlescent light. The subject was very popular among collectors of his later work.

EXHIBITING Turner's works were first shown with those of his colleagues at the **Royal Academy**, hung in tiers two or three high on the wall. From the late 1820s, Turner would submit unfinished works to the Royal Academy exhibitions and complete them during the three 'varnishing days' before the opening. A number of paintings found in a National Gallery storeroom after the Second World War raise the question of **finish**. Turner often worked spontaneously, laying in areas of light and shade and adding details later, as in *Seascape with Buoy* (c 1840).

WATERCOLOURS Take the stairs leading up from Room 41 to see a changing selection of watercolours, some of the highlights from the Turner Bequest. These might explore his time at the Royal Academy Schools, his tour of Italy in 1819, or his **influence** on later generations of artists in the 'Golden Age' of watercolour. There are more sketchbooks annotated with notes on colour, inscriptions, sky and wave studies and technical experiments including work on coloured papers.

PRINTS AND DRAWINGS STUDY ROOM Also on **Level 3** of the Clore Galleries is the Prints and Drawings Study Room, where visitors can make an appointment to see more of the Turner Bequest as well as watercolours, drawings and prints by other British artists c 1700 to 1900 and contemporary prints by British and international artists, including Pop Artists and the YBAs.

Queen's Gallery

OPEN	Daily 10.00-17.30 (timed ticket)
CLOSED	25, 26/12
CHARGES	£6.50, concessions £5, under 17s £3, under 5s free
TELEPHONE	**020 7321 2233**, credit card sales **020 7766 7301**
WWW.	**royal.gov.uk**
MAIN ENTRANCE	Buckingham Gate
UNDERGROUND	St James's Park, Victoria
DISABLED ACCESS	Wheelchair users should book through the ticket sales office

A large shop sells royal merchandise from corgi keyrings to bone china, books and videos.

The spectacular Royal Collection, reflecting the tastes of British monarchs over the centuries - especially the art-loving Charles I and George IV - is held in trust by the Queen for the nation. Many of its pictures, pieces of furniture and decorative objects can be seen in various royal palaces around the country and themed exhibitions drawn from the Collection are regularly presented around the world and at the Queen's Gallery, attached to Buckingham Palace. After a total redesign, creating much more exhibition space in appropriately sumptuous new rooms, the Gallery re-opened in 2002 to celebrate the Queen's Golden Jubilee. The first exhibition featured 450 of the most important treasures, from Rembrandt portraits to illustrated 17c Mughal manuscripts, exquisite clocks and diamond-encrusted jewellery, delicate enamels, sculpture by Antonio Canova, gold and silver tableware and porcelain, and furniture from 18c France. More intimate rooms displayed some of the Collection's most precious drawings and watercolours by artists including Leonardo da Vinci, Michelangelo, Holbein, Rubens and Canaletto. There is a reading room where printed and online catalogues of the exhibitions are available. The show in 2004 promises trinkets by Carl Fabergé.

on route

Houses of Parliament

Houses of Parliament, Parliament Square, *T* 020 7219 4272 (Commons), 020 7219 3107 (Lords), www.parliament.uk. Charles Barry's great building (1837-52), with Gothic ornament by A.W.N. Pugin, is still London's chief landmark. Queue to see debates in either house or book a guided tour for a better look at the architecture. *U* Westminster

Millbank Millennium Pier, Millbank, *T* 020 7887 8888. Origami-inspired pier by Marks Barfield, the architects responsible for the London Eye, with lighting designed by artist Angela Bulloch to change with the tide levels. Boats liveried in Damien Hirst spots provide a river link between the two Tate galleries (see above for service times). *U* Pimlico

MI6 HQ, Vauxhall Cross. This Aztec battleship (1994) by Postmodern architect Terry Farrell was built for Britain's overseas spies and had an unflattering role in the Bond movie *The World is Not Enough*. You can walk the perimeter or get a good view from Millbank. *U* Vauxhall

Museum of Garden History, Lambeth Palace Road, suggested donation £2.50, daily 10.30-17.00, *T* 020 7401 8865, www.cix.co.uk/~museumgh. Eccentric little museum housed in a former church. The Tradescants - gardeners to Charles I and II - and Captain Bligh of HMS *Bounty* are buried in the former churchyard, now a 17c garden.
U Westminster, Lambeth North

Museum of Garden History

Royal Horticultural Society Hall, 80 Vincent Square, *T* 020 7828 4125, www.horticultural-halls.co.uk. The RHS, the world's largest gardening society (founded 1804), holds regular flower shows in this building (1904) and a newer neighbour, which also host public fairs and exhibitions. *U* Victoria, St James's Park

St John's Smith Square, Smith Square, *T* 020 7222 1061, www.sjss.org.uk. Baroque church by Thomas Archer (1713-28), now deconsecrated and a major venue for classical concerts. *U* Westminster

Westminster Abbey, Broad Sanctuary, entrance charge, Mon-Fri 9.30-16.45, Sat 9.30-14.45, *T* 020 7654 4900, www.westminster-abbey.org. Pyx Chamber, chapter house and museum open daily for an additional fee. Site of coronations, weddings and other royal events, this famous Gothic church contains much magnificent statuary, Henry VII's fan-vaulted burial chapel, and the tombs of Edward the Confessor, Elizabeth I and the writers of Poets' Corner. *U* Westminster

Westminster Cathedral, Victoria Street, Sun-Fri 8.00-19.00, Sat 8.00-19.00, *T* 020 7798 9055, www.westminstercathedral.org.uk. This red-and-white striped neo-Byzantine edifice is the chief Catholic church in England and the masterpiece of John Francis Bentley (1894). In the marble interior you can see the *Stations of the Cross* (1913-18) by Eric Gill and reach the top of the campanile by lift. *U* Victoria

commercial galleries

Check opening times before visiting these Pimlico galleries: many are closed at the start of the week.

Adam Gallery, 35 Ponsonby Terrace, *T* 020 7630 0599, www.adamgallery.com. Deals in 20c work including Picasso and the St Ives painters, and exhibits current British artists including Sandra Blow and Maurice Cockrill. There is another outpost in Bath. *U* Pimlico

Barbara Behan Contemporary Art, 50 Moreton Street, *T* 020 7821 8793, www.barbarabehan.com. Devoted to paintings and sculpture by contemporary Italian artists. *U* Pimlico

Long & Ryle, 4 John Islip Street, *T* 020 7834 1434, www.long-and-ryle.demon.co.uk. Regular exhibitions by a stable of contemporary British and European painters and sculptors. *U* Pimlico

Moreton Contemporary Art, 40 Moreton Street, *T* 020 7834 7773, www.moretonart.com. More contemporary and antique art and prints sourced for corporate and private walls. *U* Pimlico

eating and drinking

AT THE MUSEUM

£ **Tate Café and Espresso Bar**. Characterless but functional café selling sandwiches, cakes, and a limited range of hot food and drinks. Self-service.

££ **Tate Restaurant**, *T* 020 7887 8825. The modern British food is pricey but the exceptional wine list good value, as is the *The Expedition in Search of Rare Meats* (1927), a mural specially commissioned from the artist Rex Whistler. Waiter service.

SURROUNDING AREA

£ **Noodle Noodle**, 312 Vauxhall Bridge Road, *T* 020 7828 8565. Plentiful, relatively inexpensive fast food from a friendly if basic outlet. *U* Victoria

Morpeth Arms, 58 Millbank, *T* 020 7834 6442. Riverside pub in a Grade II listed building (1846): good Young's beer. On the site of Millbank Prison, it is supposed to be haunted by a felon, and other spooks from MI6 HQ frequent the bar. *U* Pimlico

Vincent Rooms, Vincent Square, *T* 020 7802 8391. Untested, but why not try classic dishes prepared by the students of Kingsway College's School of Hospitality, in an Art Deco building. *U* Victoria

White Swan, 14 Vauxhall Bridge Road, *T* 020 7821 8568. Traditional boozer recommended for its very cheap pub grub and proximity to Tate and Tube. *U* Pimlico

££ **Blue Jade**, 44 Hugh Street, *T* 020 7828 0321. At the other end of Pimlico from the Tate, but worth the trek for reliable and reasonably priced Thai cooking. *U* Victoria

Brahms, 147 Lupus Street, *T* 7223 9828. Great value, simple bistro food with budget set menus for lunch and dinner make this a real find in an under-catered area. *U* Pimlico

Café Portugal, 5a-6a Victoria House, South Lambeth Road, *T* 020 7587 1962. On the other side of the Thames, this smoky Portuguese café-bar - often ruled by Brazilian soaps and football - serves reasonably priced, traditional tapas. *U* Vauxhall

Footstool, St John's Smith Square, *T* 020 7222 2779. Café-restaurant in the crypt of a famous church, handy for a pre-concert meal. *U* Westminster

Goya, 34 Lupus Street, *T* 020 7976 5309. Unpretentious tapas and wine bar, with another branch at 2 Ecclestone Place. *U* Pimlico

Lavender, 112 Vauxhall Walk, *T* 020 7735 4440. Good, reasonably priced bistro food, with choices for vegetarians. This restaurant is part of a small local chain. *U* Vauxhall

Olivo, 21 Eccleston Street, *T* 020 7730 2505. Long-established restaurant serving good-value Sardinian cooking. *U* Victoria

Pizza Express, 46 Moreton Street, *T* 020 7592 9488. This chain's rash of outlets in London means you are never far from a reliable pizza. *U* Pimlico

Pimlico Wine Vaults, 12-22 Upper Tachbrook Street, *T* 020 7233 5801. Basement wine bar with surprisingly good choice of food. *U* Victoria

Seafresh, 80-81 Wilton Road, *T* 020 7828 0747. Uninspiring décor but well-cooked, traditional fish and chips in large portions. *U* Victoria

Uno, 1 Denbigh Street, *T* 020 7834 1001. Noisy and popular pizza and pasta restaurant, rare in the neighbourhood. *U* Victoria

£££ Bank Westminster, 45 Buckingham Gate, *T* 020 7379 9797. Modern brasserie near Victoria recommended for its good-value lunch and pre- and post-theatre set menus, and its bar, Zander (see below). *U* St James's Park

Boisdale, 13-15 Eccleston Street, *T* 020 7730 6922. The meaty Scottish menu, huge choice of whisky and live jazz make this a popular, blokey venue. *U* Victoria

Cinnamon Club, Old Westminster Library, Great Smith Street, *T* 020 7222 2555. Some of the best modern Indian food (including breakfast) in Britain is served in this restaurant, located in an airy, converted building. *U* Westminster

Ken Lo's Memories of China, 67-69 Ebury Street, *T* 020 7730 7734. Pricey but extremely high-quality and consistent Chinese food in a recently refurbished restaurant. *U* Victoria

Pomegranates, 94 Grosvenor Road, *T* 020 7828 6560. You'll receive old-fashioned, personal attention at this long-established and popular restaurant. *U* Pimlico

Quirinale, 1 Great Peter Street, *T* 020 7222 7080. Prices at this elegant Italian basement restaurant reflect its location near parliament. *U* Westminster

Shepherd's, Marsham Court, Marsham Street, *T* 020 7834 9552. Traditional (grilled Dover sole, steak and kidney pud) and more modern British cooking served in a clubby atmosphere appropriate to its parliamentary surrounding. *U* St James's Park

LATE-NIGHT BARS

Cinnamon Club Bar (see above). Cool décor, Bollywood images and Indian street snacks make this bar as much of a destination as the restaurant above. Open Mon, Tue, Sun till 23.00, Wed-Sat till 1.00. *U* St James's Park

Zander, 45 Buckingham Gate, **T** 020 7379 9797. You'll build up a thirst getting here from Tate Britain, but it's worth it for the reasonably priced (for London) cocktails and a sight of the longest bar in Europe. Open Mon, Tue, Sun till 23.00, Wed-Sat till 1.00. **U** St James's Park

shopping

Pimlico, it must be admitted, is a bit of a retail desert: a few highlights and curiosities are listed here. Push westwards - walking from Pimlico or travelling one Tube stop from Victoria - for richer pickings in Belgravia and around Sloane Square.

ACCESSORIES

Philip Treacy, 69 Elizabeth Street, **T** 0207 730 3992, www.philiptreacy. co.uk. Hats and accessories by this internationally successful Irish designer. This is his London studio. **U** Victoria

BOOKS

Pimlico Bookshop, 34 Moreton Street, **T** 020 7233 6103, www.pimlico books.co.uk. Second-hand, mostly hardback, books, especially modern first editions, the writings of George Orwell and Philip Larkin, and Americana. Open Thur-Sat or by appointment. **U** Pimlico

Politico's, 8 Artillery Row, **T** 020 7828 0010, www.politicos.co.uk. Britain's only specialist political bookshop and publisher with a huge range from memoirs to manifestos, taped speeches and satirical cartoons. **U** St James's Park, Victoria

Shepherd's Bookbinders, 76 Rochester Row, **T** 020 7620 0060. Shepherd's also sells exquisite papers, leather notebooks and boxes, and bookbinding materials. **U** Victoria, Pimlico

CLOTHES

Army & Navy Stores, 101 Victoria Street, *T* 020 7834 1234. Huge department store, part of the House of Fraser chain, with plenty of fashion including Deisel, Ted Baker, DKNY. *U* Victoria

Atelier, 37 Moreton Street, *T* 020 7821 7000. Made-to-measure bridal and evening dresses. *U* Pimlico

Cornucopia, 12 Upper Tatchbrook Street, *T* 020 7828 5752. Second-hand clothes and jewellery, open daily. *U* Victoria, Pimlico

Redwood and Feller, 89 Rochester Row, *T* 020 7828 9519, www.redwoodandfeller.com. Tailors by appointment to HM, making bespoke suits and shirts for MPs and others. *U* Victoria, Pimlico

FOOD

Rippon Cheese Stores, 26 Upper Tachbrook Street, *T* 020 7931 0668. Excellent British ('Stinking Bishop', organic brie) and other cheeses. *U* Victoria, Pimlico

HOMES

Marston & Langinger, 192 Ebury Street, *T* 020 7881 5717, www.marston-and-langinger.com. Custom-made conservatories and all that goes in them. Well, you can dream. *U* Victoria, Sloane Square

Peta Smyth, 42 Moreton Street, *T* 020 7630 9898. Peta Smith specializes in antique tapestries, textiles and embroideries. *U* Pimlico

Watts and Company, 7 Tufton Street, *T* 020 7222 7169. Founded in 1874 by pupils of Gothic revivalist George Gilbert Scott (the company name comes from 'What's in a name?'), and still making handsome custom-designed and handmade church furnishings, metalwork and vestments. Worth a look. *U* Westminster

STATIONERY

History Store, 29 Churton Street, *T* 020 7976 6040. A small gallery selling a wide range of unique stationery, reprinted posters and other ephemera based on its archive, plus handmade papers and antique writing equipment. *U* Pimlico, Victoria

SOUTH
KENSINGTON

Victoria and Albert Museum

OPEN	Daily 10.00-17.45, every Wed and last Fri in month till 22.00 (selected galleries only); Print Room Tues-Fri 10.00-16.30, Sat 10.00-13.00 and 14.00-16.30; National Art Library Tues-Sat 10.00-17.00
CLOSED	1/1, 24-26/12; Print Room closed Mon and in Sept; National Art Library closed two weeks at Christmas, three weeks in summer
CHARGES	Admission free to galleries; charge for special exhibitions, with lower rates for senior citizens, full-time students, unemployed and disabled visitors
TELEPHONE	**020 7942 2000**
WWW.	**vam.ac.uk**
MAIN ENTRANCE	Cromwell Road; Exhibition Road for Henry Cole Wing
UNDERGROUND	South Kensington
DISABLED ACCESS	Level access for wheelchairs at Exhibition Road entrance; wheelchairs can be supplied by the Museum and most areas are accessible. There are four disabled parking spaces in Exhibition Road. Sound-enhancement equipment is available for talks and lectures and a touch tour on tape, in Braille or large print can be borrowed: ask at the main information desk. To book a helper to accompany you round the Museum, **T 020 7942 2197**
GUIDED TOURS	Tours introduce the history and highlights of the collection (daily at 10.30, 11.30, 13.30, 15.30, Wed also 16.30 and 19.30, free); additional tours of the new British Galleries (daily 12.30, 14.30, free). Gallery talks are held daily at 13.00
SERVICES	Information desks and cloakrooms at Cromwell Road and Exhibition Road entrances. Toilets throughout the building
SHOPS	Main shop on Level 1, left of the entrance hall, selling books, postcards and souvenirs as well as contemporary crafts; a smaller shop in the Henry Cole Wing sells children's books and gifts
EATING	Self-service restaurant in the Henry Cole Wing; cafés in the Gamble Room and in the garden in summer

The Victoria and Albert Museum presents regular special exhibitions on Level 1 (tickets from the information desk under the dome) as well as films, lectures and events.

Vivienne Westwood *Platform-soled shoes* (1993, 'mock croc'; Dress Gallery)

The Victoria and Albert Museum is an amazing treasure trove of decorative and fine arts from across the globe. Its engagingly rambling series of galleries, often lavishly ornamented themselves, contain a very important array of Italian Renaissance sculpture; Western costume from 1700; the national collections of John Constable paintings and of photographs; world-class artefacts from India and East Asia; and the award-winning British Galleries, besides vast amounts of ceramics, metalwork, furniture and glass. The whole Museum is coloured by its Victorian founders' zeal for collecting and explaining and it is still at it, acquiring everything from contemporary Japanese textiles to political protest badges and commissioning today's designers to place their work beside the inspiring examples of previous centuries.

The Museum of Manufactures was founded in 1852, in the wake of the enormously successful Great Exhibition of 1851. Merged with the School of Design and renamed the South Kensington Museum, it relocated to its present site in 1857. Its first director, Henry Cole, wanted to inspire British manufacturers with the example of fine art and supervised the Museum's collecting policy accordingly: it amassed not only the modern products that were its official brief but also historic works of art, to the extent that in 1863 the government ordered the Museum to confine its acquisitions to those that tended 'directly to improve Art applied to objects of utility'. It was ignored, of course, and the Victoria and Albert Museum, so renamed in 1899, remains an eccentric mix where you can find everything from Raphaels to office chairs.

THE BUILDING

The original buildings on this site, known unflatteringly as the 'Brompton Boilers', were by William Cubitt. In the 1860s an impressive red-brick frontage (now seen from the garden) designed by Francis Fowke was added, with courts decorated with mosaics of famous artists and architects, heroes for this 'Kensington Valhalla'. As the collections grew, so new iron-framed buildings, once considered temporary, were constructed to house them. The façade you see now on Cromwell Road was begun in 1899, the result of a competition won by Aston Webb. It is difficult to take in as a whole. The central lantern is meant to be shaped like the imperial crown and above the door are statues of Victoria and Albert by Alfred Drury, flanked by British architects and artists sculpted by students of the Royal College of Art. On Exhibition Road, the building still bears the scars of Second World War bombing.

The ground-level foyer on this side may one day be subsumed in the Spiral, designed by Daniel Libeskind as part of the Museum's FuturePlan. Under this ambitious 10-year programme, already begun, the Museum's contents will be completely reorganized, the garden relandscaped and the Victorian courtyards restored.

HIGHLIGHTS

Italian Renaissance sculpture, including works by Donatello, Rossellino and the della Robbias	Rooms 11-20
Dress, from the 17c to the 21c	Room 40
The world's greatest sculptures, in plaster	Rooms 46A-B
Raphael's huge designs for the Sistine tapestries	Room 48A
British Galleries, with re-created rooms	Rooms 52-58 and 118-125
Silver, in the lavish former ceramic galleries	Rooms 65-69

Seeing the whole Museum in a day might be possible, but not very enjoyable (for those determined on complete coverage, racks of folding stools may be found at various points). The following description is not intended as a tour but gives an overview of the different collections and picks out some highlights. The Museum's development plan means that some galleries were not open at the time of writing, and others will close for renovation and redisplay: check at the information desk for details and up-to-date maps.

The main building and Henry Cole Wing both have six floors, but communicate only at the lower levels. The principal collections are found mostly on Levels 0-3 in the main building, and are divided between those grouped by medium (ironwork, glass) and those by origin (Europe, Korea). Starting in the **main building**, on **Level 1** you can see European and North American arts in the rooms around the central garden and in the sculpture gallery to the right of the foyer; these continue on **Level 0**. The Raphael cartoons, cast courts, Asian collections, costume, photography and main temporary exhibition galleries are also on this level. **Level 2** houses the Contemporary Space and the first half of the British Galleries. Ironwork runs the length of the building on **Level 3**, where you can also find textiles, jewellery, painting, silver, and 20c design. The British Galleries continue on **Level 4**; the

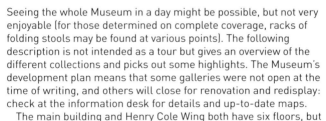

VICTORIA AND ALBERT MUSEUM
Level 0 & 1

European Collections
Asian Collections
Sculpture
Photography
Dress

◁ Entrance
ⓘ Information desk

☕ Café
↗ Stairs
⌒ Ramp
↕ Lift
Cloakroom
🚺 Women's toilet
🚹 Men's toilet
Adapted toilet
Baby changing

glass display is at the opposite end of the building. Level 5 gives
access only to the lecture theatre, but on **Level 6** you will find the
vast ceramics collection.

The **Henry Cole Wing** is being emptied of some of its exhibits but
currently has the Frank Lloyd Wright room, displays of printmaking
techniques and European ornament on Level 2; temporary
exhibitions on Levels 3 and 6; and the Print Room on Level 5.

ENTRANCE

Beyond the entrance from Cromwell Road is the **information desk**, its translucent lime-green glow almost distracting from the enormous Dale Chihuly chandelier (1999) suspended from the dome above. The meeting point for gallery talks is by the benches to the right.

On the left is the main **shop**, with a good range of art and design books and a tempting array of jewellery, stationery and gifts. The shop has its own display of architectural exhibits, including the front of Sir Paul Pindar's house from the City of London, in carved oak (c 1600). Even the gates were designed by George Gilbert Scott for Salisbury cathedral (1869-72).

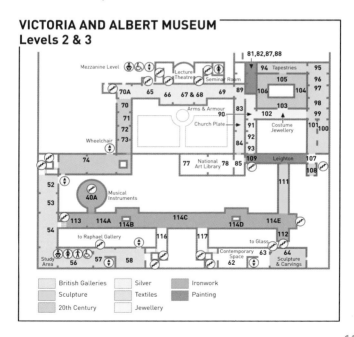

VICTORIA AND ALBERT MUSEUM
Levels 2 & 3

British Galleries	Silver	Ironwork
Sculpture	Textiles	Painting
20th Century	Jewellery	

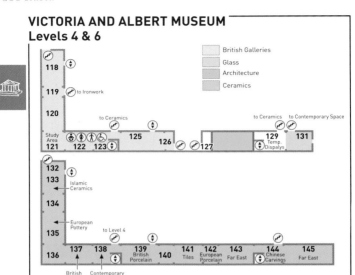

VICTORIA AND ALBERT MUSEUM
Levels 4 & 6

British Galleries
Glass
Architecture
Ceramics

118
119 to Ironwork
120
to Ceramics
Study Area 121
125 126 127
to Ceramics to Contemporary Space
129 Temp. Dispalys 131
122 123
132
133 Islamic Ceramics
134
← European Pottery
to Level 4
135
136 137 138 139 British Porcelain 140 141 Tiles 142 European Porcelain 143 Far East 144 Chinese Carvings 145 Far East
British Pottery Contemporary Ceramics

EUROPEAN COLLECTIONS

MEDIEVAL TREASURY *Room 43* The chronological displays begin
at the bottom of the steps from the foyer, with smaller objects of
the period 400-1400. Begin on the left with **Roman ivories** and
tapestry panels from Egypt (4c-7c) - with fruits and birds in still
strong colours and even a design on payprus. The Byzantines and
later dynasties preserved these skills, as in the intricately carved
Veroli casket (late 10c or early 11c) and the stunning Eltenburg
reliquary (c 1180) - a miniature temple in gold and ivory. Gothic art
spread through Europe in the 12c and 13c, often through
pilgrimages and monastic institutions. The jewel-like **stained-
glass** fragments around the walls are from major Gothic
cathedrals.

In England, Anglo-Saxon culture was affected only slowly by the Norman conquest but the great monasteries taught the smaller arts such as *opus anglicanum*, a kind of embroidery that found favour all over Europe in the 13c and 14c. Men and monkeys riot over the surface of a gilt-metal candlestick (before 1113) from Gloucester cathedral, a very rare survival from the period.

EUROPE 1100-1450 *Rooms 22-24* Emerge into Room 23, part of a long corridor. It has an array of larger **Romanesque** carving from churches including four sturdy walnut columns (1150-1200) from Italy.

Turn right into Room 24 to see **sculptures from northern Europe**. These include *St Christopher* (c 1450) carrying the Christ Child - legs comfortably crossed - on his shoulder, and some of the English alabaster carvings (early 15c) for which Nottingham was famous, with traces of the paint that once covered them. Sculpture was also used in great halls, as witnessed by three oak retainers (c 1500-25) from a Cumbrian castle.

Among smaller works in cases, look out for wooden figures from an *Entombment* (c 1440-50), crisply carved in Germany, and a charming stone group of *St Anne teaching the Virgin to read* (c 1500-30) from France.

Double back to Room 22 to see developments in **13c-15c Italy**. The workshops of the leading sculptors Arnolfo di Cambio, Nicola and Giovanni Pisano are represented: the last carved the weatherworn head from a figure on Siena cathedral and the even more powerful fragment from an ivory crucifix (c 1300). Cases contain **majolica** - a tin-glazing technique that arrived from Islamic countries in the early 13c. Look out for exquisite silks woven with lions, eagles and dragons, and for a tender terracotta group of the *Virgin and Child* (c 1425), probably from the circle of the Florentines Ghiberti, Donatello and Masaccio, all important figures from the early Italian Renaissance.

To follow the displays chronologically, you now need to retrace your steps to the east end of the corridor and turn left. Miss out Rooms 25-29 to continue with Italy.

NORTHERN EUROPE 1500-1600 *Rooms 25-29* From Room 25 a staircase leads up to the National Art Library on Level 3. The winged altarpiece is from the Tyrol (c 1500-10).

In 16c France, the Netherlands, Southern Rhineland and Spain the Reformation, expansion in trade and technological advances such as printing were turbulent influences on the arts. You may see **woodcuts** by Albrechts Dürer and Altdorfer and a copy of the *Nuremberg Chronicle* (1497), a printed history of the world. Gothic traditions and Renaissance values mingled. In Germany, Tilman Riemenschneider sculpted intense figures for an altarpiece (c 1510) and bronze-founders made classically inspired table fountains (c 1560).

Objects range from tiny, moulded clay devotional figures for mass-export from the Netherlands to lavish one-offs like the Burghley nef (1527), a salt cellar in the shape of a ship, from Paris. Rich men like the Fuggers, bankers to the Holy Roman Empire, created **cabinets of curiosities** filled with ornate examples of craftsmanship or natural wonders, from Chinese porcelain to coconuts, both given gilt mounts.

ITALY 1400-1500 *Rooms 11-20* The next suite of rooms is often unaccountably empty, given that they contain the largest collection of Italian Renaissance sculpture outside that country. The dingy paint and dusty labels will be remedied under the FuturePlan.

Room 16 focuses on **Donatello**, the most influential sculptor of the 15c, with a selection of his smaller works (copies of larger ones are in the Cast Courts) in a variety of materials: the *Ascension* (c 1428-30), in very low, 'scratched' relief on marble; the bronze *Lamentation over the Dead Christ* (c 1455-60); and a terracotta *Virgin and Child* (c 1455-60), a form which was widely copied. Antonio Rossellino's marble bust of *Giovanni Antonio Chellini* (1456), a doctor who treated Donatello, wears a marvellous smirk.

Room 15 shows delicate marble carvings by Desiderio di Settignano and Agostino di Duccio and enamelled terracottas by **Andrea della Robbia**, whose family workshop is lavishly represented in Room 14 by altarpieces, coats of arms and plaques. Prince Albert's enthusiasm for this kind of work influenced part of the Museum's decoration, as we shall see, and he donated the little figure of a *Boy playing Bagpipes* (late 15c or early 16c).

The inspiration of classical art is evident in Room 13, most importantly in two cases of bronze medallions by **Pisanello** (mid-15c) and his contemporaries. The obverses carry powerful portraits of mercenaries, churchmen and rulers, and the reverses compact allegories.

For a refreshing diversion, take the doorway off Room 13. The South Kensington Museum was the first in the world to offer its public food and drink, and in 1868 opened three rooms built to cater for them. The **Morris Room** was the earliest commission for William Morris's company. Edward Burne-Jones designed the stained glass and painted the decorative panels. The **Gamble Room** next door is a slightly indigestible riot of Minton tiles, putti, inscriptions and gilding. The tiles conceal iron pillars and the ceiling is of enamelled iron. The **Poynter Room**, designed by Sir Edward Poynter, was influenced by the Aesthetic Movement in its blue-and-white colour scheme and peacock motifs.

Room 12 is dominated by more terracotta, this time roundels of the *Labours of the Months* (c 1450-6) by Luca della Robbia. These once decorated the study of Florence's ruler Piero de Medici, and other objects that might have been found in a *studiolo* are shown in cases - Roman coins, carpets, inkstands and small antique bronzes of the kind that inspired nearby statuettes by Antico and Il Riccio.

In Room 11 you will find a linking passage to the Cole wing and restaurant and also the foot of the stupendous **Ceramic Staircase**, with moulded and coloured tiles bearing the names of leading artists from Phidias to Turner. This leads to the silver galleries above, in rooms that once housed the ceramics collection.

Turn left into Room 17, and look up at the painted ceiling (early 16c) from Cremona, showing the Muses around a *trompe l'oeil* oculus. Below it are some magnificent inlaid chests (16c). Rooms 18 and 19 have more fine **terracottas**: a charming group of the *Virgin and Child* (c 1465) by Rossellino; and a sketch for the monument of Cardinal Forteguerri (1476) by Andrea del Verrocchio, another leading Florentine sculptor. The *Lamentation over the Dead Christ* (c 1515-30) is a rare work by a female artist, Properzia dei Rossi. Room 20 has 16c **Venetian glass**, including a turquoise cup lovingly preserved by the Fairfax family since at least the 1690s.

EUROPE 1500-1600 *Room 21* Re-emerge into the main corridor. Many of the items in Rooms 21 and 21a are models which tell us a great deal about the sources and methods of **High Renaissance sculptors**. Two tiny wax figures (c 1516 and c 1520) have been attributed to Michelangelo, as has a larger terracotta torso (c 1525-30) complete with the marks of his tools. Other models were made to help painters, such as Jacopo Sansovino's *Descent from the Cross* (c 1508), made for Perugino. A selection of models by Michelangelo's follower, the Roman sculptor Giambologna, for his students includes a suitably muddy-looking river god (c 1580). His *Samson slaying a Philistine* (c 1560-2) is the only substantial work by him outside Italy. Its twisting forms show the development of Mannerism.

While in this part of the Museum, you might want to cut through Room 40 and cross a corridor to reach the Raphael gallery.

RAPHAEL GALLERY *Room 48A* This enormous room, recently refurbished, contains seven **cartoons** by Raphael of scenes from the *Lives of St Peter and St Paul* (1513). They were commissioned by Pope Leo X as designs for tapestries which still hang in the Sistine Chapel (a Mortlake tapestry of the *Miraculous Draught of Fishes* made in 1637-8 shows how they translated into silk, wool and metal thread). These beautiful drawings found early admirers and the set was acquired in 1623 by the future Charles I. While in this room, do not neglect the late fresco (1522-3) by Raphael's teacher, Perugino.

EUROPE 1600-1800 *Rooms 1-7* Take the stairs down to Level 0 from the end of Room 21, past temporary displays, and turn left. Room 1 begins with the preoccupations of **16c royal collectors**, who accumulated beautiful scientific instruments, natural curiosities or displays of craftsmanship such as an Italian spinet (1577) inlaid with ivory and 1928 precious stones, or a German altarpiece in amber (1650).

A display on **Baroque Rome** shows the Counter-Reformation in full swing, presided over by the busts of popes and cardinals, including *Cardinal Paolo Emilio Zacchia* (c 1650) by Alessandro Algardi, a terracotta whose surface quivers with life. But the greatest sculptor at this time was Gian Lorenzo Bernini: among several terracotta models by him here is the feverish deathbed scene of *Blessed Ludovica Albertoni* (1671-4). In Room 2a are smaller Baroque objects, such as a grim wax model of *Time and Death* (c 1700-40) by Caterina de Julianis, a nun. The gloom of Room 2c reveals a complete panelled room from France (late 17c), with painted decoration, filled with equally dark furniture.

A diverse selection of later 17c and early 18c objects in Room 3 features swords, tiles, flower paintings and, in Room 3d, two tall **Delftware** pyramids (late 17c) that were used to display tulips, for which there was a mania in this period; their colouring shows the influence of imported Chinese porcelains.

Room 4 is a circular space containing fine **European porcelain**: the secrets of its production were discovered in Saxony in 1708. Tablewares and ornaments from the first factory, Meissen, include wonderful parakeets (c 1740-5) and the more familiar *commedia dell'arte* shepherdesses and harlequins.

Rooms 5-7 follow the development of European taste in the 18c, with the objects on the left coming from the 19c collection of John Jones, who made his fortune as tailor to the army. Some of the earlier objects were inspired by the great palace at Versailles, and include furniture by Louis XIV's cabinetmaker, André Charles Boulle, who gave his name to a type of brass-and-tortoiseshell inlay.

The predominant style in Room 5 is **Rococo**, seen in lighter furniture and paintings of gallantry such as Nicolas Lancret's *The Swing* (c 1730), and beautiful carved wall panels (1725-50). Room 6 has small luxury objects, mainly from Paris, and in Room 7a there are French enamelled snuff boxes (1760s-80s), some with portraits of Marie-Antoinette. Among several busts, the most eccentric is the Austrian Franz Xaver Messerschmidt's *The Strong Smell* (1775-83), one of his famous physiognomical studies.

Off Room 7b is a reconstructed mirrored chamber (c 1780) with carved and gilt walls, in which candlelight is endlessly reflected. By this time **Neoclassicism** was on the rise, paring back decoration and simplifying forms. In Room 7e look out for Sèvres portrait busts of Louis XVI and Marie-Antoinette, with a strange history: given to an ambassador of Tipu Sahib (of whom more later) they were looted from Mysore by an East India Company officer in 1799.

EUROPE 1800-1900 *Rooms 8, 9* Climb a few steps into the foyer and cross it to descend into Room 8, which has been displayed in the Victorian manner, from the design of cases and light fittings to the rich colours on the walls. The 19c revived any number of **historical styles**, from ancient Egypt to French Renaissance, producing objects that directly recall some we have already seen upstairs. Standards of craftsmanship were still high, even if the results are sometimes grim, as in an armchair made of antlers (c 1860). America begins to be represented by firms such as Tiffany & Co., with a delicate silver coffee pot and creamer (c 1875-80).

By the 1890s there were widespread movements to reform design and manufacturing, from Finland to France, with a new emphasis on simplified shapes and decoration. In Room 9 objects following these principles include furniture by Hector Guimard, designer of Paris' famous Metro stations, and elevator grilles (1893-4) by Louis Sullivan. Sinuous lines on pewter and in the posters of Alphonse Mucha and Toulouse-Lautrec herald the rise of **Art Nouveau**. For more Art Nouveau furniture, see Room 126 in the British Galleries.

BRITISH GALLERIES

BRITAIN 1500-1690 *Rooms 56-58* Stairs to the left of the main Museum entrance, guarded by stone figures of kings from Bristol High Cross (c 1400), lead to the British Galleries, opened in 2001. These beautifully arranged rooms show how taste, fashion and innovation shaped British art and design over 500 years. In entertaining 'discovery areas' visitors - and not just children - can interract with (usually replica) objects, and reading rooms, touchscreens and cinemas supply the background to the exhibits. Labels for some objects are in booklets to the side of display cases. Take the opportunity to open drawers concealing embroideries, sketches and other fragile treasures.

Atmospherically dark Room 58 starts in 1500, when the **Tudor court** was the centre of taste. A portrait of *Henry VIII* (1535-40) shows the king before his makeover by Hans Holbein; a miniature of *Anne of Cleves* (1539) by that artist is thought to have deceived Henry into marriage. Gold pendants and rings and exquisite blackwork embroidery reveal the luxurious life of courtiers. A wall of pine panelling (1585-1620) with columns and pediment is one of the earliest uses of classical principles in the country. The last third of the room deals with **birth, marriage and death** in the 16c and 17c: objects range from funeral brasses to the amazing Torre Abbey jewel (1540-50), a coffin-shaped pendant with enamelled skeleton occupant.

Room 58b, a narrow gallery running down the side of this space, displays among other things charming pincushions and book covers from the Sheldon tapestry workshop, founded in 1560; and **printed books**, including a luminously beautiful page from Caxton's edition of the *Canterbury Tales* (1477) and a facsimile of John Gerard's *Generall Historie of Plantes* (1597) to leaf through.

The **Great Bed of Ware** (c 1590), which occupies a large part of Room 57, was probably made as a tourist attraction and certainly succeeded: Shakespeare mentions it in *Twelfth Night*. This room shows some of the objects that glorified the court of Elizabeth I, including **miniatures** by Nicholas Hilliard and the Drake Jewel (?1586). There are some embroideries (c 1570) by Elizabeth's *bête* *noire*, Mary Queen of Scots. In the discovery area you can try on a ruff or a gauntlet, or construct a chair. As you enter Room 56, stairs on the right lead down to the Raphael gallery, past the four **Dacre Beasts** (1507-25), apparently unique heraldic woodwork from the reign of Henry VIII, under a lick of Victorian paint.

Under the **Stuarts** the English began to put their own spin on foreign influences: Charles I was a notable patron of the arts. Contrast his marble bust (1631) by Hubert Le Sueur with Bernini's of *Thomas Baker* (c 1638), left unfinished so as not to rival the artist's portrayal of the King. A filing cabinet hides original drawings by Britain's first classical architect, Inigo Jones. Court costumes were still elaborate: there is a rare juxtaposition of a portrait, of one *Margaret Laton* (1620), and the embroidered jacket (c 1610) she is shown wearing. Much of the lavish silverware made at this time was melted down in the **civil wars** of the mid-century: this makes the Lord Keeper's Seal Cup (1626-7), recast from a discarded seal of James I, a rare survival.

After the **Restoration** of Charles II, interaction with foreign craftsmen and markets resumed. Furniture was lighter and more elaborately carved, with marquetry by French and Dutch immigrants, and Chinese porcelains and German stonewares were imported. Mezzotint printmaking, improved clocks, guns and scientific instruments arrived. On the home front, women's sewing skills were still vital: one case displays the exquisite work of young Martha Edlin (1660-1725). The small Room 56c traces Britain's growing trade with Asia and the Americas: new commodities demanded new objects, such as snuff graters and tea caddies. Elaborate security kept the goods safe: John Wilkes' 'detector lock' (c 1680) counted each time it was opened.

Room 55 is a light and comfortable **study area** with books on relevant subjects and screens on which to explore the British Galleries and leave comments. Suspended above your head is *Breathless* (2001), a circle of squashed brass instruments, by Cornelia Parker.

BRITAIN 1700-1760 *Rooms 52-54* The story resumes with **William and Mary**; propagandist prints and commemorative tankards depict the royal couple (she was popular, he wasn't) beside a modern Charles and Di mug. The **Baroque** style was spreading among the nobility, who were replacing their tapestries with painted walls and ceilings and investing in extravagant sets of silverware, like the enormous wine cooler (1719-20) here. One of the most famous craftsmen of the age was Grinling Gibbons, whose intricate limewood carving of the *Stoning of St Stephen* (1680-1710) is displayed.

Turn right into the elegant parlour from 11 Henrietta Street, Covent Garden (1727-32), designed by James Gibbs, one of the leading promoters of **Palladianism**. The style is recorded here in books, printed designs and models, showing the deep impact of Italy on early Grand Tourists. In contrast was **Rococo**, at its peak 1740-60, when fashionable C and S curves were applied to many decorative objects such as the gorgeous swirling overmantel (c 1750) in Room 53. Room 53a has Staffordshire pottery and an embroidered court dress (1740-5) with a skirt so wide the wearer had to negotiate doors sideways.

Room 52 recalls **public entertainments** such as those to be found in Vauxhall Gardens, with paintings (1741-2) from its private 'supper boxes' and a statue of the composer George Friederic Handel (1738) by Louis-François Roubiliac. Room 52a is another discovery area, where you can design a monogram or try on a hooped petticoat. A ramp skirts the Music Room from Norfolk House, St James's Square (1756), a blaze of carved and gilt emblems on white walls, brought to life on Wednesday evenings by half-hour concerts.

Finally you see a wall of portraits - 18c Britons in paint, print, marble, cut paper, ivory and wax - and items of **Chinoiserie**, a style popular 1745-65, including bedroom furnishings from Badminton House (1754) complete with dragons.

BRITAIN 1760-1830 *Rooms 118-21* Continue up the marble stairs to Level 4. Room 118 begins with the **Neoclassical** tastes that had been fired by the Grand Tour. Architects including Robert Adam designed whole buildings in the style: you can see a richly coloured section of Adam's Glass Drawing Room from

Northumberland House (1773-5) and his pastel ceiling and chimneypiece (c 1771) for the actor David Garrick's residence in the Adelphi, Adam's Thameside building development. More of Garrick's life as a fashionable Londoner is revealed in Room 118a, where there is a portrait of him and his wife, and their bedroom furniture by Chippendale. There is more on Chippendale and his famous publication, *The Gentleman and Cabinet Maker's Director* (1754), which spread his ideas far and wide; and on the collection of Horace Walpole, including the medieval stained glass he used to impart 'gloomth' to his Gothic-style house at Strawberry Hill.

Architects also designed for the new **industries** that were springing up, powered by steam and directed by entrepreneurs including Josiah Wedgwood and Matthew Boulton. Adam's work ranged from cast-iron balcony railings (c 1775) to a silver-plated 'toast machine' (c 1790).

Room 119, representing the private sculpture galleries of the 18c nobility, currently houses the *Three Graces* (1814-17) by Antonio Canova. The statue is shared with the National Gallery of Scotland in Edinburgh on a three-year cycle.

Salisbury Cathedral (1823) by Constable and objects commemorating the victories of Nelson, Wolfe and Wellington introduce the idea of 'Britishness' in Room 120. Until about 1830 **Classicism** - as seen in the type of woman's gown (c 1800) a Jane Austen heroine might wear - was the well-established national style but classical good taste was not universal. *Bashaw* (1832-4), a sculpture of the Earl of Dudley's faithful dog in coloured marble, is a case in point. The highly romantic bust of *George IV* (1831, a year after his death) by Samuel Joseph flatters this enthusiastic if inconstant patron of the arts.

Gothic forms had been rediscovered from the mid-18c by Walpole, the extravagant collector William Beckford and others, and after 1800 they entered mainstream design. The pretty little 'Strawberry Room' from Lee Priory in Kent (1783-94), with a fan-vaulted plaster ceiling, designed by James Wyatt, shows the overall effect.

Room 121 is another study area, with a view down on Cornelia Parker's installation.

BRITAIN 1840-1900 *Rooms 122-26* The full-blown **Gothic Revival** is displayed in Room 122: it became the 19c's most popular style from about 1840. The perception that it was a Christian form explains its enthusiastic adoption by architects responsible for a wave of church-building. A.W.N. Pugin was its most famous practitioner: his designs for church plate and inlaid earthenware tiles came to be used in domestic as well as religious spaces; and when the Houses of Parliament were rebuilt in the 1840s, he designed their wallpapers, flooring and furniture. A literary element to the revival is also seen in an extraordinary, Dante-inspired washstand (1880) by William Burges.

The next part of the main gallery concentrates on the **Great Exhibition** of 1851, and centres on a model of Joseph Paxton's Crystal Palace, where it was held. (His design for the building, rapidly sketched on blotting paper, hangs nearby.) The enterprise was intended to show off the best of all kinds of manufacturing, so knitted underwear is included beside elaborate porcelains among the exhibits shown here. Room 122c deals with the new technologies that made many of these items possible and transformed the Victorians' everyday world - pressed glass dishes, textiles coloured with bright, synthetic dyes, mass media publications churned out on steam presses, and photography, including some fascinating scenes from *Street Life in London* (1877-8). Room 122b is a discovery area where you can try on a crinoline or view stereographs.

The Great Exhibition was copied throughout the world and one of its committee members, **Sir Henry Cole**, was the first director of the Victoria & Albert Museum's ancestor on this site. Cole had previously attempted to reform British design through Felix Summerlee's Art Manufacturers (1847): a case of its products and those of contemporary firms is shown to demonstrate the axiom that decoration should not detract from form or function. Another Kensington building was devoted to British art - works by J.M.W. Turner, David Roberts and Sir Edwin Landseer are included here - and working people were encouraged to visit, all part of a grand educational programme.

The next gallery displays on one side items celebrating **Queen Victoria**, from a fold-out panorama of her coronation procession (1838) to some madly patriotic Golden Jubilee wallpaper (1887). On the other side, 'Understanding objects' encourages us to identify materials and techniques and spot fakes.

Room 124 examines the impact of Japanese art in Britain from the 1850s. Bamboo leaves and peacock feathers appeared everywhere and screens became fashionable; a sideboard (1867-70) by E.W. Godwin looks very modern in its angularity. By the 1870s the craze had spawned the **Aesthetic Movement**, which advocated 'art for art's sake'.

Chôkôsai Eishô *The Courtesan Yosooi of the Matsuba-ya House* (1795–1800, colour woodcut)

The aesthetes' clothes and manners were mocked by the general public, but Liberty & Co. was able to sell rolls of its 'Peacock Feathers' textile (1887).

The side gallery, Room 125c, covers further influences from the Islamic world, China and India; and training schools for British designers, set up to compete with European rivals. Ceramics, textiles and metalwork (including some very contemporary-looking teapots) by Christopher Dresser illustrate the career of one of the first professional designers.

Room 125b examines birth, marriage and death in the Victorian age. A gentleman's wardrobe has every outfit convention demanded for different social occasions; the white wedding dress (1865) was popularized by the Queen herself; and there is a sober display of mourning costume (1894-6), jewellery and stationery.

The larger gallery ends with the **Arts and Crafts Movement** and styles that grew out of it. William Morris dominates the first part: here is his only painting, *La Belle Iseult* (1858); items by Morris, Marshall, Faulkner and Co. (founded 1861), with stained glass, carpets, and still-familiar designs including the 'Strawberry Thief' textile (1883) and 'Acanthus' wallpaper (1874); and lavishly produced books from his Kelmscott Press. From the **Scottish School**, a high-backed chair (1897) and fireplace for the Willow Tea Rooms (c 1904) by its leader Charles Rennie Mackintosh manage to be elegant and robust. For almost the first time, named women designers are represented, with candle sconces (1896) by Frances and Margaret Macdonald and embroideries (c 1900) by Jessie Newbery.

The landing on which you emerge is overlooked by mosaic portraits (1862-71) of artist and architect heroes from the 'Kensington Valhalla', originally in the South Court of the Museum.

ASIAN COLLECTIONS

INDIA *Rooms 41, 47a, 47b* The earliest pieces are in Room 47b, part of the corridor beyond the entrance hall. They begin with small terracotta figurines (1c BC) but include sculptures in stone - including a swaying sandstone torso of *Buddha Avalokitesvara* (c 900) - ivory and wood, and examples of the famous **Chola bronzes**.

Room 41 is an airy space mainly devoted to the arts of the subcontinent after 1500, the achievements of the Muslim **Mughal dynasty**, and the incursions by European colonists. A chart at the front of the gallery defines themed areas. The beautiful displays are introduced by an elegant colonnade (first half 17c) from Ajmer, mixing Hindu and Near Eastern forms; otherwise, the Mughals' grandiose architectural projects have to be extrapolated from coloured tiles, stone screens pierced with geometrical patterns (*jali*), and watercolours made for East India Company employees. A particularly impressive example of the Mughal jeweller's art is the white jade wine cup (1657), with a ram's-head handle, linked to the emperor Shah Jahan.

In the 18c the empire began to collapse and **provincial courts** asserted themselves. There are displays of the distinctive paintings and textiles of Rajasthan and the Punjab; Bidri ware - zinc alloy vessels with complex inlay of silver or brass - from the Deccan; and very bold watercolours by Kalighat painters from 19c Calcutta. The Sikhs, allies of the British, are also represented: note the conical Akali turban (mid-19c), handy for carrying deadly steel quoits. One of the most remarkable objects in the whole Museum is 'Tippoo's Tiger' (1790s), an automaton of a life-sized beast devouring a European. It was made for the ruler of Mysore, Tipu Sultan, the last opponent of the British in southern India. An organ added authentic screams and roars.

Back in the corridor, turn right to the end of Room 47a for the arts of **South-east Asia**. These include sculptures from Nepal, closely related to those in India, including a huge, eye-popping head of Bhairava, the wrathful Shiva (17c), crowned with snakes and skulls. There are more Buddhist and Hindu figures from Tibet, Sri Lanka, Burma, Cambodia, Vietnam and Indonesia.

ISLAM *Rooms 42, 47c* Most of the spectacular **tile panels** in Room 47c were made in **Iznik** (16c), part of the Ottoman empire, in blue and white sometimes accented with dabs of red (green and purple are seen in wares made in Syria). The main displays in Room 42 will be closed for refurbishment until 2006. They include the astounding **Ardabil carpet** (1539-40), 10.5m in length; brilliant turquoise-glazed Iranian earthenwares (early 13c); enamelled glass **mosque lamps** (c 1313) from Syria that were copied by Europeans in the 19c; and delicate illustrations by Riza Abbasi (1632) for a manuscript of the romance of *Khusraw and Shirin*. During the closure, parts of the collection will be on tour, but you can still see superb examples of Islamic glass, ceramics and textiles in the relevant galleries on the floors above.

CHINA *Rooms 44, 47e, 47f* Two large marble figures (c 1400-1600), possibly of Korean envoys, in robes incised with delicate cloudbands, introduce the arts of China in Room 47e. Continue into Room 47f to see **items made for export** to the West, especially in the southern port of Canton, from around 1550.

The main part of the collection is in Room 44, which is divided into themes. The central zone relates to the material splendour of the **imperial family**, and includes a massive throne (1775-80) and a red table (1426-36), the only surviving major piece from the Ming lacquer works called the Orchard Factory. The emperor's role as a collector and promoter of the arts is exemplified in some exquisite jade, porcelain and enamel objects in a lacquer display cabinet (1760-80). Lesser, but still wealthy, mortals used solid, elegant furniture including wooden armchairs, tables and a coffer for storing clothes (1550-1600). Pottery vessels and utensils were divided according to the type of food they were used to prepare or serve - grains and starch (*fan*) or vegetables and meat (*cai*) - with others for wine or tea. Pastimes included 'encirclement chess', or writing with extensive sets of equipment.

The displays at the end of the room follow burial practices from the stone age to the Ming dynasty, with a selection of **grave goods**. In the Han period (206 BC-AD 220), jade was thought to preserve the body, which was also sent into the afterlife with cooking equipment and terracotta models of people and animals to replace live sacrifice. Tang period (618-906) burials had even more elaborate animal entourages of glazed terracotta, and fierce tomb guardians, to ensure no loss of status in death; later the dead were buried with objects they had used in life. **Ancestor portraits**, such as those of Qing military and civil officials and their wives (1700-1800), would be brought out on special occasions. Of two Bodhissatva figures, one in a relaxed seated pose is of the Jin period (1115-1234), the other an upright, elongated, Ming figure (1368-1644).

Some of the items in the last case are fakes, made to satisfy the Chinese market for antiquities that arose as early as the 11c. They are now valuable in themselves.

JAPAN *Room 45* The exquisite artefacts of Japan are arranged by date or according to material or use. Sue stonewares were made in imitation of Chinese and Korean techniques and styles, with simple glazes and flaring shapes (c 500-750). **Porcelain** began to be made at Arita around 1600 and enamelled wares for export at Kakeimon. A display charts the course of the tea ceremony (*chanoyu*) which began to be formalized around 1400 and demanded a wide range of utensils - caddies, whisks, bowls and kettles. Other leisure pursuits might merit beautiful, specialized objects such as a picnic set of gold and black lacquer (1800-50), which certainly outdoes tupperware. A display explains the different types of **lacquer decoration**.

Netsuke and inro, fittings on a man's belt, are some of the most familiar and popular Japanese artefacts and the Museum has a large collection (1700-1900), demonstrating brilliant carving and often a sense of humour. Textiles, prints of Kabuki theatre, swords and sinister samurai armour of the Edo period (1615-1858) are also shown. Artefacts of the Meiji period (1868-1912) combined traditional craft skills with responses to Western influences. The Museum still collects Japanese ceramics, textiles and woodwork.

KOREA *Room 47g* The end of the corridor focuses on the arts of Korea from 300 AD to the present, including pieces made by contemporary artists using traditional means. Highlights include **green-glazed ceramics** of the Koryo dynasty (935-1392), with restrained floral or animal decoration - look out for the ewer shaped like a bamboo shoot (1100-50) - and exquisitely coloured modern variations on traditional female costume. Dragons, symbols of water and royal power, are found on many items, from a slate burial chest (1150-1250) to wide-bodied porcelain jars of the Choson dynasty (1392-1910).

SCULPTURE

SCULPTURE AND ARCHITECTURE *Rooms 50a, 50b* The long, light-filled gallery opposite the main shop is devoted to European sculpture. For a chronological view, start at the end furthest from the foyer, occupied by a complete **chapel** from a Florentine church (c 1493-1500), designed by Giuliano da Sangallo. Another wall is dominated by an enormous equestrian monument (c 1430-5), towering over carved well-heads from Italy (9c-16c).

The centrepiece of Room 50b is Bernini's ***Neptune and Triton*** (c 1620-2), a marble group made for a fountain and once owned by Sir Joshua Reynolds. The wall ahead is actually the back of a vast roodloft (1610-13) from a church in the Netherlands, complete with balustrade and alabaster statues.

Now you enter the main part of the gallery, a forest of still white figures. The imposing **effigies** in the centre are those of Sir Moyle Finch and Elizabeth, Countess of Winchilsea (c 1630), by England's foremost sculptor of the 17c, Nicholas Stone. Of the 18c works, some of the most appealing are **terracotta models**, from tiny sketches by Joseph Nollekens to Roubiliac's more finished idea for Shakespeare's monument in Westminster Abbey (1757). The influence of Rome is everywhere, and the chief personality is Antonio Canova, whose ***Theseus and the Minotaur*** (1782) is the focal point for the other end of the gallery. (For his ***Three Graces***, see the British Galleries.)

CAST COURTS *Rooms 46a, 46b* Across the corridor from Room 50b are two of the most fantastic spaces in this or any museum, containing the largest collection of **plaster reproductions** of sculpture to survive, a testament to the didactic drives of the Victorians. Room 46a has been repainted in its original colour scheme and has works from Northern Europe and Spain. Walk beside the enormous portal of Santiago da Compostela, Anglo-Saxon crosses, Viking doorways and royal effigies from Westminster to Trajan's Column, its 38m chopped in two, and preserving details now lost to pollution on the original. You can look closely at sculptures one might not get near in reality, and notice new details, such as the snails supporting the 'bronze' tomb of St Sebaldus by Peter Vischer the Elder. Room 46b concentrates on Renaissance Italy, from Ghiberti's prize-winning panel for the doors on Florence's baptistery (1401) to Michelangelo's ***David*** (c 1501-4): look round the back of the plinth to see the fig leaf the Museum kept handy in case Queen Victoria visited.

FAKES AND FORGERIES *Room 46* Running between the Cast Courts is a fascinating display of pastiches, altered originals and outright fakes. Many show high levels of skill but are betrayed by modern materials or mixed-up imagery.

SMALL-SCALE SCULPTURE *Room 64* From Room 50b climb a short flight of stairs to Level 2. At the top is a small display of **wax models**, especially portraits, popular in England, Germany and Italy from the 16c to 19c. In Room 64 a daunting array of display cases contain small sculptures and carvings. Among the bronzes there are interesting demonstrations of the lost-wax casting method used in Giambologna's 16c studio, and of cameo-carving. Ivories range from Byzantine plaques (10c-12c) to a *Virgin and Child* (1916-24) by Eric Gill.

RODIN *Room 111, 108* Stairs from the Korean displays lead up to Level 3, where Room 111 is set to reopen in February 2004 with a display of sculpture. It also gives a wonderful view over the Cast Courts, with Trajan's Column as you'll never see it in Rome.

At the end, go down the steps and turn right to the East Staircase, where a collection of bronzes and one marble by the French sculptor Auguste Rodin are now displayed. Most were given to the Museum by the artist in 1914. Downstairs are relatively conventional bust portraits (1890s) and his *St John the Baptist*, acquired in 1902. Above are more expressionist figures from his later projects.

OTHER COLLECTIONS

ARMS AND ARMOUR *Room 90* A compact display on Level 3 ranges from a crumbly iron sword (c 1380) to Italian parade armour decorated with classical figures and gold ornament (16c), and intricately carved German rifle stocks and inlaid powder flasks (16c and 17c).

CERAMICS *Rooms 132-45* Climb the West Stairs to Level 6 to wonder at the Museum's vast collection of ceramics, beginning with **Ancient Egyptian fragments** with blue glaze and some Greek pottery including black- and red-figure vases, all in Room 132.

Room 133 has **Islamic ceramics**: vividly patterned Iznik dishes from the Ottoman empire and sparsely decorated Iranian pieces glazed in subtle celadon, white or opaque turquoise (17c).

Rooms 134-136 have **European pottery**, including Delft tiles, lustre-glazed dishes from Spain and case upon case of Italian majolica. A smaller display of northern European ceramics includes salt-glazed tankards from Germany. Turn into the next room: the entire length of the building lies ahead, and it is full of pots.

In Room 137, **British pottery** ranges from rustic 16c earthenware to 18c and 19c Staffordshire figurines, Toby jugs to Wedgwood jasperware. Clarice Cliffe, Charlotte Rhead and Susie Cooper, three prominent 20c female commercial potters are represented, as are studio potters Lucie Rie and Bernard Leach (1950s-60s). Room 138 showcases sculptural **contemporary ceramics**, and pieces made by Picasso at Vallauris. **British porcelain** fills Rooms 139 and 140, with all the famous manufacturers - Derby, Chelsea, Coalport, Worcester - represented amid the crowds of figurines.

Room 141 features **European tiles** and Room 142 has delicate 18c **Continental porcelains** including exquisite cups and tea pots.

The final suite of galleries celebrates **Far Eastern ceramics**. Room 143 has Thai and Vietnamese stoneware and hundreds of Chinese pots, from elegant grey-green celadons (10c) to a striking display of the clear coloured glazes derived from iron, copper and manganese. Room 144 has **Chinese carving**, in materials from rose quartz to bamboo root as well as jade, producing simple bi discs (2000-1500 BC) or ornate ornaments, brush rests, cups and boxes; and Chinese glass in striking, strong colours and shapes. Lastly, Room 145 has more Chinese ceramics. A few modern pieces, such as a crystal-glazed jar (1988) from Taiwan, demonstrate the continuing skill of Eastern potters, and there are even political objects, including a snuff bottle with transfer portraits of Mao and Nixon (1972).

Pottery diehards can take the stairs on the right of the main entrance, past 17c and 18c sculptures, to Level 4. The stoneware **Doulton Frieze** (1939), showing pottery's appreciation by great civilizations, hangs here. It was modelled by Gilbert Bayes, whose most famous work is probably the 'Queen of Time' clock on Selfridge's, and was rescued from demolition in 1971. Room 128 will re-open as a new **architecture gallery** in autumn 2004.

DRESS *Room 40* This huge domed space on Level 1 contains an entertaining display of **Western costume** from 1700 (see also the rooms on India, China, Japan and Korea and the textile galleries). Individual designers - recently Jean-Paul Gaultier, Ossie Clark - are showcased and there are displays of shoes, fans, parasols, bridal headgear and other accoutrements. Relics of the recent past like platform shoes and puffball skirts seem as outlandish as the crinoline.

GLASS *Rooms 129, 131* The **glass** collections on Level 4 are best accessed via the end of the ironwork display (Room 114e). Cross a bridge over the sculpture galleries to Room 112 to see *Old Woman* (1990), a striking drawing on glass by Czech artist Dana Zamecnikova, and a suitably vitreous sign by students of the RCA.

The first thing you see in Room 131 is a Venetian glass chandelier (18c-19c), and then a glittering sculpture, *A Moment in Time* (1998) by Peter Aldridge, in 'Starphire' glass. The staircase with glass steps and balustrade by Danny Lane leads up to the study collections: metal drawers contain many fragments and allow closer inspection.

The historical tour starts in the wall cases on your left. Following the discovery of glass-making in Mesopotamia about 4500 years ago, it was adopted by ancient peoples for luxury goods: a tiny unguent jar from Egypt (1400-1336 BC) still has beautifully clear colours. By 500 AD the ability to make blown-glass had spread across the Roman Empire to the Gauls and Anglo-Saxons. There is a wonderful display of **Islamic cut glass** (9c-10c) and later lustre-painted fragments: it is no surprise that a delicately enamelled Syrian beaker (13c) was considered a talismanic 'fairy goblet' by its Crusader owner.

Venetian glass was famous by the 15c, especially clear *cristallo* glass, which was fused with opaque white threads to make filigree wares (16c). Venetians perfected enamelling and gilding and sold their expertise as well as their goods across Europe. Ever more elaborate decoration was produced in northern Europe, as Bohemian glassmakers found deeper colours and the Dutch perfected diamond-engraving.

The other side of the room, including a case entirely filled with drinking glasses, charts British achievements. 'Glass for the million' became possible after the development of press-moulding in America in the 1820s but some makers could use even **mass-production** methods for artistic ends, as Lalique's vases with human figures, thistles and abstract patterns (1910-20s) prove. There are vases copying plant forms by Emile Gallé (1902) and Daum Frères, and lustrous favrile glass by Louis Comfort Tiffany (1896).

Room 129 currently shows part of the Museum's collection of **art glass** by the likes of Dale Chihuly. It may soon close for refurbishment.

IRONWORK *Rooms 113, 114* On Level 3 a long, white-painted gallery houses the national collection of ironwork, with over 2000 pieces from Britain and Europe dating from the 12c to recently commissioned items, such as Albert Paley's bench (1994) ending in whiplash tangles. It appears daunting but the sheer variety of shapes and applications soon becomes mesmerizing. You may want to read the useful glossary in Room 113 before embarking on the displays of bells, candlesticks, firedogs, garden furniture, railings and gates, roasting hooks, tradesmen's signs, weathervanes and fittings for doors and chests. At the midpoint is the glittering **Hereford Cathedral screen** (1862), designed by George Gilbert Scott. Weighing in at over 8 tons, its iron frame and ornament of mosaic, brass, copper and paint took five months to make and 13 to restore.

JEWELLERY *Rooms 91-93, 102* From Room 109 on Level 3 you can enter the jewellery collection. The one-way route, starting from Room 93, is guarded by a narrow turnstile, so leave your surfboard in the cloakroom. Inside are copies of the catalogue to consult as you view the closely packed cases. The first room has boxes in gold, enamel and precious stones (16c-19c), watches, swords, and the **Londonderry jewels**, including a necklace of huge amethysts. Room 92 has exquisite Greek gold filigree jewellery (2nd millennium BC), medieval enamels, extravagant Renaissance pendants, black Berlin iron jewellery (1804-55), Art Nouveau plaques and brooches, and contemporary pieces; and Room 91 adornments from Africa, pre-Columbian America and Celtic Ireland, including a gold collar (7c), and rings, including some set with enormous precious stones (15c, 16c).

On emerging, turn right into Room 102 to see part of the **costume jewellery** collection (18c-20c). A mosaic portrait of Prince Albert marks the start of the Prince Consort Gallery over the South Court: a window allows a peep at its elaborate decoration, soon to be restored under FuturePlan.

LEIGHTON FRESCOS *Rooms 107, 102* From the ironwork displays, take Room 111 to Room 107 to see a now somewhat darkened fresco, *Arts of Industry applied to Peace*, one of two painted 1878-86 by Frederic Leighton, the celebrated Royal Academician, to adorn the South Court. *Arts of Industry applied to War* is in Room 102. The display includes preliminary drawings and a full-sized cartoon.

MUSICAL INSTRUMENTS *Room 40a* A mezzanine above the dress gallery has a small but pleasing display of instruments, from a French glass flute (1815) to an upright piano painted with scenes of *Death and the Maiden* (c 1860) by Edward Burne-Jones. There are also cases of clocks and astronomical devices such as astrolabes.

NATIONAL ART LIBRARY *Rooms 77, 78, 85* At the top of the stairs from Room 25, presided over by more figures from the 'Kensington Valhalla' and Edward Burne-Jones' unfinished *Car of Love* (1890s), is Room 85. Small exhibits, often of artist's books and other printed matter, are regularly held here. Beyond is the National Art Library.

PAINTING *Rooms 81, 82, 87, 88* These were the original painting galleries (built in the 1850s) and have been restored to show 200 works from the Museum, which contains the national collections of paintings by John Constable and of watercolours. One room is densely hung with typically literary Victorian scenes by Landseer, Etty and Millais; and the last is devoted to the 19c Ionides collection, with Botticelli's portrait of **Smeralda Bandinelli** (1471), Millet's **Wood Sawyers** (c 1849) and Degas' **Ballet Scene** (1876), complemented by French sculpture and Oriental ceramics.

PHOTOGRAPHY *Room 38a* This gallery draws on the national collection of over 300,000 British and international photographs, which the prescient Museum began acquiring in 1852: the earliest is a daguerrotype view down Whitehall (1839). The first part of the gallery shows changing highlights from the collection: you might see Julia Margaret Cameron's portraits and tableaux of Victorian worthies, experimental photograms by Laszlo Moholy-Nagy, scenes from urban America in saturated colour by William Eggleston, or 'untitled film stills' by Cindy Sherman. The small space beyond has themed shows.

SILVER *Rooms 65-69, 83, 84* The study collection of **church plate** on Level 3 is soon to be redisplayed with stained glass. Room 84 has relatively austere English pieces, Room 83 more elaborate Continental crosiers, reliquaries and crucifixes.

You will emerge in Room 89, the start of the magnificent new **silver** galleries, with a huge group of **Lions**, an electrotype copy of a set (1670) guarding the Danish royal throne at Rosenborg Castle. Room 69 displays European silver from 1400 to 1800, Room 67 international silver from 1800 to the present, and Room 65 British silver from 1400 to 1800, with a copy of a **Leopard** (1600-1). Room 68 is a study area with touchscreens exploring techniques, while in Room 66 you have the opportunity to identify mystery silver objects and rub or stamp hallmarks. Among a huge range of glittering exhibits are spectacular church plate from 16c and 17c Spain, drawers of nutmeg graters, bottle labels and cutlery, and an enormous silver-gilt table centrepiece (1824-5). Text panels discuss everything from the world's sources of silver to the craftsmen's guilds who worked it. At the end, two columns clad in

Minton 'Renaissance' tiles, and the nearby staircase, indicate the original contents of the galleries. The decoration of the walls and ceiling (c 1870) by Frank Moody was recently restored.

TEXTILES *Rooms 94-101* From the East Stairs or the Leighton gallery, turn into Room 101, which displays **recent textile acquisitions**: these might include clothing, printed fabrics or collaged wall-hangings. Room 100, which runs beside it, has hundreds of European embroideries and printed textiles, late antique (4c-5c) and medieval fabrics, Italian damasks and Iranian and Turkish silks (16c), all in frames which can be pulled from the racks for study. Hung on the walls are designs by Raoul Dufy and Vanessa Bell, and a sampler (after 1830) worked with her pitiful life story by one Elizabeth Parker.

Room 99 has historical textiles including a woven linen shirt (c 1370-1352 BC) from Tutankhamen's tomb and minutely stitched Turkish embroideries. Costumes from Siberia, Iran, Macedonia and elsewhere line this room and Room 96. In Room 98 you can attempt to try on a *kimono* and *obi* (sash) and see a range of other **Japanese costumes**, in angular traditional shapes but contemporary textiles, and 18c Chinese robes. Room 96 has exquisite old **lace**, net and equally fragile work made with straw.

Perhaps the highlight of this section is Room 94, hung with medieval **tapestries**. They include a series known as the *Devonshire Hunts* (1420s-40s), in fact from several sets perhaps made in Arras, which preserve fascinating details of courtly costume and manners.

20C DESIGN *Rooms 103-106, 70-74* The jewellery and textile galleries encircle a utilitarian display of **20c furniture** and smaller objects. The circuit begins in Room 103 with British Arts and Crafts designs, Secessionist furniture from Vienna (1900-10), and pieces from the Omega Workshops hand-painted by Roger Fry and Duncan Grant. Work by German and Dutch Modernists include Mies van der Rohe's cantilevered armchair (1927). Entertaining Surrealist objects by Meret Oppenheim and Cecil Beaton are followed by severe Utility designs (1940s) and iconic chairs by Scandinavians and Americans including Charles and Ray Eames. Colourful Pop icons of the 1960s by the likes of Verner Panton and Arne Jacobsen outshine some 1980s office furniture, no longer looking very hi-tech; Postmodern chairs have clashing upholstery; there are even shelves from IKEA.

Cut through the silver galleries or take the West Stair to Rooms 70-74. In Room 74, objects are arranged to examine particular periods and themes, such as Modernism or the impact of machines. The presentation is rather dry but many of the exhibits are iconic, such as Dalí's sofa in the shape of Mae West's lips (1936) or Marcel Breuer's chairs for the Bauhaus. The uses of **typography**, in everything from newspapers to road signs and packaging, is examined at the end.

Room 73 looks at **mass consumption** through designs that really caught on, like Melamine tableware or the Olivetti typewriter. In Room 72, form and function are analysed through furniture including Ettore Sottsass's 'Casablanca' sideboard (1971) for the Memphis design group, and Ron Arad's 'Little Heavy Chair' (1993); and design used for political ends in an array of badges, mugs and sloganeering T-shirts. Finally, Room 71 samples some continuing craft traditions and **technological advances** from Lycra to a Dyson vacuum cleaner (1986) in nauseating pale pink.

The Museum's new **Contemporary Space** on Level 2, reached by stairs to the right of the main foyer, has a changing programme of exhibitions and events that include further aspects of 20c design.

HENRY COLE WING

The wing is undergoing major changes as part of the FuturePlan, and amenities and displays may have changed.

ROOMS 202, 206-9, 220 Opposite the lifts on Level 2, Room 203 is a temporary exhibition space. Go through it and right to reach a small display on the American architect **Frank Lloyd Wright** (1867-1959), its fascinating centrepiece the office (1935-7) he designed for Edgar J. Kaufmann of Philadelphia, his only work this side of the Atlantic. Angular woodwork panels and cubic armchairs give a cosy, ship's cabin feel.

Retrace your steps through Room 203 to Room 220, on **European ornament** from 1450 to the present, crammed with objects and lots of reading. It takes in natural patterns and their copies (from acanthus leaves on Roman candelabras to Victorian floral wallpaper and 1920s' snakeskin shoes), classical originals and their sometimes strange later interpretations, the influences of China, India, Japan and Egypt, and the rediscovery of medieval styles. The 19c love of classification provided the backdrop to the creation of the Victoria and Albert Museum itself.

Return to the lifts and turn left into Room 206 for the start of a sequence of detailed displays on **printmaking techniques** and finished results, from the West and from Japan. Contemporary prints are often shown here.

LEVELS 3-6 The rooms on Level 3 host temporary displays from the graphics collections. Level 4 is now empty, awaiting reassignment. On Level 5 in the **Print Room** you can see printed ephemera, photographs or original works such as Beatrix Potter watercolours. Level 6 has more temporary exhibition space.

on route

Albert Memorial, Hyde Park, tours Sun 14.00, 15.00, *T* 020 7495 0916. You can't miss this tribute to the Prince Consort, built (1863-72) near the site of his Great Exhibition. The best sculptors of the day were employed to sculpt the Continents and Industries, and the golden Prince himself. The glittering Gothic shrine of bronze, glass mosaic and granite was lovingly restored in the 1990s. *U* South Kensington, High Street Kensington

Brompton Oratory, Brompton Road, *T* 020 7808 0900, www.brompton-oratory.org.uk. This very Roman-looking church (1880-4) is the second largest Catholic church in London. Its interior has many side chapels with sculptures and paintings including the only known religious work by

Rex Whistler, and its famous choir can be heard at sung masses.
U South Kensington

Chelsea Physic Garden, 66 Royal Hospital Road (but entrance in Swan Walk), entrance charge, April-Oct only, Wed 12.00-17.00, Sun 14.00-18.00, *T* 020 7352 5646, www.chelseaphysicgarden.co.uk. Founded in 1673 to train apothecaries in the use of medicinal plants, the garden was given a secure future at its sheltered riverside site by Sir Hans Sloane and continues its educational work to this day. *U* Sloane Square

Kensington Palace, Kensington Gardens, entrance charge, Mar-Oct daily 10.00-18.00, Nov-Mar 10.00-17.00, *T* 0870 751 5170, www.kensington-palace.org.uk. Favourite retreat of William III and Mary, the palace has impressive state rooms and a museum of royal dress. The Orangery in the gardens is a restaurant. *U* High Street Kensington, Queensway

Natural History Museum,
Cromwell Road (level access in Exhibition Road), Mon-Sat 10.00-17.50, Sun 11.00-17.50, *T* 020 7942 5000, www.nhm.ac.uk. Award-winning Darwin Centre joins comprehensive displays on the planet's structure (Earth) and inhabitants (Life), in a wonderfully ornamented building (1881) by Alfred Waterhouse.
U South Kensington

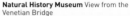
Natural History Museum View from the Venetian Bridge

Royal Albert Hall, Kensington Gore, guided tours to recommence in 2004, *T* 020 7589 8212 (bookings), www.royalalberthall.com. Another offshoot of the Great Exhibition, the arena-like hall (1871) was designed by Francis Fowke. Originally called the Central Hall for Arts and Sciences it has hosted events from motor shows to ice-skating but is best known for concerts, including the Proms, and remains the largest concert hall in England. *U* South Kensington, High Street Kensington

Royal Geographical Society, 1 Kensington Gore, *T* 020 7591 3000, www.rgs.org. Founded in 1830, the Society supports exploration and the public understanding of geography through lectures, films and other events. A new project, scheduled to open in early 2004, will provide full access to the archives of maps, photographs and manuscripts for the first time. *U* South Kensington, Knightsbridge

Science Museum, Exhibition Road, daily 10.00-18.00, *T* 0870 870 4868, www.sciencemuseum.org.uk. Steam engines compete with spacecraft

171

on the ground floor; above you can explore scientific issues from materials to food technology, health and weather. The basement has child-friendly hands-on activities and the futuristic new Wellcome Wing (by Richard MacCormac) interactive displays on key issues in modern science, and an IMAX cinema (charge). **U** South Kensington

Serpentine Gallery, Kensington Gardens, daily 10.00-18.00, **T** 020 7402 6075, www.serpentinegallery.org. Originally built as a tearoom (1934), the Serpentine is now one of London's leading public galleries for modern and contemporary art. Each summer a leading architect designs a pavilion for the leafy setting. **U** Knightsbridge, Lancaster Gate, South Kensington

commercial galleries

Ackermann & Johnson, 27 Lowndes Street, **T** 020 7235 6464, email ackermannjohnson@btconnect.com. 18c-20c British paintings and watercolours, especially of sporting subjects, landscapes and maritime scenes. **U** Knightsbridge

The Andipa Gallery, 162 Walton Street, **T** 020 7589 2371, www.andipa.com. These 'dealers in fine art for over 400 years' sell Old Masters, antiquities, Russian, Greek, Romanian and Serbian icons, and even Pop Art. **U** Knightsbridge

Cadogan Contemporary Art, 108 Draycott Avenue, **T** 020 7581 5451, www.artcad.co.uk. Paintings and sculptures by young British and international artists. **U** South Kensington

Coskun & Co. Limited, 93 Walton Street, **T** 020 7581 9056, www.coskunfineart.com. Prints by Matisse, Picasso, Warhol and other 20c masters. The website is entertaining and informative. **U** South Kensington

Crane Kalman, 178 Brompton Road, **T** 020 7584 7566, www.cranekalman.com. Long-running, family-run gallery selling Modern British, international and contemporary art. **U** Knightsbridge

Mathaf Gallery, 24 Motcomb Street, **T** 020 7235 0010, www.mathafgallery.com. 19c 'Orientalist' paintings of the Middle East;

also a stable of British artists who will undertake commissions on the same subject. *U* Knightsbridge

eating and drinking

AT THE MUSEUM

£   **New Restaurant**, spacious restaurant providing snacks, hot and cold meals and cakes. On the expensive side for what you get. Serves suppers from 18.00 on late-night openings. Self-service.

Garden Restaurant and Café, open in summer only, the restaurant has waiter service and hot meals, the café sandwiches and drinks.

Gamble Room, tea, coffee and light snacks amid the over-the-top decoration of this original Museum refreshment room. Self-service.

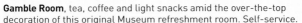

SURROUNDING AREA

£   **Bosphorus**, 59 Old Brompton Rd, *T* 020 7584 4048. Great value kebab house, locally popular. *U* South Kensington

Caffè Nero, 66 Old Brompton Road, *T* 020 7589 1760. One of the best of the coffee bar chains, also selling juices and smoothies, panini and other snacks. *U* South Kensington

Fileric, 57 Old Brompton Road, *T* 020 7584 2967. Friendly patisserie popular with French ex-pats, also serving light meals and coffee. *U* South Kensington

Maison Blanc, 11 Elystan Street, *T* 020 7584 6913. Upmarket sandwiches and mouth-watering patisserie. *U* South Kensington

Orangery, Kensington Palace, *T* 020 7376 0239. Atmospheric venue for a champagne tea or a light lunch. *U* High Street Kensington

Patisserie Valerie, 215 Brompton Road, *T* 020 7823 9971. Boost your blood sugar with a cake or three at this popular French patisserie and café. *U* South Kensington

££ **Admiral Codrington**, 17 Mossop Street, *T* 020 7581 0005. Busy posh-person's pub in a back street, with a restaurant at the back. Recommended Sunday roasts. *U* South Kensington

Bangkok, 9 Bute Street, *T* 020 7584 8529. The oldest Thai restaurant in Britain and still locally favoured. *U* South Kensington

Bibendum Oyster Bar, 81 Fulham Road, *T* 020 7589 1480. Trendy place for a seafood snack, below the famous restaurant and in the foyer of the Conran Shop. *U* South Kensington

La Bouchée, 56 Old Brompton Road, *T* 020 7589 1929. Small, popular local restaurant serving good, typically French cuisine. *U* South Kensington

Brasserie St Quentin, 243 Brompton Road, *T* 020 7589 8005. Authentic-looking French brasserie, one of London's oldest and best. Set lunches change weekly. *U* South Kensington

Café Lazeez, 93-95 Old Brompton Road, *T* 020 7581 9993. Stylish, traditional and modern Indian food. *U* South Kensington

Crescent, 99 Fulham Road, *T* 020 7225 2244. The huge wine list is the main attraction at this diner serving Mediterranean-style food. Set brunch menus and often deals on wine. *U* South Kensington

Daquise, 20 Thurloe Street, *T* 020 7589 6117. Shabby but atmospheric and much-loved outpost of Poland, founded in 1947, serving appropriately warming food, or just coffee and cake. *U* South Kensington

Elistano, 25-27 Elystan Street, *T* 020 7584 5248. Atmospheric (noisy) Italian trattoria, good-value in this area. *U* South Kensington

Fifth Floor Café, Harvey Nichols, Knightsbridge, *T* 020 7823 1839. Better value than the restaurant, with set menus lunch and evening and great afternoon tea. The store also has a handy branch of Wagamama. *U* Knightsbridge

Gaucho Grill, 89 Sloane Avenue, *T* 020 7584 9901. Reliable chain serving Argentinian steaks to dedicated carnivores. *U* South Kensington

Good Earth, 233 Brompton Road, *T* 020 7584 3658. Chinese restaurant, predictable but with some good vegetarian options and set lunches on weekdays. *U* South Kensington

Hugo's Café, Goethe Institute, 51 Princes Gate, Exhibition Road, *T* 020 7596 4006. Of interest for its dedication to sourcing local, seasonal and organic produce. *U* South Kensington

Joe's, 126 Draycott Avenue, *T* 020 7225 2217. Recommended for burgers and people-watching, if not for value. **U** South Kensington

Khan's of Kensington, 3 Harrington Road, **T** 020 7581 2900. Organic Indian food right by the Tube station. **U** South Kensington

Maroush, 38 Beauchamp Place, **T** 020 7581 5434. Part of a small chain serving authentic Lebanese food: this café gives the best value and is open very late. **U** Knightsbridge

Noor Jahan, 2a Bina Gardens, **T** 020 7373 6522. Good-value, traditional Indian cooking from a long-established restaurant. Also takeaway. **U** Gloucester Road

Polish Hearth Club, 55 Princes Gate, Exhibition Road, **T** 020 7589 4635. Old-fashioned Polish grub served in an atmospheric, chandeliered dining-room, or on the terrace in summer.
U South Kensington

Racine, 239 Brompton Road, **T** 020 7584 4477. New and welcoming restaurant serving good French food including rustic dishes such as tête de veau. **U** South Kensington

Spago, 6 Glendower Place, **T** 020 7225 2407. Busy place serving basic pizzas and Italian café food. No cards. **U** South Kensington

Tootsies, 107 Old Brompton Road, **T** 020 7581 8942. Diner serving unpretentious burgers and breakfasts. **U** South Kensington

£££ Bibendum, 81 Fulham Road, **T** 020 7581 5817. Modern European food, served in a Conran-styled dining room. Very expensive but the Sunday set lunch offers good value. **U** South Kensington

Cambio de Tercio, 163 Old Brompton Road, **T** 020 7244 8970. Award-winning and very popular restaurant serving modern Spanish food, with a good wine list. **U** Gloucester Road

Capital, 22-24 Basil Street, **T** 020 7589 5171. Superb modern French food. Go for the set Sunday lunch to avoid scary expense, and remember your jacket and tie. **U** Knightsbridge

Già, 62-64 Fulham Road, **T** 020 7589 2232. Cool modern Italian with an Asian twist (spices, seafood carpaccios). **U** South Kensington

Gordon Ramsay, 62-64 Royal Hospital Road, **T** 020 7589 2232. Ramsay's classic French food won him 3 Michelin stars in 2001 and confirmed him as Britain's top chef. **U** Sloane Square

Lundum's, 119 Old Brompton Road, **T** 020 7373 7774. Good Danish cooking (lots of fish and cream) well served in charming premises. **U** Gloucester Road, South Kensington

Sandrini, 260-262 Brompton Road, *T* 020 7584 1724. Long-established Italian in a very trendy area. *U* South Kensington

LATE-NIGHT BARS

Eclipse, 113 Walton Street, *T* 020 7581 0123. Japanese-style nibbles and fruit juice-based cocktails. Open Mon-Sat till 1.00, Sun till 0.30. *U* South Kensington

Townhouse, 31 Beauchamp Place, *T* 020 7589 5080. Invitingly cosy bar set out over three floors of an ivy-clad building. Its 26-page cocktail menu is expensive but worth it. Open Mon-Sat till 24.00, Sun till 23.30. *U* Knightsbridge

Zuma, 5 Raphael Street, *T* 020 7584 1010. Elegant bar next to the excellent restaurant, serving up Japanese-style sake cocktails and the occasional celebrity. Open Mon-Sat till 23.30, Sun till 10.30. *U* Knightsbridge

shopping

ACCESSORIES

Bentleys Vintage Luggage, 204 Walton Street, *T* 020 7584 7770. Cases for every occasion. The whole interior of this shop seems to have acquired the patina of antique leather. *U* Knightsbridge

Accessorize, 29 Brompton Road, *T* 020 7581 1408. The Monsoon chain offers relatively cheap and always temptingly colourful costume jewellery, hats, bags, scarves and belts. *U* South Kensington

BOOKS & STATIONERY

The French Bookshop, 28 Bute Street, *T* 020 7584 2840. Caters for local Francophiles drawn by the Institut Français nearby. *U* South Kensington

Book Ends Papercraft, 25-28 Thurloe Place, *T* 020 7589 2285. Children's books, origami papers and a great array of paper theatres, automata and dolls, plus art materials sold in the basement. *U* South Kensington

Bookthrift, 22 Thurloe Street, *T* 020 7589 2916. Remaindered art, architecture and design titles. *U* South Kensington

Medici Galleries, 26 Thurloe Street, *T* 020 7589 1363. Good selection of greetings cards, wrapping and posters, with a framing service. *U* South Kensington

CLOTHES

Amanda Wakeley, 80 Fulham Road, *T* 020 7584 4009. Elegant evening wear and accessories for special occasions from a designer who once dressed the Princess of Wales. *U* South Kensington

Bruce Oldfield, 28 Beauchamp Place, *T* 020 7584 1363. Designer specializing in evening wear, in this very exclusive little shopping haven. *U* Knightsbridge

Harvey Nichols, 109-125 Knightsbridge, *T* 020 7235 5000, www.harveynichols.com. The department store for fashionistas, made even more famous by *Absolutely Fabulous*. It sells international designer names and its own clothes line, as well as perfumes, cosmetics and jewellery. The frequently held sales can produce bargains. *U* Knightsbridge

Hilditch and Key, 131 Sloane Street, *T* 020 7823 5683. Long-established makers of high-quality gentlemen's shirts. *U* Knightsbridge

Jean Paul Gaultier, 171-175, Draycott Avenue, *T* 020 7584 4648. Refurbished store designed by Philippe Starck. *U* South Kensington

Katharine Hamnett, 20 Sloane Street, *T* 020 7823 1002. Clothes from a top British designer, from sequinned dresses to the famous T-shirts with political slogans, and now watches and eyewear. *U* Knightsbridge

Paul Costelloe, 156 Brompton Road, *T* 020 7589 9480. Suits, linen clothes and knits for men from Ireland's most famous designer, with collections in three price ranges. *U* Knightsbridge

Uniqlo, 163-169 Brompton Road. *T* 0845 100 0390. A far cry from the designer boutiques all around, this Japanese store sells very cheap basics. *U* Knightsbridge, South Kensington

Whistles, 303 Brompton Road. Part of the trendy boutique chain, mixing own-label and designers including Dries van Noten, plus a good range of accessories. *U* South Kensington

COSMETICS & HEALTH

Jo Malone, 150 Sloane Street, **T** 020 7730 2100, www.jomalone.co.uk. All
the familiar fragrances (lime, basil and mandarin) to be combined,
plus face creams and bath oils. **U** Sloane Square

FLOWERS

Grovers, 7-9 Exhibition Road, **T** 020 7584 5090. Large, friendly florists,
also selling potted citrus trees, close to Tube. **U** South Kensington

Fake Landscapes, 164 Old Brompton Road, **T** 020 7835 1500,
www.fake.com/flowers.htm. Artificial flowers and plants from
topiary pigs to traditional bouquets. **U** South Kensington

FOOD

Baker and Spice, Milner Street, entrance on Mossop Street, **T** 020 7589
4734. Ruinously expensive but delicious pastries. **U** South
Kensington

La Bonne Bouchée, 22 Bute Street, **T** 020 7584 9839. Bread, cakes and
confectionary. **U** South Kensington

Harrods, 87-135 Brompton Road, **T** 020 7730 1234, www.harrods.com.
The always crowded Food Hall is worth visiting for the décor alone.
U Knightsbridge

La Grande Bouchée, 31 Bute Street. Stock up on essentials including foie
gras, caviar and good French and British cheeses. **U** South
Kensington

HOMES

Conran Shop, 81 Fulham Road, **T** 020 7589 7401. Designer and own-
range furniture, pricier than its founder's more famous chain,
Habitat. **U** South Kensington

Chelsea Gardener, 125 Sydney Street, **T** 020 7352 5656,
www.chelseagardener.com. Pricey but pukka gardening togs,
tools and containers, and a greenhouse full of bonsai and citrus.
U Sloane Square, South Kensington

Divertimenti, 139-141 Fulham Road, **T** 020 7581 8065,
www.divertimenti.co.uk. Stocks a vast range of kitchenalia and
tableware, from elegant designer oil drizzlers to robust pots and
pans and knives the professionals wield. **U** South Kensington

Locks and Handles, 4-8 Exhibition Road, *T* 020 7581 2401, www.doorhandles.co.uk. A bewildering array of locks, doorknobs, window catches and other brass hardware, just the thing if you've just staggered from the ironwork display at the Victoria & Albert. *U* South Kensington

Monogrammed Linen Shop, 168 Walton Street, *T* 020 7589 4033, www.monogrammedlinenshop.co.uk. A wide range of products from bedsheets to babyclothes, in Egyptian cotton to silk. You can design your own embroidered monogram. *U* Knightsbridge

V.V. Rouleaux, 54 Sloane Square, *T* 020 7730 3125, www.vvrouleaux.com. Treasure house of trimmings, with braids, ribbons, tassels and feathers. *U* Sloane Square

JEWELLERY

Cox and Power, 95 Walton Street, *T* 020 7589 6355, www.coxandpower.com. Sensuous and sculptural modern jewellery made on site, commissions undertaken. *U* South Kensington

Hamilton and Inches, 52 Beauchamp Place, *T* 020 7589 3215, www.hamiltonandinches.com. Traditional and funkier modern jewellery, watches and small silver gifts from Scotland's leading jeweller. *U* South Kensington

McKenna & Co., 28 Beauchamp Place, *T* 020 7584 1966. Dealers in antique and period jewellery. *U* Knightsbridge

Van Peterson Designs, 194-96 Walton Street, *T* 020 7584 1101, www.vanpeterson.com. Fashionable modern designs. *U* South Kensington

KIDS

Caramel, 291 Brompton Rd, *T* 020 7589 7001. A 'hip designer boutique' for 0-10 year-olds. *U* South Kensington

Dragons, 23 Walton Street, *T* 020 7589 3795, www.dragonsltd.co.uk. Wonderful, hand-painted traditional toys. *U* South Kensington

The Nursery Window, 83 Walton Street, *T* 020 7581 3358, www.nurserywindow.co.uk. Everything for the new baby, from soft toys to furniture and accessories. *U* South Kensington

Traditional Toys, 53 Godfrey Street, *T* 020 7352 1718. Wooden toys and dressing-up outfits from France with characters such as D'Artagnan, Robin Hood and Little Red Riding Hood. *U* South Kensington

LINGERIE

Janet Reger, 2 Beauchamp Place, *T* 020 7584 9360,
www.janetreger.co.uk. Famous brand of sexy lingerie and nightwear,
with a colourful history (see the website). *U* Knightsbridge

Rigby and Peller, 2 Hans Road, *T* 020 7589 9293. Corsetières to the
Queen. Famous for their made-to-measure bras, they also sell off-
the-peg briefs, bras, slips and other underpinnings. *U* Knightsbridge

MUSIC

Music Discount Centre, 46 Thurloe Street, *T* 020 7584 3338,
www.mdcmusic.co.uk. Part of a small chain dedicated to classical
music, with well-informed staff to guide you to the recording you
need. *U* South Kensington

SHOES

Emma Hope, 53 Sloane Square, *T* 020 7259 9566, www.emmahope.co.uk.
It's worth a footslog out of the area to see this designer's exquisitely
pointy shoes, often with beaded or embroidered decoration, truly
'regalia for feet'. *U* Sloane Square

Jimmy Choo, 160 Draycott Avenue, *T* 020 7584 6111. Sophisticated store
for this ever-more fashionable range of women's shoes and
handbags (the eponymous Jimmy is a fiction). *U* South Kensington

Manolo Blahnik, 49-51 Old Church Street, *T* 020 7352 3863. Original
Chelsea outlet for the now world famous sexy shoes, recently given
their own retrospective at the Design Museum. *U* Sloane Square,
South Kensington

Patrick Cox, 129 and 30 Sloane Street, *T* 020 7730 8886. Chunky heeled,
square-toed shoes for women, cheaper Wannabe loafers for men
too, plus accessories. *U* South Kensington

entertainment

INFORMATION
TICKETS
CINEMA
THEATRE, OPERA AND DANCE
MUSIC
COMEDY
CLUBS

INFORMATION

Details and reviews of London theatre, cinema, exhibitions, nightclubs, sporting fixtures and other events are published each Wednesday in the magazine *Time Out*, available at most newsagents and newsstands. Its website previews monthly highlights. More limited but still useful listings can be found in most broadsheet newspapers and in the *Evening Standard*, the local paper for London.

Time Out, www.timeout.com

Evening Standard, www.thisislondon.com

Also useful for listings is www.londonnet.co.uk

TICKETS
BUYING IN PERSON

If possible, buy tickets from the venue's box office rather than ticket agencies, which charge a fee. The **Society of London Theatre** sells half-price tickets (plus a small handling fee) on the day of performance from the *tkts* booth in Leicester Square. The **London Tourist Board** can also book tickets to events and popular shows.

tkts, Leicester Square, open Mon-Sat 10.00-19.00, Sun 12.00-15.00, www.tkts.co.uk

London Tourist Board, *T* 020 7932 2000, www.londontouristboard.com

TICKET AGENCIES

First Call, *T* 0870 840 1111, www.firstcalltickets.com

Ticketmaster, *T* 020 7344 0055, www.ticketmaster.co.uk

Last Minute, www.lastminute.com

CINEMA

BFI London IMAX, South Bank, *T* 020 7902 1234, www.bfi.org.uk/imax. 3-D films on Britain's biggest screen. *U* Waterloo

Curzon Soho, 93-107 Shaftesbury Avenue, *T* 020 7734 2255, www.curzoncinemas.com. Comfortable, central cinema with good repertory programme. *U* Leicester Square

Empire, Leicester Square, *T* 0870 0102 030, www.uci-cinemas.co.uk. Once a theatre where the Lumière brothers showed films in the 1890s, now a major cinema. *U* Leicester Square

National Film Theatre, South Bank, *T* 020 7928 3232, www.bfi.org.uk. Repertory, themed seasons, festivals and lectures for the film buff, and a riverside café/bar. *U* Embankment, Waterloo

Odeon, Leicester Square, *T* 0870 505 0007, www.odeon.co.uk. London's largest cinema, for gala screenings, and flagship of a nationwide chain. *U* Leicester Square

Other Cinema, Rupert Street, *T* 020 7437 0757, www.picturehouse.co.uk. Small and central independent, with a bar, showing foreign and indie films. *U* Piccadilly Circus

Prince Charles, 7 Leicester Place, *T* 020 7494 3654, www.princecharlescinema.com. Bargain repertory, not to mention the 'sing-along Sound of Music'. *U* Leicester Square

Renoir, Brunswick Square, *T* 020 7837 8402. Foreign-language and arthouse films. *U* Russell Square

THEATRE, OPERA AND DANCE

Performances in the West End are generally at 19.30, with Wednesday and Saturday matinees. Check in advance for discounts and accessibility. The Society of London Theatre website can help you find a show by category or theatre; returns may be available at theatre box offices on the day of performance.

Society of London Theatre, www.officiallondontheatre.co.uk

THEATRE

Donmar Warehouse, 41 Earlham Street, *T* 020 7240 4882, www.donmarwarehouse.com. Former banana depot, then ballet studio, now highly regarded for new productions and classics. *U* Covent Garden

Old Vic, The Cut, *T* 020 7928 7616, www.oldvictheatre.com. Historic theatre, once the home of the National, attracts star actors. *U* Waterloo

National Theatre, South Bank, *T* 020 7452 3000, www.nationaltheatre.org.uk. National company performing new work, classics, musicals and children's shows. Frequent small-scale performances and concerts are often free. *U* Embankment, Waterloo

Royal Court, Sloane Square, *T* 020 7565 5000, www.royalcourttheatre.com. Focusing on new writers and plays. *U* Sloane Square

OPERA

English National Opera, St Martin's Lane, *T* 020 7632 8300, www.eno.org. Works performed in English at the Coliseum, currently being revamped. *U* Charing Cross, Leicester Square

Royal Opera House, Floral Street, Covent Garden, *T* 020 7304 4000, www.roh.org.uk. The nation's premiere company: expensive tickets but look out for last-minute deals. *U* Covent Garden

DANCE

Sadlers Wells, Rosebery Avenue, *T* 020 7863 8000, www.sadlerswells.com. Based on a 17c music hall rebuilt at the end of the 1990s, and now a centre for international dance, opera and music. *U* Angel

Royal Ballet, Royal Opera House, Floral Street, Covent Garden, *T* 020 7304 4000, www.roh.org.uk. Classical ballet and new work by the company founded by Ninette de Valois and Frederick Ashton. *U* Covent Garden

MUSIC
CLASSICAL

Barbican Centre, Silk Street, *T* 020 7638 8891, www.barbican.org.uk. Home of the London Symphony Orchestra, also hosts jazz and world music and theatrical productions. *U* Barbican, Moorgate

Queen Elizabeth Hall, South Bank, *T* 020 7960 4242, www.rfh.org.uk. Smaller South Bank venue, with the Purcell Room, for recitals and choral concerts. *U* Embankment, Waterloo

Royal Albert Hall, Kensington Gore, *T* 020 7589 8212,
www.royalalberthall.com. Varied programme, including the BBC Proms
in summer, in this Victorian landmark. *U* South Kensington

Royal Festival Hall, Belvedere Road, *T* 020 7960 4242, www.rfh.org.uk.
Part of the South Bank arts complex with a wide-ranging music
programme and the Meltdown festival in summer. *U* Waterloo

Wigmore Hall, Wigmore Street, *T* 020 7935 2141, www.wigmorehall.org.uk.
Chamber music and recitals. *U* Oxford Circus

JAZZ

100 Club, 100 Oxford Street, *T* 020 7636 0933, www.the100club.co.uk.
Long-established club with a great jazz pedigree, also played its part in
punk and indie scenes. *U* Oxford Circus, Tottenham Court Road

Jazz Café, 5 Parkway, *T* 020 7916 6060, www.meanfiddler.com. Major
venue for improvised music, including soul and blues, and club nights.
U Camden Town

Pizza Express Jazz Club, 10 Dean Street, *T* 020 7439 8722,
www.pizzaexpress.co.uk/jazzsoho. Intimate venue with live music seven
nights a week. *U* Tottenham Court Road

Pizza on the Park, 11-13 Knightsbridge, *T* 020 7235 5273. Attracts some
world famous names. *U* Hyde Park Corner

Ronnie Scott's, 47 Frith Street, *T* 020 7439 0747, www.ronniescotts.co.uk.
Historic jazz club featuring international (mainly US) and British acts.
U Tottenham Court Road, Leicester Square

ROCK AND POP

Astoria, 157 Charing Cross Road, *T* 020 7434 9592,
www.meanfiddler.com. Large, central venue for big-name rock acts.
U Tottenham Court Road

Borderline, Orange Yard, off Manette Street, *T* 020 7734 2905,
www.borderline.co.uk. Tucked-away venue with a very varied
programme. Often hosts small names destined to become big.
U Tottenham Court Road

Brixton Academy, 211 Stockwell Road, *T* 020 7771 3000, www.brixton-
academy.co.uk. Atmospheric old Art Deco cinema, now an important
venue for rock and pop. *U* Brixton

Carling Apollo, Queen Caroline Street, *T* 0870 606 3400,
www.carlinglive.com. Large venue for international acts.
U Hammersmith

Shepherd's Bush Empire, Shepherd's Bush Green, *T* 020 8354 3300, www.shepherds-bush-empire.co.uk. Grand theatre opened in 1903, once a BBC studio and now major live rock venue. *U* Shepherd's Bush

Wembley Arena, Empire Way, *T* 020 8902 8833, www.wembley.co.uk. Enormodome for superstar concerts by the likes of Tom Jones, Elton John. *U* Wembley

FOLK AND WORLD

12 Bar Club, 22-23 Denmark Place, *T* 020 7916 6989, www.12barclub.com. Venue with a tiny stage, focusing (of neccessity) on singer/songwriters but also acoustic groups. *U* Tottenham Court Road

Union Chapel, Compton Terrace, *T* 020 7226 1686, www.unionchapel.org.uk. Victorian church hosting wide-ranging musical events with a multicultural emphasis. *U* Highbury & Islington

COMEDY

Comedy Store, 1A Oxendon Street, *T* 020 7344 0234, www.thecomedystore.co.uk. Britain's first full-time comedy club, with nationally famous stand-ups and improv twice weekly. *U* Piccadilly Circus

Jongleurs, Dingwalls Building, Camden Lock, *T* 0870 787 0707, www.jongleurs.com. National chain of comedy clubs (others in Battersea and Bow). *U* Camden Town

CLUBS

Coronet, 24-28 New Kent Road, SE1, *T* 020 7701 1500, www.coronet-london.co.uk. Restored music hall venue for live music and film as well as regular club nights. *U* Elephant & Castle

Fabric, 77a Charterhouse Street, EC1 *T* 020 7336 8898, www.fabriclondon.com. Very popular. In the city, with three dancefloors and three bars. *U* Farringdon

Heaven, Under the Arches, Craven Street, WC2, *T* 020 7930 2020, www.heaven-london.com. Well-established gay club. *U* Charing Cross

Ministry of Sound, 103 Gaunt Street, SE1, *T* 020 7740 8600, www.ministryofsound.com. Centre of the global dance music brand. *U* Elephant and Castle

Pacha, Terminus Place, SW1, *T* 020 7833 3139, www.pachalondon.com. More sophisticated than some; centrally located. *U* Victoria

Turnmills, 63b Clerkenwell Road, EC1 *T* 020 7250 3409, www.turnmills.co.uk. House and techno. *U* Farringdon

planning

TOURIST OFFICES

For help in planning your trip and obtaining tickets for London transport and attractions, contact the **British Tourist Authority** in your country. Not all offices are open to callers in person but all can supply free brochures and other information.

IN CANADA
Visit Britain, 5915 Airport Road, Suite 120, Mississauga, Ontario L4V 1T1, **T** (888) 847 4885 or 1 888 VISIT UK (toll free), **F** (905) 405 1835, www.visitbritain.com/ca. Visitors are welcome Mon-Fri 9.00-17.00, telephone enquiries 10.00-18.00.

IN THE REPUBLIC OF IRELAND
Visit Britain, 18/19 College Green, Dublin 2, **T** 00 353 (1) 670 8000/8100, **F** 00 353 (1) 670 8244, www.visitbritain.com/ie. Visitors and telephone enquiries welcome Mon, Wed, Thur 9.00-17.30, Tues 10.00-17.30, Fri 9.00-17.00; in person only Sat 10.00-14.00.

IN THE UNITED STATES
Visit Britain, 551 Fifth Avenue, Suite 701, New York, NY 10176-0799, **T** (212) 462 2748 or 1 800 GO 2 BRITAIN (toll-free), **F** (212) 986 1188, www.travelbritain.org. Visitors welcome Mon-Fri 9.00-18.00, telephone enquiries 10.00-18.00.

Visit Britain, 625 North Michigan Avenue, Suite 1001, Chicago, IL 60611. In-person enquiries only Mon-Fri 9.00-17.00.

IN THE UK

Once in London, you can get further information, tickets and advice (in person only) covering England, Scotland and Wales at the **Britain Visitor Centre**, 1 Regent Street. Open Mon 9.30-18.30, Tues-Fri 9.00-18.30, Sat, Sun 10.00-16.00.

The **London Tourist Board** provides recorded information on sightseeing, eating out, shopping etc, *T* 09068 663 344 (premium rate), www.londontouristboard.com. Through the LTB and Tourist Information Centres at Heathrow Terminal 1, 2, 3, Liverpool Street Tube, Waterloo International Terminal and Victoria Station you can search for and book accommodation and buy tickets for transport, sightseeing and shows.

GETTING THERE
BY AIR
FROM OTHER UK CITIES

Competition between discount airlines means that it is increasingly affordable to fly to London. easyJet, for example, fly from Aberdeen, Inverness, Edinburgh, Glasgow, Newcastle and Belfast; their rivals Ryanair have routes from Derry, Glasgow, Blackpool and Newquay. Bear in mind the extra cost of reaching London from the more distant airports (see below) where most budget flights land.

   British Midland operate from the airports above and from Teesside, Manchester and Leeds, mostly to Heathrow; British Airways have an extensive network from these and other airports, including the Channel Islands.

British Airways, *T* 0845 773 3377, www.ba.com

British Midland, *T* 0870 6070 555, www.flybmi.com

easyJet, *T* 0870 600 0000, www.easyjet.com

Ryanair, *T* 0871 246 0000, www.ryanair.com

FROM THE REPUBLIC OF IRELAND

Aer Lingus, T 0818 365000 (in Ireland), *T* 0845 084 4444 (in UK), www.aerlingus.com. Departures from Dublin, Shannon and Cork.

British Airways, *T* 1 800 626 747 (in Ireland), *T* 0845 7733 377 (in UK), www.ba.com. Departures from Cork, Dublin, Knock and Shannon.

British Midland, *T* 44 1332 854 854 (from Ireland), *T* 0870 60 70 555 (in UK), www.flybmi.com. Departures from Dublin.

Ryanair, *T* 0818 303 030 (in Ireland), *T* 353 818 303 030 (from overseas), *T* 0871 2460 000, www.ryanair.com. Departures from Cork, Dublin, Kerry, Knock and Shannon.

FROM THE USA AND CANADA

Air Canada, *T* 888 247 2262 (in USA and Canada), *T* 0870 5247 226 (in UK), www.aircanada.ca

American Airlines, *T* 800 433 7300 (in USA), *T* 020 7365 0777 (in London), *T* 0845 7789 789 (from rest of UK), www.aa.com

British Airways, *T* 800-AIRWAYS (in USA and Canada), *T* 0845 773 3377 (in UK), www.ba.com

Delta Airlines, *T* 800 241 4141 (in USA and Canada), *T* 0800 414 767 (in UK), www.delta.com

United Airlines, *T* 800 538 2929 (in USA and Canada), *T* 0845 844 4777 (and in UK), www.ual.com

Virgin Atlantic, *T* 800 862 8621 (in USA and Canada), *T* 01293 450 150 (in UK), www.virgin-atlantic.com

GETTING TO THE CITY CENTRE FROM THE AIRPORTS

London is served by five airports:

Heathrow, *T* 020 8759 4321, www.baa.com

Gatwick, *T* 0870 000 2468, www.baa.com

Stansted, *T* 01279 680 500, www.baa.com

Luton, *T* 01582 405 100, www.london-luton.com

City, *T* 020 7643 0000, www.londoncityairport.com

From Heathrow: **Heathrow Express** trains to Paddington station run from approximately 5.00 to 23.30 and take 15-20 minutes, *T* 0845 600 1515, www.heathrowexpress.co.uk. **Piccadilly Line** trains run from two Tube stations, Terminals 1, 2, 3 and Terminal 4, every few minutes from approximately 5.00 (5.50 Sundays) to 23.45 (22.50 Sundays), taking 50 minutes to central London. **Airbus A2** goes to King's Cross, with stops in central London; at night the **N97** runs every 30 minutes to Trafalgar Square, *T* 020 7222 1234. **Black cabs** can be hired at the airport: only fares for journeys in the Greater London area will be metered; otherwise, negotiate the fare in advance, extra at evenings and weekends. Drivers expect a tip.

From Gatwick: **Gatwick Express** trains to Victoria station run from 5.35 to 0.50 and take 30 minutes, *T* 0845 850 1530, www.gatwickexpress.co.uk. **Thameslink trains** run from Gatwick to London Bridge, Blackfriars and King's Cross stations and take 40 minutes, *T* 020 7620 6333, www.thameslink.co.uk. Gatwick Airport station is in the south terminal, which you can reach by a shuttle from the north terminal. **Airbus A5** runs to Victoria and takes 1 hour 30 minutes. You can book a taxi for a fixed price from Chequer Cars in the north terminal, *T* 01293 501377.

From Stansted: **Stansted Express** trains run to Liverpool Street station every 15 minutes from 8.00 to 17.00 weekdays and every 30 minutes early mornings, evenings and weekends, taking 40 minutes, *T* 0845 850 0150, www.stanstedexpress.co.uk. National rail services take the same route. **Airbus A6** goes to Victoria via stops in central London, taking 1 hour 40 minutes, *T* 0870 5747 777.

From Luton: **Thameslink** operates regular rail services to central London from approximately 7.00 to 22.00 Monday to Friday and 9.00 to 20.00 on Sunday, taking 25-35 minutes. A shuttle bus between the airport and rail station takes around 5 minutes. **Greenline 757** bus goes to Victoria with stops in central London, *T* 0345 788 788, www.greenline.co.uk.

From City: **Airport Shuttle** buses link the airport to Canning Town, Canary Wharf (both Jubilee Line) or Liverpool Street stations. Or walk to Silvertown station for regular trains to Fenchurch Street station.

BY TRAIN

Eurostar runs from Paris Gare-du-Nord to Waterloo International in 2 hours 35 minutes, from Brussels in 2 hours 20 minutes; there are 17 trains daily from Paris and some stop at Lille or Calais. Book ahead for reduced fares, *T* 090 186 186 (from outside UK 44 1233 617 575), www.eurostar.com

Rail Europe, 179 Piccadilly, has information and bookings on all European rail services, *T* 0870 5848 848, www.raileurope.co.uk.

Le Shuttle carries cars, caravans and motorbikes through the Channel Tunnel between Calais and Dover in 20 minutes. The UK terminal is just over an hour from London via the M20. For more details from Eurotunnel, *T* 0870 535 3535, www.eurotunnel.com.

Britrail passes for train travel in Britain are available only to foreign visitors. Buy from travel agents or online, www.britrail.net

National Rail Enquiries, *T* 0845 7484 950, www.nationalrail.co.uk

Train tickets can be bought in Britain at stations and online at www.thetrainline.com or www.qjump.co.uk

BY COACH

Regular coach services from mainland Europe to London are operated by Eurolines, represented in Britain by National Express, who operate a scheduled coach network around the country. International arrivals and National Express services terminate at Victoria coach station.

Eurolines, (from the UK *T* 01582 404 511), www.eurolines.com

National Express, *T* 0870 580 8080, www.nationalexpress.com

BY SEA

From Dover, Folkestone, Ramsgate and Newhaven, take trains to London Victoria; from Harwich, take trains to Liverpool Street.

Brittany Ferries, *T* 0870 3665 333, www.brittany-ferries.com

Hoverspeed, *T* 0870 2408 070, www.hoverspeed.co.uk

P&O Ferries, *T* 0870 600 0611, www.poferries.com

SeaFrance, *T* 0870 571 1711, www.seafrance.co.uk

From Ireland, the fastest routes for ferry crossings are from Dublin and Dun Laoghaire to Holyhead and Liverpool.

Irish Ferries, *T* 0870 5171 717, www.irishferries.com

Norse Merchant, *T* 0870 6004 321, www.norsemerchant.com

Stena Line, *T* 0870 5707 070, www.stenaline.com

GETTING AROUND

The Tube, buses, DLR, tram and river transport are all controlled by Transport for London. **London Travel Information Centres** give out advice, maps and timetables, and sell tickets for travel and to many attractions: you'll find them at Heathrow Terminal 1 arrivals hall; national rail stations Euston, Paddington and Victoria; bus and coach stations at Hammersmith, West Croydon, Uxbridge and Victoria; and Tube stations Liverpool Street, Oxford Circus,

Piccadilly Circus, St James's Park and Heathrow Terminals 1, 2, 3, and 4. Maps for the Tube network, ticket and access guides, and excursion ideas are also available from most Tube stations.

Transport for London, information *T* 020 7222 1234, textphone 020 7918 3015, www.tfl.gov.uk

TRAVEL PASSES AND TICKETS

The Tube network is divided into Zones 1-6, with Zone 1 covering central London. A single adult ticket currently costs £2 within Zone 1 and £2.20 between Zones 1 and 2. Tickets and Travelcards can be bought at all Tube stations, mainline rail stations and many newsagents also sell Travelcards. The **Oyster card**, a cashless ticketing system designed to cut queues, has to be applied for at Tube stations or online, www.oystercard.com, *T* 0845 330 9876. Eventually it will replace most paper tickets. Touch the card to the circular reader on Tube gates and by bus doors. If you decide to make a journey further than permitted by your Travelcard, you must buy a ticket extension before travelling or face a fine.

Any single bus journey costs £1 for adults; children under 11 travel free on buses. In Zone 1, you'll need a ticket before you board (see below).

Visitor Card: a weekly card valid on Tube, bus, DLR and most national rail within Zones 1-6, or just Zone 1, available in advance to visitors from Australia, New Zealand, South Africa, Republic of Ireland and the USA, www.ticket-on-line.com

Travelcard: a ticket valid on Tube, DLR, national rail and bus services for a day, weekend, week or month; you can buy a card for Zones 1 and 2 or more. Cards for travel before 9.30 Mon-Fri are more expensive. Cards for a month or more will soon be phased out and replaced by Oyster (see above). Family Travelcards give discounts for one or two adults travelling with up to four children.

Carnet: a book of 10 single tickets for use on the Tube in Zone 1 only. A book of 6 single 'Saver' tickets can be used on the whole bus network.

LT Card: valid on Tube, bus, DLR and tram services but not on national rail across Zones 1-6, including peak times (though for travel within Zones 1-4 a Peak Day Travelcard will be cheaper).

DLR Rail & River Rover: combines one day's travel on City Cruises riverboats (running between Westminster, Waterloo, Tower and Greenwich piers) and the DLR. Group and family tickets should be bought a week in advance, *T* 020 7363 9700.

BY TUBE

The Underground or Tube runs between approximately 5.30 and 1.00: check the times of last trains at the relevant station. At almost all stations you need to pass your ticket through an automatic barrier to validate it and reach the platforms: staff will be on hand if you have any difficulties. The various lines - and often platforms, too - are colour-coded and indicators should show the train's destination. Maps of the network will be displayed in ticket halls and on platforms.

Bear in mind that, despite the presence of escalators, there may still be stairs to climb, especially when making connections. Avoid travelling alone late at night and beware of pickpockets.
London Underground, *T* 0845 330 9880, www.thetube.com

BY BUS

Bus services begin at about 5.00. On traditional **Routemasters**, board at the back and pay the conductor. On **driver-only buses**, however, you board at the front and, if travelling in Zone 1, must have a ticket already, either a Travelcard or a single ticket or pass bought from a machine at the bus stop (exact money only). Bendy-buses introduced on two routes from Waterloo to Victoria and London Bridge are also cashless. Once on board, press the bell once to stop the bus. **Night buses**, with route numbers prefixed N, take over at about 00.30.

Many bus stops display route maps and timetables, though London's traffic may render these theoretical. A leaflet available at Tube stations, *Map out your day*, shows key bus routes linking tourist attractions in central London: for example, the new RV1 links 47 sites, most along the South Bank, between the Tower and Covent Garden.

BY TAXI

Licensed taxis or **black cabs** can be hired at taxi ranks (often outside national rail stations) or on the street if the yellow taxi sign is illuminated.The cost of the journey is metered and displayed inside the vehicle, as are extra charges for evening and weekend journeys, and luggage. Cab drivers expect a tip, about 10 per cent of the total fare. They are not obliged to accept a hiring of over six miles. Make any complaints to the Public Carriage Office, *T* 020 7230 1631.

Minicabs do not have meters and you should negotiate the fare in advance. Never take a minicab that touts for hire on the street.

Computacab, *T* 020 7286 0268

Radio Taxis, *T* 020 7272 0272

BY CAR

London's roads are overloaded, to the extent that a **congestion charge** of £5 per day for each car entering the central zone (roughly equivalent to Zone 1) has been introduced: see www.cclondon.com to see if you are exempt. If you do drive in, parking space will be hard to find.

MUSEUM PASSES

All five of the major museums and galleries featured in this guide are free to enter, charging only for special exhibitions. Concessions may be available to children, senior citizens, the disabled, students and the unemployed on entrance tickets for these shows.

London Pass, free entry to over 50 attractions and activities over 1, 2, 3 or 6 days, with an option for travel on buses, Tube and trains. Current prices (excluding VAT and transport) are £23, £36, £44 or £62 for adults and £15, £25, £29 or £41 for children. *T* 020 7287 6020, www.londonpass.com

London for Less, reductions at over 200 attractions, including theatre, concert, opera and ballet tickets, for 8 days for up to four people. Current cost £12.95 from bookshops and the Britain Visitor Centre, www.for-less.com

OTHER ESSENTIALS
DISABLED TRAVELLERS

Access to public institutions such as museums is often excellent, and hotels are catching up, but transport may still cause problems.

Access from the airports: from Heathrow, the Airbus and Heathrow Express are both accessible, but only some Connex South Central and Gatwick Express routes to Victoria are, so call ahead *T* 01293 535 353. From Stansted, the Skytrain to Liverpool Street, where there is a level exit, is the best option. London City Airport has disabled car parking facilities, and accessible buses run to Liverpool Street, operated by Stagecoach, *T* 0870 608 2608, www.stagecoach-london.co.uk.

Public transport: the relatively new Docklands Light Railway and Tramlink services are fully accessible but do not run in the most central areas. Many newer buses can be lowered to allow level boarding and accessible Stationlink buses run between the major rail stations: route 501 clockwise from Paddington hourly, route 502 anti-clockwise. Only about 90 Tube stations have alternatives to escalators and stairs (Jubilee Line stations between Westminster and Stratford all have lifts and step-free access to trains). Download the *Tube access guide* at http://tube.tfl.gov.uk or get the printed version at Tube stations. *Access to the Underground* is free from the Access & Mobility office (see below). All new black cabs are wheelchair accessible and many have other facilities (ramps, induction loops, intercom).

Accommodation: the London Tourist Board website has a database of hotels that have been inspected and graded for access under the Tourism for All system, and lists a few that allow guide dogs and hearing dogs. The LTB site also has advice on parking for disabled drivers, shopping at major stores and centres, access to entertainment venues, and specialist tour guides.

Access & Mobility office (Transport for London), *T* 020 7941 4600 within office hours, textphone 020 7918 3014, www.tfl.gov.uk

Access Project, 39 Bradley Gardens, West Ealing, London W13 8HE, publishes *Access In London*, a comprehensive review of attractions, transport, and facilities for the disabled. Large-print version available.

Disabled Living Foundation, Heathrow Travelcare service, *T* 020 8745 7495, minicom 08745 7565.

Holiday Care Service, 2 Old Bank Chambers, Station Road, Horley RH6 9HW, *T* 01293 774 535. Publishes *Accessible Britain*, a guide to accommodation and facilities for disabled people; £5.99 from the English Tourism Council, **T** 0870 606 7204.

Radar, 12 City Forum, 250 City Road, London EC1V 8AF, **T** 020 7250 3222. Publishes *Holidays in Britain & Ireland: a Guide for Disabled People* (£8.00) and *Getting There*, a guide to airport facilities (£5), from bookshops.

Royal National Institute for the Blind, 224 Great Portland Street, London W1N 6AA, **T** 020 7388 1266. Maps of London for the blind. Publishes a *Hotel Guide Book* for blind and partially sighted people (£4.99).

Tripscope, Vassall Centre, Gill Avenue, Bristol BS16 2QQ, **T** 08457 585 641 (also for minicom). Free travel and transport information.

EMBASSIES AND CONSULATES

Australian High Commission, Australia House, Strand, London WC2B 4LA, **T** 020 7379 4334, www.australia.org.uk

Canadian High Commission, Macdonald House, 1 Grosvenor Square, London W1K 4AB, **T** 020 7258 6600, www.dfait-maeci.gc.ca/london

Irish Embassy, 17 Grosvenor Place, London SW1X 7HR, **T** 020 7235 2171, www.irlgov.ie

New Zealand High Commission, New Zealand House, 80 Haymarket, London SW1Y 4TQ, **T** 020 7930 8422, www.nzembassy.com

US Embassy, 24 Grosvenor Square, London W1A 1AE, **T** 020 7499 9000, www.usembassy.org.uk

HEALTH
MEDICAL SERVICES

Citizens of the EU, Australia and New Zealand receive free NHS health care. Visitors from Canada, South Africa and the USA are only eligible for free treatment in accident and emergency departments at NHS hospitals; if you are admitted to the hospital as an in-patient, sent to an out-patient clinic, or choose one of many private hospitals, you will have to pay. Travel insurance to cover this is essential.

Minor injuries units exist at most hospitals and are staffed by nurses. In case of emergency, go to the accident and emergency department of the nearest public hospital. Those running 24-hour services in central London are:

Chelsea and Westminster Hospital, 369 Fulham Road,
T 020 8746 8000

Guy's Hospital, St Thomas Street, Southwark, *T* 020 7955 5000

Royal London Hospital, Whitechapel Road, *T* 020 7377 7000 ext. 2067 or 2070 (for dental emergencies)

St Mary's Hospital, Praed Street, Paddington, *T* 020 7886 6666

St Thomas' Hospital, Lambeth Palace Road, *T* 020 7922 8020

University College Hospital, Grafton Way, Bloomsbury, *T* 020 7387 9300

For confidential medical advice from a nurse, available 24-hours a day, contact **NHS Direct**, *T* 0845 46 47, www.nhsdirect.nhs.uk

LATE-NIGHT CHEMISTS
Bliss Chemist, 5-6 Marble Arch, *T* 020 7723 6116, open Mon-Sun 9.00-24.00, *U* Marble Arch.

Zafrash Pharmacy, 233-235 Old Brompton Road, *T* 020 7373 2798, open 24 hours every day of the year, *U* Edgware Road

NHS Walk-in Centre, 1 Frith Street (off Soho Square), *T* 020 7534 6500, *U* Tottenham Court Road

LOST OR STOLEN PROPERTY
CREDIT CARDS AND TRAVELLER'S CHEQUES
American Express, card *T* 01273 696 933, cheques *T* 0800 521 313

Diner's Club, card and cheques *T* 0800 460 800

Mastercard, *T* 0800 964 767

Thomas Cook cheques, *T* 0800 622 101

Visa, card *T* 0800 891 725, cheques *T* 0800 895 078

LOST PROPERTY
Report the theft or loss of valuables immediately to the police. Mislaid **passports** or **visas** should be reported both to the police and your country's embassy or high commission in London.

Airports: each airport has its own lost property office. Gatwick, *T* 0870 0002 468; Heathrow, *T* 020 8745 7727; Luton, *T* 01582 395 219; Stansted, *T* 01279 663293; City, *T* 020 7646 0088. For items left on the plane, contact the airline directly.

Bus, Tube and DLR: write to or visit the Transport for London Lost Property Office, 200 Baker Street, open Mon-Fri 9.00-14.00, or

F 020 7918 1028; or send a lost property enquiry form (available from any Tube station).

Train: contact either the train operating company or that in charge of the overground station. Obtain numbers from National Rail Enquiries, *T* 08457 484950.

Taxi: items left in licensed black cabs are handed in at local police stations, logged and forwarded to the Transport for London Lost Property Office (see above).

OPENING HOURS

Shops are generally open Mon-Sat 9.30-18.00, and Sun 11.00-17.00: in Knightsbridge on Wednesday and the West End on Thursday they may not close until 20.00, and many big supermarkets open 24 hours in the week. **Banks** open Mon-Fri 9.30-16.30 and larger branches open Sat 9.30-12.30; post offices open Mon-Fri 9.00-17.30 and some Sat 8.30-12.00. Hours for **restaurants** vary widely, many being closed Sunday or Monday; most pubs are open 11.30-23.30 but **clubs**, which often open around 17.00, can have later licences. For **museums**, see the individual chapters.

PUBLIC HOLIDAYS

New Year's Day, 1 January

Good Friday (9 April 2004, 25 March 2005)

Easter Monday (12 April 2004, 28 March 2005)

May Day (3 May 2004, 2 May 2005)

Spring Bank Holiday (31 May 2004, 30 May 2005)

Summer Bank Holiday (30 August 2004, 29 August 2005)

Christmas Day, 25 December

Boxing Day, 26 December

SIGHTSEEING
BY BUS

The following companies run tours with commentaries in a choice of languages: you can join or leave the open-topped bus at various points on the circular routes, at clearly marked stops. Buy tickets in advance - there are discounts for online booking - or when you board.

Big Bus Company, tickets valid for 24 hours, *T* 020 7233 9533, www.bigbus.co.uk

Original LondonSightseeing Tour, tickets valid for 24 hours, *T* 020 8877 1722, www.theoriginaltour.com

BY BIKE

You can also tour London by bike, either with a guide or on your own. Transport for London publishes *London Cycle Guides*, and the London Cycle Network maps and other information for cyclists, *T* 020 7721 7254, www.londoncyclenetwork.org

London Bicycle Tour Co., themed guided tours by bike, or hire a rickshaw, *T* 020 7928 6838

BY BOAT

A number of commuter and tourist services now run on the Thames. All the tourist cruises provide commentary. Holders of LT Travelcards can get a third off many river fares.

Catamaran Cruises, to Greenwich via Waterloo and Bankside, circular trips, and lunch and dinner cruises, all from Embankment Pier, *T* 020 7925 2215, www.bateauxlondon.com.

City Cruises, from Westminster Pier to Tower of London and Greenwich, *T* 020 7740 0400, www.citycruises.com

Thames River Services, from Westminster Pier to Greenwich and Thames Barrier, *T* 020 7930 4097, www.westminsterpier.co.uk

Westminster Passenger Services, from Westminster Pier to Kew, Richmond and Hampton Court, *T* 020 7930 2062, www.wpsa.co.uk

London Waterbus Company runs trips in the summer along the Regent's Canal, from Little Venice to Camden via the Zoo, *T* 020 7482 2660, www.camdenlockmarket.com

BY TAXI

There are other ways to get the benefit of the London cabbie's legendary 'Knowledge' of the city streets.

Black Taxi Tours, 2-hour tour for a maximum of five passengers £75-85, *T* 020 7935 9363, www.blacktaxitours.co.uk

ON FOOT

London has literally hundreds of guided walks to choose from, often with literary, historical or architectural themes.

Blue Guides, personal tours, often by specialists, half-day (up to 4 hours) £89, full day (up to 9 hours), *T* 020 7403 2962, www.aptg.org.uk

Original London Walks, a wide range of guided walks, often in large groups, £5 adults, £4 concessions, *T* 020 7624 3978, www.walks.com

PLACES TO STAY

The English Tourism Council, AA or RAC inspect accommodation annually and award either star **ratings** (hotels, town houses, self-catering, campus and hostel accommodation) or diamond ratings (bed-and-breakfast and guest accommodation). In hotels, one star denotes a good standard of cleanliness, friendly service and almost certainly an en-suite or private bathroom, while five stars can mean luxurious decor and haute cuisine. Within these categories, prices vary according to location and season. They are generally quoted per room, as here, and VAT (17.5 per cent) is normally included, but check this. Breakfast is not usually included in the room rate, except in bed-and-breakfast hotels. Hostels start at about £20 per person, B&Bs from £45 for a double room. A three-star hotel may cost between £80-£100 and a five-star hotel upwards of £200. Book well in advance for the best deals: a deposit is sometimes payable. Business hotels often offer special rates for weekend guests, and rooms may be cheaper if booked online.

The hotels listed below are intended to give an idea of the choice available, and are not personal recommendations.

£   up to £100 for a double room

££   £100-£200

£££ £200 and above

HOTELS
STRAND, COVENT GARDEN, WC2
£   **Seven Dials Hotel**, 7 Monmouth Street, *T* 020 7681 0791, *F* 020 7681

0792, giovanni@dipopolohotels.fsnet.co.uk. Small bed-and-breakfast hotel in Covent Garden. Rooms from £55 single, £65 double.
U Covent Garden

Citadines ApartHotel Trafalgar, 18-21 Northumberland Ave,
T 0800 376 3898, www.citadines.com. A variety of self-catering accommodation, with hotel services available, including a breakfast lounge. Rooms from £70. Very central. *U* Charing Cross

Royal Adelphi Hotel, 21 Villiers Street, *T* 020 7930 8764, *F* 020 7930 8735, www.royaladelphi.co.uk. Small bed-and-breakfast in a busy but very central location. No lift. Rooms from £50 single, £68 double.
U Charing Cross

££ **Thistle Trafalgar Square**, Whitcomb Street, *T* 0870 333 9119,
F 0870 333 9219, www.thistlehotels.com.trafalgarsquare. A modern chain hotel, with a restaurant and pub, behind the National Gallery. Rooms from £96. *U* Charing Cross

Le Meridien Waldorf, Aldwych, *T* 0870 400 8484, *F* 020 7836 7244, www.lemeridien.com. Grand Edwardian hotel. Recently updated, it has a health club and pool but weekend tea dances are still held in the famous Palm Court. Rooms from £130. *U* Temple

Savoy Hotel, Strand, *T* 020 7836 4343, *F* 020 7240 6040, www.savoy-group.com/savoy. Shining Art Deco institution, now with a refurbished Savoy Grill. Rooms from £149 single.
U Embankment, Temple

£££ **Hazlitt's**, 6 Frith Street, *T* 020 7434 1771, www.hazlittshotel.com. Atmospheric hotel in the heart of Soho, named after the writer who lived there until 1830. Rooms from £175 single, £205 double.
U Leicester Square, Tottenham Court Road

One Aldwych, 1 Aldwych, *T* 020 7300 1000, *F* 020 7300 1001, www.onealdwych.com. Award-winning contemporary style hotel, with a swimming pool, gymnasium, and its own art collection. Rooms from £295 single, £315 double. *U* Temple

St Martin's, 45 St Martin's Lane, *T* 020 7300 5500, *F* 020 7300 5501, www.ianschragerhotels.com. Philippe Starck fitted out this hip hotel (guests can change the lighting to suit their mood) in a 60s office block. Rooms from £225. *U* Leicester Square

BLOOMSBURY, WC1

£ **The Generator**, Compton Place, 37 Tavistock Place, *T* 020 7388 7666, *F* 020 7388 7644, www.generatorhostels.com. Hostel with a futuristic design, bar and restaurant and games area. Rooms from £35 single, £20 twin, including breakfast. **U** Russell Square

Gower House, 57 Gower Street, **T** and **F** 020 7636 4685. Small bed-and-breakfast near the British Museum. Rooms from £40 single, £45 double. **U** Goodge Street

Gresham Hotel, 36 Bloomsbury Street, **T** 020 7580 4232. British Museum next door. Rooms from £40. **U** Tottenham Court Road

George Hotel, 58-60 Cartwright Gardens, **T** 020 7387 8777, **F** 020 7387 8666, www.georgehotel.com. Traditional English bed-and-breakfast hotel in a quiet but central location, overlooking gardens. Rooms from £60 single, £89 double. **U** Russell Square

££ **The Academy**, 21 Gower Street, **T** 020 7631 4115, **F** 020 7636 3442, www.etontownhouse.com. Housed in five Georgian townhouses. Rooms from £130 single, £185 double. **U** Goodge Street, Russell Square

Grange Holborn Hotel, 50-60 Southampton Row, **T** 020 7242 1800, **F** 020 7404 1641, www.grangehotels.com/holborn. Large, modern hotel. Rooms from £95. **U** Holborn

Radisson Edwardian Kenilworth Hotel, 97 Great Russell Street, **T** 020 7637 3477, **F** 020 7631 3133, www.radisson.com. Recently refurbished, with lots of wood and neutral fabrics. Rooms from £105 double. **U** Tottenham Court Road

Myhotel Bloomsbury, 11-13 Bayley Street, Bedford Square, **T** 020 7667 6000. East meets West in this newish hotel fitted out on feng shui principles. Rooms from £150 single, £185 double. **U** Tottenham Court Road

£££ **Blooms Town House Hotel**, 7 Montague Street **T** 020 7323 1717, **F** 020 7636 6498, www.bloomshotel.com. Very close to the British Museum, with a walled garden. Rooms from £175 single, £205 double. **U** Holborn, Russell Square

Charlotte Hotel, 15-17 Charlotte Street, **T** 020 7907 4000, **F** 020 7806 2002, www.charlottestreethotel.com. All mod-cons in individually designed rooms and suites. Rooms from £195 single, £220 double. **U** Tottenham Court Road

BANKSIDE, SE1

£ **Tower Bridge Travel Inn**, Tower Bridge Road, **T** 0870 238 3303, **F** 020 7940 3719, www.travelinn.co.uk. Note there is an extra charge for car drivers. All rooms £74.95 Mon-Thur, £69 Fri-Sun.
U London Bridge, Borough, Tower Hill

Express by Holiday Inn, 103-109 Southwark Street, *T* 020 7401 2525, *F* 020 7401 3322, www.hiexpress.com/lon-southwark. Modern budget hotel, handy for Tate Modern. £69 single, £92 double. *U* Southwark

Bankside House, 24 Sumner Street, *T* 020 7107 5750, *F* 020 7107 5757, www.lse.ac/uk/vacations. Student accommodation on the South Bank, next to Tate Modern. £43 single, £58 double. *U* Southwark

County Hall Travel Inn, Belvedere Road, *T* 0870 238 3300, *F* 020 7902 1619, www.travelinn.co.uk. Basic hotel housed in an architectural landmark. No on-site parking. All rooms £79.95 Mon-Thur, £74.95 Fri-Sun. *U* Waterloo

Mad Hatter Hotel, 3-7 Stamford Street, *T* 020 7401 9222, *F* 020 7401 7111, www.fullershotels.com. New hotel over a pub, a minute's walk from Blackfriar's Bridge. Rooms £99.50, £79 Fri, Sat. *U* Blackfriars

££ **Mercure London City Bankside**, 75-79 Southwark St, *T* 020 7902 0800, F 020 7902 0810, www.mercure.com. Business and tourist chain hotel. Rooms from £89. *U* Southwark

Southwark Rose Hotel, 43-47 Southwark Bridge, *T* 020 7015 1480, *F* 020 7015 1481, www.southwarkrosehotel.co.uk. Business-orientated and therefore well-equipped boutique hotel. Rooms from £95. *U* London Bridge

London Bridge Hotel, 8-18 London Bridge Street, *T* 020 7855 2200, *F* 020 7855 2233, www.london-bridge-hotel.co.uk. Four-star hotel with 1915 frontage and luxury two-bedroom apartments. Weekend rates £110 single, £140 double. *U* London Bridge

£££ **London Marriott Hotel County Hall**, *T* 020 7928 5200, *F* 020 7928 5300, www.marriott.com. Luxury hotel with views across the river to the Houses of Parliament. Not to be confused with the Travel Inn (see above). Rooms from £150. *U* Waterloo

WESTMINSTER, SW1

£ **Cheviot Hotel**, 8 St George's Drive, *T* 020 7834 6017, *F* 020 7834 6018, www.cheviothotel.co.uk. Closest bed-and-breakfast to Victoria station. Rooms from £55 single, £65 double. *U* Victoria

Vandon House Hotel, 1 Vandon Street, *T* 020 7799 6780, *F* 020 7799 1464, www.vandonhouse.com. Bed-and-breakfast hotel minutes from the Houses of Parliament. Rooms from £42 single, £66 double. *U* St James's Park

Victor Hotel, 51 Belgrave Road, *T* 020 7592 9853, *F* 020 7592 9854, www.victorhotel.co.uk. Small, family hotel in a white-stuccoed Edwardian building. Rooms from £70 single, double £90. *U* Pimlico

Victoria Inn, 65-67 Belgrave Road, *T* 020 7834 6721, *F* 020 7931 0201, www.victoriainn.co.uk. Simple hotel, with free breakfast. Rooms from £64 single, £79 double. *U* Pimlico

Windermere Hotel, 142-144 Warwick Way, *T* 020 7834 5163, *F* 020 7630 8831, www.windermere-hotel.co.uk. The LTB's best bed-and-breakfast 2003, friendly and well-equipped. Rooms from £64 single, £89 double. *U* Victoria

££ Dolphin Square Hotel, Chichester Street, *T* 020 7834 3800, *F* 020 7798 8735, www.dolphinsquarehotel.co.uk. Comfortable hotel with a spa and private gardens. Suites from £120. *U* Pimlico

Grange Rochester Hotel, 69 Vincent Square, *T* 020 7828 6611, *F* 020 7233 6724, www.grangehotels.com. Well-appointed hotel in a quiet square. Rooms from £105. *U* Victoria

Melita House Hotel, 35 Charlwood Street, *T* 020 7828 0471, *F* 020 7932 0988, www.melita.co.uk. Family-run bed and breakfast. Rooms from £66 single, £90 double. *U* Pimlico

Quality Hotel Eccleston, 82-83 Eccleston Square, *T* 020 7834 8042, *F* 020 7630 8942, www.qualityinn.com. In a quiet square but close to mainline rail. Rooms from £90. *U* Victoria

£££ Goring Hotel, Beeston Place, *T* 020 7396 9000, www.goringhotel.co.uk. Handsomely refurbished, historic hotel run by the Goring family since 1910, with a large garden. Rooms from £220 single, £280 double. *U* Victoria

SOUTH KENSINGTON

£ Swiss House Hotel, 171 Old Brompton Road, *T* 020 7373 2769, *F* 020 7373 4983, www.swiss-hh.demon.co.uk. Well-situated, cosy bed-and-breakfast. Rooms from £55 single, £90 double. *U* South Kensington

££ Aster House, 3 Sumner Place, *T* 020 7581 5888, *F* 020 7584 4925, www.asterhouse.com. Voted best bed-and-breakfast in 2002 by the LTB. Homely accommodation, pond and pet ducks. No smoking. Rooms from £85 single, £125 double. *U* South Kensington

Five Sumner Place Hotel, 5 Sumner Place, *T* 020 7584 7586, *F* 020 7823 9962, www.sumnerplace.com. Award-winning small hotel in a listed Victorian building, handy for the museums. Rooms from £85 single, £130 double (not including VAT). **U** South Kensington

Harrington Hall, 5-25 Harrington Gardens, **T** 020 7396 9696, **F** 020 7396 9090, www.harringtonhall.co.uk. Privately owned, luxury hotel near museums. Rooms from £100. **U** Gloucester Road

Pelham Hotel, 15 Cromwell Place, **T** 020 7589 8288, **F** 020 7584 8444, www.firmdale.com. On busy Cromwell Road, but very close to the museums and filled with antiques. Rooms from £150 single, £180 double. **U** South Kensington

£££ Basil Street Hotel, 8 Basil Street, **T** 020 7581 3311, **F** 020 7581 3693, www.thebasil.com. Family-run establishment built in 1910, with Edwardian comforts and excellent service. Rooms from £145 single, £205 double. **U** Knightsbridge

Blake's Hotel, 33 Roland Gardens, **T** 020 7370 6701, **F** 020 7373 0442. Designed by Anouska Hempel, with opulent fantasy decor, a fine restaurant, and celebrity clientele. Rooms from £200.
U Gloucester Road

Capital Hotel, 22-24 Basil Street, **T** 020 7589 5171, **F** 020 7225 0011, www.slh.com/capitalhotel. Award-winning small hotel in the heart of Knightsbridge. Rooms from £190 single, £245 double. **U** Knightsbridge

Milestone Hotel, 1 Kensington Court, **T** 020 7917 1000, **F** 020 7917 1010, www.milestonehotel.com. Voted best small hotel by the LTB in 2002, with a range of individually decorated rooms and suites. Overlooks Kensington Gardens. Rooms from £195 (not including VAT). **U** High Street Kensington

HALLS OF RESIDENCE

Very good value accommodation, at a variety of central locations, is on offer outside term times from universities. Try the following:

University College London, **T** 0707 387 7050

King's College London, **T** 020 7836 5454

London School of Economics, **T** 020 7405 7686

HOSTELS

Youth Hostel Association (YHA), locations include St Pancras, stpancras@yha.org.uk; City of London, city@yha.org.uk; Holland House, hollandhouse@yha.org.uk; Earl's Court, earlscourt@yha.org.uk

St Christopher's Inns, five locations, at Greenwich, Southwark, Camden, St Christopher's Orient Expresso (near St Christopher's Southwark) and The Village on the South Bank, www.st-christophers.co.uk

HOMESTAYS

Many agencies provide accommodation in London homes.

At Home in London, *T* 020 8748 1943, www.athomeinlondon.co.uk. Properties in Kensington, Knightsbridge and other parts of West London.

Best Bed & Breakfast in London, *T* 020 8742 9123, toll free from US *T* 011 800 852 26320, from Australia *T* 0011 800 852 26320, www.bestbandb.co.uk. Wide selection of rooms, catalogue available.

Uptown Reservations, *T* 020 7351 3445, www.uptownres.co.uk. Focuses on more expensive areas in Kensington, Chelsea, Knightsbridge, all rooms with private bathrooms

Welcome Homes & Hotels, *T* 020 8265 1212, www.welcomehomes.co.uk. Also finds budget apartments and hotels.

CAMPING

London's campsites are situated within easy reach of the centre and some are even open all year. The **Lee Valley Leisure Centre**, located on Meridian Way N9, has camping all year with 160 pitches. Daily prices are £10.70 per pitch and £2.85 for an electrical hook-up.

ART CALENDAR

JANUARY

London Art Fair, Business Design Centre, 52 Upper Street, *T* 020 7359 3535, www.londonartfair.co.uk. Britain's largest contemporary art fair, showing famous and collectable artists and unknowns. *U* Angel

MARCH

Affordable Art Fair, Battersea Park, *T* 020 7371 8787, www.affordableartfair.com. Friendly twice-yearly event selling contemporary art by young graduates and established names alike, all under £2500. *U* Sloane Square (for free shuttle)

Spring Olympia Fine Art & Antiques Fair, Olympia, *T* 020 7370 8211, www.olympia-antiques.com/FAAF. An eclectic mix of decorative art and antiques shown by British and international dealers, with lectures and other events. *U* Kensington Olympia

APRIL

London Original Print Fair, Royal Academy of Arts, Piccadilly, *T* 0118 932 0960, www.londonprintfair.com. The longest-running specialist print fair in the world has hundreds of works by artists from Rembrandt to Hockney, and at a wide range of prices. *U* Green Park, Piccadilly Circus

Beck's Futures, ICA, The Mall, *T* 020 7930 3647, www.ica.org.uk. Recent graduates are nominated to win Britain's biggest arts prize. The accompanying ICA exhibition often involves conceptual, installation and performance art. *U* Charing Cross, Piccadilly Circus

JUNE

Royal Academy Summer Exhibition, Piccadilly, *T* 020 7300 8000, www.royalacademy.org.uk. The world's largest open exhibition hangs work by amateurs beside that of distinguished Academicians and invited artists. Most is for sale. Always enjoyably controversial. *U* Green Park, Piccadilly Circus

Grosvenor House Art & Antiques Fair, Le Meridien Grosvenor House, Park Lane, *T* 020 7496 6406, www.grosvenor-fair.co.uk. Prestigious fair where dealers sell furniture, paintings, sculpture, glass, ceramics, jewellery, textiles, books, even garden statuary. *U* Hyde Park Corner, Green Park

Summer Olympia Fine Art & Antiques Fair, as for the spring event

JULY

Fresh Art, Business Design Centre, 52 Upper Street, *T* 020 7359 3535, http://198.170.232.22/. The only fair where independent artists and studio groups sell their work. Your chance to spot new talent. *U* Angel

OCTOBER

Affordable Art Fair, Battersea Park. The galleries at this autumn show (see above) will be different from those featured in spring. *U* Sloane Square and then a long walk

Chelsea Craft Fair, Chelsea Old Town Hall, King's Road, *T* 020 7278 7700, www.craftscouncil.org.uk. Europe's biggest crafts fair, held over two weeks, features a huge range of high-quality work by talented makers. *U* South Kensington, Sloane Square

NOVEMBER

Winter Olympia Fine Art & Antiques Fair, as for the spring event

art glossary

Ackroyd, Peter (born 1949). Critic, novelist and biographer. Ackroyd has written about many of London's key characters, from Sir Thomas More to Dickens and Dan Leno. He has also produced a rich 'biography' of the city and says London has always provided 'the landscape of my imagination'.

Albert of Saxe-Coburg-Gotha (1819-61). Consort of Queen Victoria. Best known for promoting the Great Exhibition of 1851, he also wielded considerable political influence as Britain's 'uncrowned king', despite the anti-German suspicions of his subjects. His scheme for a series of educational establishments to carry on the Exhibition's work resulted in the South Kensington Museums and he is commemorated in the Royal Albert Hall, Albert Memorial, Albert Bridge, and so on.

Barfield, Julia (born 1952) and David Marks (born 1952). Architects and designers of the London Eye. Their vast observation wheel on the South Bank proved the popular choice to mark the millennium. Originally intended as a temporary structure, it has been granted a 20-year stay on its site opposite the Houses of Parliament. Their practice also designed the new Millbank Pier.

Barry, Charles (1795-1860). Architect. Built the Renaissance-style Travellers' Club, the Reform Club, and most famously the Houses of Parliament (1839-52), combining a classically symmetrical ground plan and river façade with a Gothic skyline of towers, clad in Perpendicular detail by Augustus Pugin.

Bazalgette, Joseph (1819-91). Engineer. He was responsible for the development of London's sewerage system in the 1860s, thanks to which a repeat of the 'Great Stink' of 1858 and the cholera outbreaks that had periodically devastated the city were avoided. His work involved the building of the Victoria, Albert and Chelsea Embankments on the Thames, Battersea Bridge, and major roads including Charing Cross Road.

Beck, Harry (1903-74). Designer of the Tube map. Originally rejected by the Underground's publicity office when first suggested, Beck's design was based on circuit diagrams, abandoning geographical realities. After its first publication in 1933 it became one of the most useful and widespread images of London ever made.

Betjeman, John (1906-84). Poet and architectural critic. Born in Highgate, Betjeman celebrated London's suburbs and its - at the time unfashionable - Victorian landmarks. In the 1960s he was central to the campaign to save St Pancras Chambers, which is now to be restored to its former spendour.

Blake, William (1757-1827). Artist and writer. Blake was truly a Londoner, born near Oxford Street and a long-term resident of Lambeth, where he liked to sunbathe naked in the garden. Though his city largely rejected his unique visionary engravings and books, he drew inspiration from it to produce some of his most famous poems, including 'London'.

Cole, Henry (1808-82). Founding Director of the Victoria and Albert Museum. An official at the Public Records Office, writer on art, children's book editor and designer under the pseudonym Felix Summerlee, Cole became a committee member for the Great Exhibition of 1851 and was later closely involved in the development of the South Kensington Museums. He also instigated the production of the first Christmas card in 1843.

Classicism Architectural style first developed during the Italian Renaissance, when the writings of the Roman Vitruvius were rediscovered. From the 1750s a more authentic interpretation of ancient Greek and Roman principles and accurate use of details resulted in Neoclassical buildings, to be replaced in the 19c by a more heavily decorated imperial manner.

Coade, Eleanor (1733-1821). Manufacturer of Coade stone. This special type of hard-wearing ceramic could be moulded to form detailed architectural ornaments and statuary which can still be seen across London (for example, the lion on Westminster Bridge). It was made in Lambeth until the 1840s.

Conran, Terence (born 1931). Designer and entrepreneur. With his affordable modern furniture and household accessories, Conran influenced generations of London domestic interiors: he created the Design Museum below Tower Bridge in 1989. As a restaurateur he has also provided Londoners with a range of fashionable eateries.

Dickens, Charles (1812-70). Novelist and journalist. Dickens' books chronicled the teeming life of 19c London. Of his various London addresses his house in Doughty Street survives as a museum, and many of the places featured in his work can still be visited.

Gilbert and George (Gilbert Proesch born 1943, George Passmore born 1942). Artists. Perhaps the ultimate urban artists, Gilbert & George met at St Martin's School of Art in the 1960s and have lived and worked together in London's East End ever since. An early performance turned them into a 'Singing Sculpture' and they still appear in many of their instantly recognizable photographic works. Their matching, conservative suits and deadpan expressions contrast with the often graphic content of the images (*Spit on Shit*, for example), which are meant to communicate to everyone.

Foster, Norman (born 1935). High-tech architect. Foster has augmented some long-standing buildings - slotting the Sackler Galleries into the Royal Academy, roofing over the Great Court of the British Museum - and created new London tourist sites including the Millennium Bridge, the helmet-like London Assembly building, and the cavernous Tube station at Canary Wharf. He has changed the City skyline with the SwissRe Building, instantly dubbed the 'Gherkin'. He is perhaps the most internationally renowned British architect at the turn of the 21c.

Gothic Revival Architectural movement of the later 18c and 19c, at first manifested as a fashion for sham medieval castles and follies. In the 19c it was accepted as the only suitable style for churches but was also applied to many other public buildings, most famously the Houses of Parliament. It is recognizable by its verticality, with pointed arches, rib vaults and flying buttresses.

Greek Revival Architectural style at its peak in Britain in the 1820s and 30s, though ancient Greek buildings had been studied from the 1750s. It is characterized by austerity and seen in the work of Robert Smirke and James 'Athenian' Stuart.

Herzog, Jacques (born 1950) and **Meuron, Pierre de** (born 1950). Architects. This successful Swiss partnership is responsible for a number of acclaimed buildings in Europe. Best-known in Britain for their conversion of a power station into Tate Modern, they also designed the rainbow-coloured Laban Centre, a dance school, in Deptford.

Hogarth, William (1697-1764). Painter and engraver. Hogarth's satirical depictions of London's rakes and prostitutes still vividly evoke the 18c city. An energetic art theorist and entrepreneur, he was an early member of the Royal Academy and a trustee of the Foundling Hospital. Good examples of his work can be seen at Tate Britain and the National Gallery, and his house at Chiswick survives.

Johnson, Samuel (1709-84). Lexicographer, critic and poet. Dr Johnson is closely associated with the capital through his assertion that 'when a man is tired of London, he is tired of life', though his poem 'London' was a satire on its vices. He compiled his *Dictionary* (1755) at a house near Fleet Street that can still be visited.

Jones, Inigo (1573-1652). Britain's first classical architect. Jones was ahead of his time in his Italianate designs for the Queen's House at Greenwich, the Banqueting House in Whitehall and Covent Garden Market - London's first square - with St Paul's Church, the 'handsomest barn in all England'. He also designed Baroque staging and costumes for court entertainments.

Jopling, Jay (born 1963). Art dealer. Eton-educated, ex-fire extinguisher salesman Jopling was one of the most influential figures in the 1990s revival of Britain's contemporary art scene. A mastery of publicity allowed him to sell the art of the YBAs to both collectors (among them Charles Saatchi) and an initially sceptical public. His White Cube galleries, first in traditional St James's and now in trendy Hoxton Square, show among others Marc Quinn, Damien Hirst and older artists including Anthony Gormley. He is married to YBA Sam Taylor-Wood.

Libeskind, Daniel (born 1946). American architect, now famous for his Jewish Museum in Berlin and plans for the redeveloped World Trade Centre in New York. His design for the new Spiral extension to the Victoria and Albert Museum will be a spectacular addition to South Kensington's buildings.

Mayhew, Henry (1812-87). Journalist and playwright. In *London Labour and the London Poor* (1851-62), he exposed the dreadful living conditions of most of the city's Victorian population and helped inspire reform. He was also a founder and editor of the humorous magazine *Punch*.

Nash, John (1752-1835). Architect and urban planner. A favourite of George IV, he laid out Carlton House Terrace, Trafalgar Square and Regent Street and the graceful crescents and terraces around Regent's Park. Nash began work on Buckingham Palace (later altered) but after George's death in 1830 was sacked over the spiralling costs and died in disgrace.

Palladianism Architectural style based on the writings of Andrea Palladio (1508-80), with its foundations in the symmetry and harmonious proportions of ancient Roman buildings. Inigo Jones saw his work in Italy and transferred its principles to English architecture.

Paoletti, Roland Project architect for Jubilee Line Extension. Paoletti hired internationally recognized and relatively unknown architects to design the 11 new stations (1990-2000). The emphasis is on space and natural light and an appealing overall aesthetic of exposed grey concrete, glass walls and brushed steel.

Pearsall, Phyllis (1906-96). Creator of the *A-Z*. A portrait artist frustrated by out-of-date maps, she researched and - more importantly - indexed 23,000 streets to produce the indispensable tool for navigating London. She founded a successful company to publish her atlas in 1936, and became a millionaire.

Pepys, Samuel (1633-1703). Diarist and naval official. Vivid first-hand accounts of the Great Plague and Fire and the court of Charles II make Pepys' diaries, which he kept from the year of the Restoration until 1669, a uniquely valuable record of 17c London.

Reynolds, Joshua (1723-92). Painter and first President of the Royal Academy of Arts. He produced many portraits and allegorical pictures and campaigned to establish painting as a profession. His statue in the courtyard of Burlington House is garlanded to celebrate every Summer Exhibition.

Rogers, Richard (born 1933). Hi-tech architect. First worked in partnership with Norman Foster, but after making his name with the Pompidou Centre in Paris formed his own practice. Lloyd's (1978-86) is his best-known work in the capital but he was also responsible for the Millennium Dome (not its dreary contents).

Saatchi, Charles (born 1943). Art collector. Saatchi was largely responsible for the soaring fame and fortunes of the Young British Artists in the 1990s. Although his wealth was made from advertising, he is shy of personal publicity and has directed attention to his collection, now on display in its own museum in County Hall.

Scott, George Gilbert (1811-78). Gothic Revival architect. Scott specialized in full-blown decorative Gothic churches, even working on 'restorations' at Westminster Abbey, but also built the great red hotel at St Pancras and designed the Albert Memorial. His grandson Giles Gilbert Scott (1880-1960) built Waterloo Bridge and the power station that now houses Tate Modern.

Serota, Nicholas (born 1946). Museum director. Serota's influential terms as director of the Whitechapel Gallery and now of the Tate have made him an important advocate of contemporary British art. He oversaw the Tate's expansion into the Bankside power station and instigated its innovative hanging policy.

Sickert, Walter (1860-1942). Artist. Sickert was an Impressionist, but a London Impressionist, favouring shabby interiors and very dark colours rather than fresh air and light. He celebrated London's boarding houses and music halls and their inhabitants, and founded the Camden Town and London groups.

Sinclair, Ian (born 1943). Poet, novelist and essayist. Sinclair writes about London's less well-trodden ways (which he treads personally, often with photographer Marc Atkins) and its obscure personalities - Jack the Ripper, second-hand-book dealers, fellow London obsessives - in a knotty, visionary style.

Sloane, Hans (1660-1753). Doctor, plant collector and President of the Royal Society. At Sloane's suggestion his art, antiquities and library were acquired for the nation after his death, which led to the foundation of the British Museum. He was also instrumental in establishing the Chelsea Physic Garden. Sloane Square and other streets built on his estate are named after him.

Smirke, Robert (1780-1867). Greek Revival architect. In his twenties, Smirke travelled through Greece and Italy drawing ancient buildings, and later became one of Victorian England's leading classical architects. His Covent Garden Theatre (1808) was the first Doric building in Britain and his General Post Office (1824-9) was on the same scale as the British Museum: both have since been destroyed.

Smirke, Sydney (1798-1877). Architect. He took over the building of the British Museum after the retirement of his brother Robert and created its circular Reading Room. He built the exhibition galleries of the Royal Academy in Burlington House and with George Basevi designed the Carlton Club in St James's.

Stirling, James Frazer (1926-92). Architect. Stirling's earlier buildings were Brutalist but the Clore Galleries (1980-4) he designed for Tate Britain with Michael Wilford are in a more colourful Postmodern style. His most controversial building, at Number One Poultry, in the City, was completed posthumously in 1998.

Venturi, Robert (born 1925). Postmodern architect. The American partnership of Venturi and Denise Scott Brown was responsible for the Sainsbury Wing of the National Gallery (1986-91).

Webb, Aston (1849-1930). Edwardian architect. A very successful designer of public buildings at the turn of the century, Webb was not only responsible for the Cromwell Road façade of the Victoria and Albert Museum but also for the present front of Buckingham Palace, Admiralty Arch and the Mall that runs between them.

Wren, Christopher (1632-1723). Scientist, mathematician, astronomer and architect, Oxford professor and MP. After the Great Fire in 1666 he planned to rebuild London on utopian lines: this scheme was rejected but he went on to build St Paul's Cathedral (1675-1709) and Greenwich Hospital (from 1696), and supervised the construction of 51 City churches. He died aged 91, after a lifetime of public service.

Cover pictures

The front cover features a detail of William Blake's Newton (c 1795), the inside front cover shows the painting in full: reproduced by kind permission of the Tate Gallery (picture kept at Tate Britain). The back cover, courtesy of the British Museum, shows the Great Court at the British Museum, with a Hellenistic lion (late 4c–early 3c BC).

Inside illustrations

For permission to reproduce the pictures throughout the book, grateful thanks are due to the following: The British Library (p 74); The British Museum (pp 45, 54, 59, 61, 65); The Museum of Garden History (p171); The National Gallery (pp 7, 14, 18, 22); The National Portrait Gallery (p 30: Jeremy Dixon/Edward Jones © Dennis Gilbert/VIEW); The Natural History Museum (p 171); The Saatchi Gallery (p 99); Somerset House (p 29: © James Brittain); The Tate Gallery (pp 83, 97, 113, 125, 127); The Victoria and Albert Museum (pp 139, 156); Visit London (pp 101, 102, 108, 130, 171).

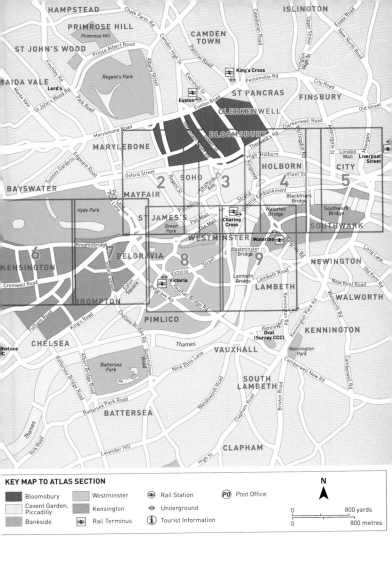

HAMPSTEAD

ISLINGTON

PRIMROSE HILL

Primrose Hill

CAMDEN TOWN

ST JOHN'S WOOD

Prince Albert Road

Chalk Farm Rd

Caledonian Road

Upper Street

Essex Road

New North Road

Regent's Park

Camden High St

Pancras Road

King's Cross

Pentonville Rd

City Road

Finchley Rd

Albany Street

Eversholt St

MAIDA VALE

Lord's

Euston

Euston Road

ST PANCRAS

FINSBURY

St John's Wood Rd

Park Road

CLERKENWELL

Old Street

Marylebone Road

BLOOMSBURY

Clerkenwell Road

Aldersgate St

Moorgate

BAYSWATER

MARYLEBONE

Tottenham Court Rd

Theobald's Rd

London Wall

Liverpool Street

Sussex Gardens

Edgware Road

Oxford Street

2

SOHO

High Holborn

HOLBORN

4

CITY

5

Gower St

Regent St

3

Kingsway

Fleet St

MAYFAIR

Shaftesbury Ave

Strand

Blackfriars Bridge

Southwark Bridge

SOUTHWARK

Hyde Park

Park Lane

ST JAMES'S

Piccadilly

Pall Mall

Victoria Embankment

Waterloo Bridge

6

Green Park

Charing Cross

KENSINGTON

7

Knightsbridge

WESTMINSTER

Waterloo

9

NEWINGTON

Cromwell Road

BELGRAVIA

Sloane Street

8

Westminster Bridge

Waterloo Rd

Long Lane

Old Kent Rd

Eaton Square

Victoria

Lambeth Bridge

Lambeth Road

New Kent Road

WALWORTH

BROMPTON

Belgrave Rd

Vauxhall Bridge Rd

LAMBETH

Kennington Rd

Walworth Rd

PIMLICO

Chelsea Bridge Rd

King's Road

Kennington

Kennington Park Rd

KENNINGTON

Chelsea C

CHELSEA

Thames

VAUXHALL

Oval (Surrey CCC)

Kennington Park

Camberwell Rd

Albert Bridge Road

Queenstown Road

Battersea Park

Battersea Park

Nine Elms Lane

SOUTH LAMBETH

Camberwell New Rd

Battersea Bridge Road

York Road

Battersea Park Road

Wandsworth Road

Clapham Road

Brixton Road

BATTERSEA

Lavender Hill

CLAPHAM

High St

KEY MAP TO ATLAS SECTION

N

Bloomsbury

Covent Garden, Piccadilly

Bankside

Westminster

Kensington

Rail Terminus

Rail Station

Underground

Tourist Information

PO Post Office

0 800 yards

0 800 metres

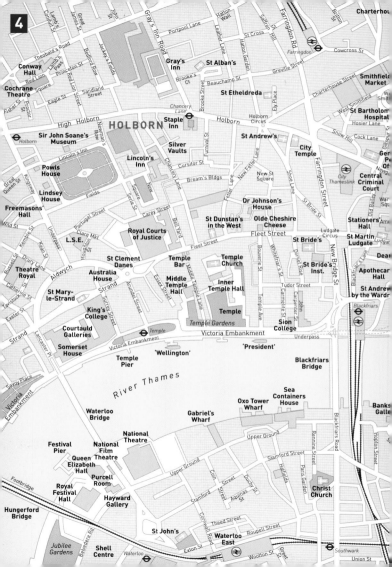

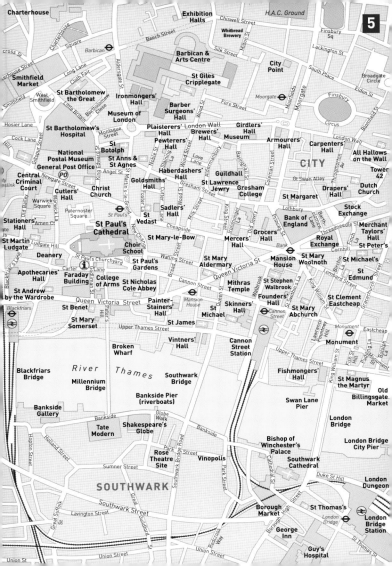

Charterhouse
Exhibition Halls
H.A.C. Ground
Chiswell Street
Whitbread Brewery
Finsbury Sq
cross St
Charterhouse Square
Beech Street
Silk Street
Lackington St
Barbican
Barbican & Arts Centre
City Point
South Place
Broadgate Circle
Eldon St
Smithfield Market
Long Lane
Cloth Fair
Aldersgate Street
St Giles Cripplegate
City Point
Finsbury Circus
Blomfield St
West Smithfield
St Bartholomew the Great
Little Britain
Moorgate
Fore Street
Moorfields
Moorgate
Smithfield
Museum of London
London Wall
Girdlers' Hall
London Wall
Hosier Lane
Montague Street
Plaisterers' Hall
Brewers' Hall
Armourers' Hall
CITY
Cock Lane
St Bartholomew's Hospital
Angel St
St Botolph
St Anns & St Agnes
Pewterers' Hall
Wood Street
Love Lane
Basinghall Street
Carpenters' Hall
All Hallows on the Wall
Hill
National Postal Museum
General Post Office
Newgate Street
Goldsmiths' Hall
Haberdashers' Hall
St Lawrence Jewry
Guildhall
Coleman Street
Tower 42
Dutch Church
Central Criminal Court
PO
St Martin's-le-Grand
Foster Lane
Gutter Lane
Gresham Street
Gresham College
Gt Swan Alley
Drapers' Hall
Cutlers' Hall
Christ Church
Cheapside
St Margaret
Lothbury
Stock Exchange
Warwick Square
Paternoster Square
St Vedast
Sadlers' Hall
Milk Street
King Street
Poultry
Bank of England
Bartholomew Lane
Throgmorton Street
Merchant Taylors' Hall
St Peter's
Stationers' Hall
Amen Ct
St Paul's
St Paul's Cathedral
Cheapside
St Mary-le-Bow
Mercers' Hall
Grocers' Hall
Royal Exchange
Threadneedle St
Cornhill
St Michael's
St Martin Ludgate
Ludgate Hill
Choir School
Watling Street
St Mary Aldermary
Bank
St Mary Woolnoth
Lombard Street
St Edmund
Blackfriars
Deanery
St Paul's Churchyard
Carter Lane
St Paul's Gardens
Bread Street
Queen Victoria St
Mansion House
Walbrook
King William Street
St Clement Eastcheap
Apothecaries' Hall
Faraday Building
College of Arms
St Nicholas Cole Abbey
Cannon Street
Mithras Temple
St Stephen Walbrook
St Mary Abchurch
St Andrew by the Wardrobe
Queen Victoria Street
Painter-Stainers' Hall
Mansion House
Queen St
Skinners' Hall
Founders' Hall
St Mary Abchurch
Eastcheap
St Benet
St Mary Somerset
St James
St Michael
Cannon St
Monument
Monument
Upper Thames Street
Vintners' Hall
Cannon Street Station
Lawrence Pountney Hill
Fish St Hill
Pudding La
River   Thames
Broken Wharf
Southwark Bridge
Upper Thames Street
Fishmongers' Hall
King William Street
St Magnus the Martyr
Blackfriars Bridge
Millennium Bridge
Swan Lane Pier
London Bridge
Old Billingsgate Market
Bankside Gallery
Bankside
Bankside Pier (riverboats)
Globe Walk
Bankside
London Bridge City Pier
Holland Street
Hopton Street
Tate Modern
Shakespeare's Globe
Park Street
Southwark Bridge Road
Bankside
Bishop of Winchester's Palace
Southwark Cathedral
Cathedral St
Duke St Hill
London Dungeon
Rose Theatre Site
Vinopolis
Sumner Street
SOUTHWARK
Southwark Street
Great Suffolk St
Lavington Street
Redcross Way
Borough High Street
Borough Market
St Thomas's
London Bridge
London Bridge Station
St Thomas St
George Inn
Guy's Hospital
Union St
Union Street
Union Street
George Inn

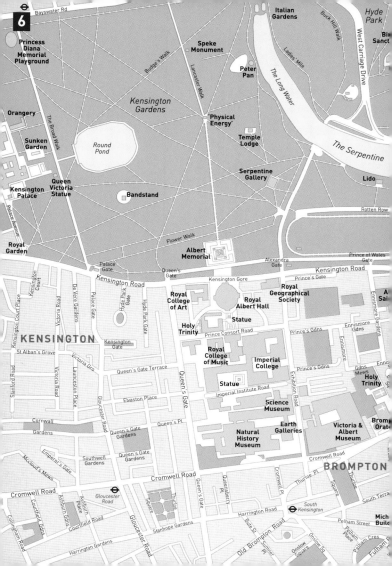

Bayswater Rd

Princess
Diana
Memorial
Playground

Italian
Gardens

Buck Hill Walk

Hyde
Park

Bi
Sanct

West Carriage Drive

Speke
Monument

Budge's Walk

Lancaster Walk

Peter
Pan

Ladies' Mile

The Long Water

Orangery

Kensington
Gardens

The Broad Walk

Sunken
Garden

'Physical
Energy'

Round
Pond

Temple
Lodge

The Serpentine

Kensington
Palace

Queen
Victoria
Statue

Serpentine
Gallery

Lido

Palace Avenue

Bandstand

Rotten Row

Royal
Garden

Flower Walk

Albert
Memorial

Palace
Gate

Alexandra
Gate

Prince of Wales
Gate

Kensington Road

Queen's
Gate

Kensington Gore

Kensington Road

Prince's Gate

Kensington Court Place

Kensington
Court

De Vere Gardens

Palace Gate

Hyde Park Gate

Royal
College
of Art

Royal
Albert Hall

Royal
Geographical
Society

A
Sai

Ennismore Gardens

St Alban's Grove

KENSINGTON

Kensington
Gate

Holy
Trinity

Statue

Prince Consort Road

Prince's Gdns

Ennismore
Gdns

Ennismore

Stanford Road

Victoria Road

Launceston Place

Victoria Gro.

Queen's Gate Terrace

Royal
College
of Music

Imperial
College

Prince's Gdns

Gdns
Mews

Ennis

Holy
Trinity

Gloucester Road

Elvaston Place

Queen's Gate

Statue

Imperial Institute Road

Exhibition Road

Cornwall
Gardens

Queen's Pl.

Science
Museum

Victoria &
Albert
Museum

Brom
Orat

Queen's Gate
Gardens

Queen's Gate
Gardens

Earth
Galleries

Emperor's Gate

McCleod's Mews

Southwell
Gardens

Natural
History
Museum

Cromwell Road

BROMPTON

Cromwell Road

Ashburn Gdns

Gloucester
Road

Stanhope Gardens

Queen's Gate

Thurloe
Square

Queensberry
Pl.

Cromwell Pl.

Thurloe Pl.

Pelham Cres.

South Terra

Courtfield Gdns

Ashburn Place

Courtfield Road

Columbham Road

Harrington Gardens

Bute St.

Harrington Road

Onslow
Square

South
Kensington

Pelham Street

Pelham
Place

Pelham Cres.

Mich
Build

Onslow Sq.

Sumner Pl.

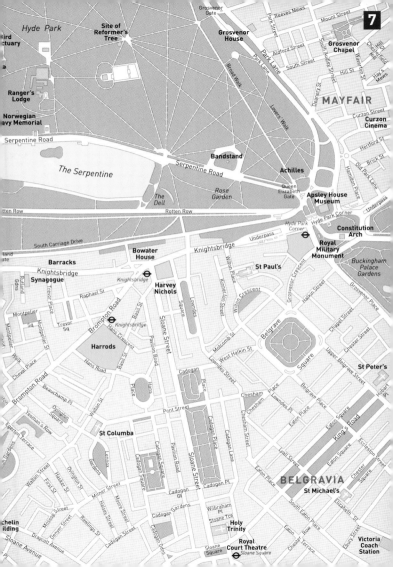

Hyde Park

Site of Reformer's Tree

ird ctuary

a

Ranger's Lodge

Norwegian avy Memorial

Grosvenor Gate

Grosvenor House

Reeves Mews

Mount Street

Park Street

Aldford Street

South Audley Street

Broad Walk

Park Lane

South Street

Hill Street

Grosvenor Chapel

Hay's Mews

Waverton St

Chesterfield Hill

Hill St

Lovers' Walk

Deanery St

MAYFAIR

Serpentine Road

Curzon Street

Curzon Cinema

The Serpentine

Bandstand

Serpentine Road

Achilles

Queen Elizabeth Gate

Hertford St

Brick St

Old Park Lane

Hamilton Place

Underpass

The Dell

Rose Garden

Apsley House Museum

tten Row

Rotten Row

Hyde Park Corner

Hyde Park Corner

Constitution Arch

South Carriage Drive

Knightsbridge

Underpass

Royal Military Monument

Buckingham Palace Gardens

land ate

Barracks

Bowater House

St Paul's

Grosvenor Crescent

Grosvenor Place

Knightsbridge

Synagogue

Knightsbridge

Harvey Nichols

Wilton Place

Halkin Place

Chapel Street

Chester Street

Rutland Gdns

Trevor Place

Raphael St

Square

Lowndes

Kinnerton Street

Wilton Crescent

Belgrave

Upper Belgrave Street

St Peter's

Montpelier Sq

Trevor Sq

Brompton Road

Basil St

Hans Crescent

Knightsbridge

Montpelier Walk

Montpelier St

Cheval Place

Harrods

Hans Road

Pavilion Road

Sloane Street

Montcomb St

West Halkin St

Square

Belgrave Place

Hobart Place

Brompton Road

Beauchamp Pl

Walton St

Cadogan Place

Lowndes Street

Chesham Place

Eaton Place

Eaton Square

Chester Square

Egerton Place

Ovington Square

Yeoman's Row

Hans Place

Pont Street

Chesham Street

Eaton Square

Eccleston Street

Egerton Terrace

Ovington Gardens

Walton St

Lennox Gardens

Cadogan Place

Cadogan Lane

Chesham Place

St Columba

Pavilion Road

Sloane Street

King's Road

Gardens

Cadogan Square

Cadogan Square

Milner Street

Moore Street

Halsey Street

Cadogan Street

Cadogan Gdns

Cadogan Gt

Pont Street

Cadogan Gt

Cadogan Place

Epton Place

Lyall Street

Eaton Square

Chester Square

Elizabeth St

Chester Row

BELGRAVIA

St Michael's

ichelin ilding

SLOANE AVENUE

Draycott Avenue

Mossop Street

Denyer Street

Rawlings St

First St

Hasker St

Cadogan Gardens

Wilbraham Pl

Sloane Tce

South Eaton Place

Eaton

Chester Terrace

Ebury Street

Holy Trinity

Royal Court Theatre

Sloane Square

Sloane Square

Victoria Coach Station

Charles St
Berkeley Street
Dover Street
Albemarle Street
Arlington St
Burlington House
Fortnum & Mason
Jermyn Street
Duke Street
St James
Regent Street
Charles II St
Haymarket
Pall Mall East
Cockspur St
Her Majesty's
Nels Colu

Bolton St
Clarges St
Stratton St
Green Park
Mayfair Theatre
London Library
King Street
St James's Square
Pall Mall
Carlton Gdns
Waterloo Pl
ICA
Duke of York's Column
Admir Arch
Ne Adm

Curzon St
Half Moon St
White Horse St
Curzon Cinema
Green Park
ST JAMES'S
Spencer House
St James's Pl
Cleveland Row
St James's St
Ryder Street
Bury Street
Arlington St
Queen's Chapel
Carlton House
Carlton Gdns
The Mall

Brick St
Down St
Piccadilly
Bridgewater House
York House
St James's Palace
Marlborough House
Nels Colu

Green Park
Lancaster House
Clarence House
St James's Park
Fo O
Tre

Buckingham Palace Gardens
The Horse Ride
Constitution Hill
Queen Victoria Memorial
Cabinet War Rooms
Gt Geo
Middl Guild

Buckingham Palace
Birdcage Walk
Queen Anne's Gate
Old Queen St
Lewisham St
Central Hall
Westmins
Westmi Scho

Queen's Gallery
Wellington Barracks
Guard's Chapel Museum
National Trust HQ
Dartmouth
St James's Park
Westminster Abbey

Royal Mews
Buckingham Gate
Buckingham Gate
Petty France
Palmer St
Caxton Hall
Broadway
Tothill Street
New Scotland Yard
St Ann's St

Lower Grosvenor Pl
Catherine Pl
Wilfred St
Stafford Pl
Palace Street
Castle Lane
Passport Office
Caxton Street
P O
Orchard St
Gt Smith St

Grosvenor Place
Buckingham Palace Rd
Warwick Row
Bressenden Place
Stag Place
Westminster City Hall
Victoria Street
Old Pye Street
Perkins Rents
St Matthew
Great Peter Street

Hobart Pl
Grosvenor Gdns
Beeston Pl
Palace Place
WESTMINSTER
Francis's Place
Howick Pl
Artillery Row
Strutton Ground
Monck Street

Lower Belgrave Street
Victoria St
Westminster Cathedral
Morpeth Terrace
Thirleby Road
Ambrosden Ave
St Matthew Street
Great Peter Street

Bury St
Eccleston St
Victoria
Victoria Palace Theatre
Cardigan Place
Greencoat Place
Rochester Row
St Stephen
Manck Street

Buckingham Palace Rd
Victoria Station
Apollo Victoria
Wilton Road
Vauxhall Bridge Road
Willow Place
Francis Street
Vincent Square
Royal Horticultural Society
Marsham
Page Street
Horseferry Road

P O
Eccleston Bridge Street
Gillingham St
Warwick Way
Rutherford Street
Vincent Street
Regency Street

Victoria Coach Station
Elizabeth Bridge Street
Eccleston
Longmore St
Warwick Way
Guildhouse St
Denbigh St
Belgrave Road
Churton Street
Tachbrook St
Vincent Square
Hide Place
Douglas Chapter St
Erasmus Stre
Ta Bri

Warwick Way
PIMLICO
St James the Less
Lupus Street & Pimlico Tube Station

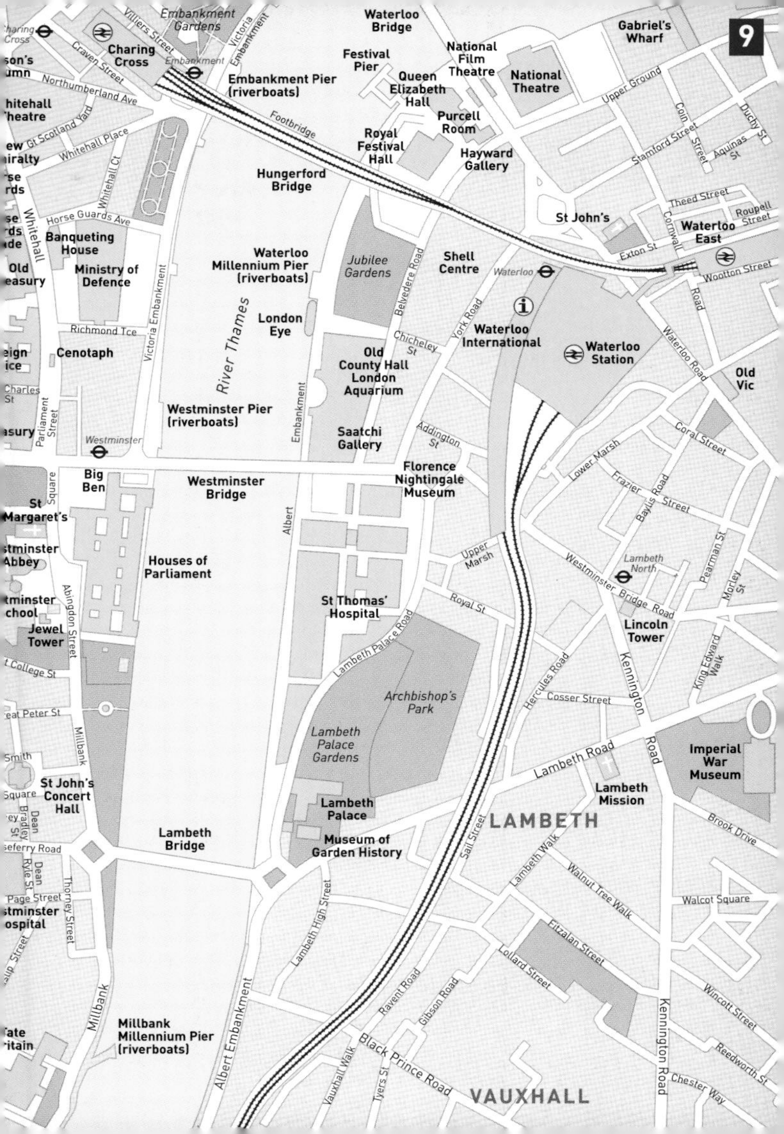
9
Embankment Gardens
Villiers Street
Charing Cross
Craven Street
Northumberland Ave
Embankment
Victoria Embankment
Waterloo Bridge
Festival Pier
Embankment Pier (riverboats)
National Film Theatre
Queen Elizabeth Hall
National Theatre
Gabriel's Wharf
Upper Ground
Purcell Room
Royal Festival Hall
Hayward Gallery
Footbridge
Hungerford Bridge
Gt Scotland Yard
Whitehall Place
Whitehall Theatre
Whitehall Ct
Horse Guards Ave
Whitehall
Banqueting House
Ministry of Defence
Old Treasury
Richmond Tce
Cenotaph
Charles St
Parliament Street
Westminster
Victoria Embankment
River Thames
Waterloo Millennium Pier (riverboats)
London Eye
Westminster Pier (riverboats)
Jubilee Gardens
Belvedere Road
Shell Centre
Chicheley St
Old County Hall London Aquarium
Embankment
Saatchi Gallery
York Road
Waterloo
Waterloo International
Waterloo Station
Stamford Street
Coin Street
Duchy St
Aquinas St
Theed Street
Roupell Street
St John's
Cornwall
Exton St
Waterloo East
Wootton Street
Road
Waterloo Road
Old Vic
Coral Street
Lower Marsh
Frazier Street
Baylis Road
Addington St
Big Ben
Square
St Margaret's
Westminster Bridge
Florence Nightingale Museum
Albert
Westminster Abbey
Houses of Parliament
Upper Marsh
Westminster Bridge Road
Lambeth North
Pearman St
Morley St
Royal St
St Thomas' Hospital
Westminster School
Abingdon Street
Jewel Tower
Lambeth Palace Road
Lincoln Tower
Kennington
King Edward Walk
College St
Archbishop's Park
Hercules Road
Cosser Street
Great Peter St
Millbank
Lambeth Palace Gardens
Lambeth Road
Road
Imperial War Museum
Smith Square
St John's Concert Hall
Lambeth Palace
Lambeth Mission
LAMBETH
Sail Street
Brook Drive
Bradley St
Dean
Horseferry Road
Lambeth Bridge
Museum of Garden History
Lambeth Walk
Walnut Tree Walk
Dean Ryle St
Page Street
Westminster Hospital
Thorney Street
Lambeth High Street
Walcot Square
Fitzalan Street
Lollard Street
Ravent Road
Gibson Road
Millbank
Albert Embankment
Kennington Road
Wincott Street
Millbank Millennium Pier (riverboats)
Tate Britain
Black Prince Road
Vauxhall Walk
Tyers St
VAUXHALL
Reedworth St
Chester Way

For Simon

First edition 2004
Published by A&C Black Publishers Ltd
37 Soho Square, London W1D 3QZ

ISBN 0-7136-6695-1

Published in the United States of America by
WW Norton & Company, Inc
500 Fifth Avenue, New York, NY 10110, USA

ISBN 0-393-32593-8

Published simultaneously in Canada by
Penguin Books Canada Limited
10 Alcorn Avenue, Ontario M4V 3B2

Series devised by Gemma Davies
Series designed by Jocelyn Lucas
Editorial and production: Gemma Davies, Jocelyn Lucas, Lilla Nwenu-Msimang, Miranda Robson, Kim Teo, Judy Tither

Maps by Mapping Company Ltd. Maps based upon the Ordnance Survey mapping with the permission of The Controller of Her Majesty's Stationery Office ©Crown Copyright 398454. Map of the London Underground reproduced by permission of Transport for London.

Printed and bound in Singapore by Tien Wah Press (Pte.) Ltd.